Emotional Intelligence for Project Managers

The People Skills You Need to Achieve Outstanding Results

ANTHONY C. MERSINO, PMP

AMACOM

American Management Association

New York | Atlanta | Brussels | Chicago | Mexico City
San Francisco | Shanghai | Tokyo | Washington, D. C.

This publication is designed to provide accurate and authoritative information in regard to the subject matter covered. It is sold with the understanding that the publisher is not engaged in rendering legal, accounting, or other professional service. If legal advice or other expert assistance is required, the services of a competent professional person should be sought.

Project Management Institute (PMI). *PMI Today.* Project Management Institute, Inc. 1993, 1994, 1995, 1996, 1997, 1998, 1999, 2000, 2001, 2002, 2003, 2004, 2005. Copyright and all rights reserved. Material from this publication has been reproduced with permission of PMI.

Project Management Institute (PMI). *A Guide to the Project Management Body of Knowledge (PMBOK® Guide), Third Edition.* Project Management Institute, Inc., 2004. Copyright and all rights reserved. Material from this publication has been reproduced with permission of PMI.

"PMI" and the PMI logo are service and trademarks registered in the United States and other nations; "PMP" and the PMP logo are certification marks registered in the United States and other nations; "PMBOK", "PM Network", and "PMI Today" are trademarks registered in the United States and other nations; and "Project Management Journal" and "Building professionalism in project management" are trademarks of the Project Management Institute, Inc.

Library of Congress Cataloging-in-Publication Data

Mersino, Anthony C.
    Emotional intelligence for project managers : the people skills you need to achieve outstanding results / Anthony Mersino.
        p.   cm.
    Includes index.
    ISBN-13: 978-0-8144-7416-7
    ISBN-10: 0-8144-7416-0
    1. Project management—Psychological aspects.   2. Emotional intelligence.
3. Teams in the workplace—Management.   I. Title.
HD69.P75M475   2007
658.4'04019—dc22   2007008599

Printing number

10 9 8 7

Contents

■ **PART TWO**
Project Management Begins with
Self-Management   31

■ **PART THREE**
Building Project Stakeholder Relationships   81

■ PART FOUR
Using EQ to Lead Project Teams   155

■ Acknowledgments

Writing a book was a lot more work than I imagined, and it is not something that I could have done on my own. I am extremely grateful to all those people who graciously invested their time and energy to help me with my personal growth and with this book.

The support of two published authors eventually convinced me to start writing. Jim Taylor gave me the idea to write on emotional intelligence and project management. Rajesh Setty was instrumental in pointing out that I was better off to begin writing than to continue planning to write.

Rich Blue and Nancy Rollins of the Center for Life Enrichment taught me about emotions and how to recognize what I was feeling. I am particularly grateful to Rich for his unwavering belief and constant encouragement during my personal growth work over the last five years. Two wonderful support groups at CLE taught me about relationships and pushed me to do my very best. My coed group included Meredith, Laura, Beth, Tom, Jo, Mike, Kim, Jane, and Barry. Ramp it up, guys! My men's group included Tim, Barry, Rick, Bill, Cortney, Stephen, Tim, Neale, Dennis, and Jim. My brother Ted also helped me to define how to apply emotional intelligence to project management.

My editor, Christina Parisi, was a tremendous help in writing something that made sense to others. Steve Cohn was also a great coach and an inspiration during the writing process. Jim Friel, Chris Samp, Don Knapp, Barbara Brown, and various others read early chapters and provided valuable feedback and encouragement.

I would be remiss not to recognize the great support of my home team. My children, Jack and Krista, gave me the space and support to work at home. And most of all, my wife, Norma, was helpful in too many ways to list here. Thank you for our unwavering belief in me and your support while I was working on this. I love you!

Finally, thanks to God for the ability to write and for the desire to learn and grow and become a better person. With God, all things are possible.

PART 1

An Introduction to Emotional Intelligence

My Growth in Emotional Intelligence

■ A Dangerous Situation

"Do you have any idea how dangerous it is not to be in touch with your feelings?" This question was posed to me in the summer of 2001 by Rich, a therapist who has since become my career coach and mentor. His words stopped me in my tracks. *Dangerous?* That was a curious word choice. What could be dangerous about not being in touch with my feelings? I was thirty-nine years old and had been a successful project manager (PM) for over seventeen years. I had a record of slow but steady career progression. I had been certified as a Project Management Professional (PMP) since 1995. I owned my own project management consulting business and lived, taught, and even breathed project management. No one had ever asked me about feelings before. No one had ever mentioned that there might be danger involved. What could be dangerous? What was so important about feelings?

Rich's question resonated with me but I wasn't sure why. It didn't feel dangerous to be out of touch with my emotions. However, I had a nagging sense that he saw or knew things that I didn't. On some level I recognized that the way I approached work wasn't always effective. Hard work did not always make the difference in the outcomes of the projects I managed. I wondered how others seemed to succeed with less effort. I also felt insecure about the lack of personal and professional relationships I had built, and I suspected that it was hurting me. As much as I wanted to deny that my career and relationship challenges might be related to my emotions, I began to suspect that Rich might be right.

The truth was that I wasn't aware of my feelings or emotions. I was about as emotionally aware as a small green soap dish. If I could have taken an emotional intelligence test at that time, I would have been considered the village idiot.

With Rich's help, I began to see a connection between my lack of emotional awareness and my limited success in project management. Up to that point, my project management career had been a bumpy road. While not quite a dead end street, my career path hadn't exactly taken a superhighway either. Lately that road didn't seem to be taking me anywhere. I had recently been passed over for a key promotion at Unisys. My career ladder had literally run out of rungs. Perhaps I had been promoted to my level of incompetence and was therefore living proof of the Peter Principle.

Eventually I found I could no longer ignore Rich's question about the danger, and I decided to do something about it. I knew I needed to make some changes. I was ready to make more of an investment in my emotions and relationships. Initially it wasn't for personal reasons. It was all about ROI, my return on investment for improving my emotional intelligence. I believed that my career would benefit from it. And after spending most of the last five years working on my emotional intelligence, I am happy to report that my career has benefited significantly.

As I grew, I learned how my work relationships reflected my world view. Up to that point, my relationships with my project teams and other stakeholders were weak or non-existent. That was largely the result of my project management style as a taskmaster. I was all business. Unfortunately, I placed a higher value on tasks, productivity, and outcomes than on relationships. I lacked empathy. I had a way of driving the people on my project teams that was hostile and irresponsible. My coworkers may have called me driven but they would never have characterized me as a warm and fuzzy relationship person. At best people warmed up to me over time.

My big shift came when I began to recognize the value of emotions and relationships in the workplace. I became aware of feelings and learned to trust them as a source of information. I learned to recognize and acknowledge when I felt angry, scared, or happy. I also began to pay attention to what those around me were feeling and to consider that information when making decisions. By doing this I was able to better manage my projects, and to be a better leader of people.

I learned the importance of stakeholder relationships and invested in relationships with friends, co-workers, and other leaders. I learned how critical relationships and support were to be successful on large projects. My relationships began to grow as did my ability to lead others.

The results were nothing short of impressive. The investment and changes I made began to improve my effectiveness as a PM. Within a year of beginning my work on emotions and relationships, I was asked to lead a fast-moving project of twelve people. As I demonstrated success with this team, my responsibilities grew until I was managing seventy-five people across the United States and internationally. As I continued to learn and apply my skills in this area, I was able to effectively lead large teams, build strong relationships with project stakeholders, and achieve the goals of the projects I was managing.

■ Emotional Mastery for Project Managers

I am quite sure that many of you are thinking "of course, you idiot" when I talk about mastery of emotions leading to success as a PM. You were probably among the five million people that bought one of Daniel Goleman's books on emotional intelligence and then actually read it. Yes, of course emotions play a role at work, no matter what your position. They are of special concern to those of us in project management and leadership. Emotions play a direct role in our success as PMs and leaders.

I was not one of the five million people who bought Goleman's first book, *Emotional Intelligence: Why It Can Matter More Than IQ* when it came out in 1997. In fact, I wasn't even sure what emotional intelligence was when I first began working on my emotional awareness. It wasn't until I decided to include emotional intelligence as part of the curriculum for the project management course I taught at Northwestern University that I began to read the published materials on the topic. By then I had accepted the fact that I lacked emotional intelligence; proving, I suppose, that admitting I had a problem was the first step toward recovery. More than that, I had begun to grow and make changes and to experience greater success as a project manager.

After my own powerful experience with emotional intelligence, I conducted some research to see what experience other PMs had with emotional intelligence. In late 2005, I conducted a survey of over 100 PMs to determine their beliefs and attitudes about emotional intelligence. The results were very interesting (see Appendix K for details). Most of the PMs I surveyed thought that emotional intelligence was important to success as a PM and were interested in learning more. However, the survey also indicated that most PMs didn't know very much about emotional intelligence.

Was this surprising? Not really. Sure, PMs understand basic project management techniques and the contents of the *Guide to the Project Management Body of Knowledge (PMBOK® Guide)*. They have also pursued PMP certification and become black-belt masters of project scheduling tools like MS Project, Artemis, or NIKU. In fact, those are prerequisites for success even as a junior PM; consider them entry criteria. But in order to advance your career, you will need strong interpersonal skills or soft skills. Emotional intelligence provides the framework for those interpersonal skills.

Do you see a connection between emotional intelligence and your own success as a PM? Are you trying to advance your career? Do you ever feel frustrated by lack of opportunity even though you have done all you can to improve your technical project management skills? Perhaps you are doing things the hard way as I did, working harder to make up for soft skills.

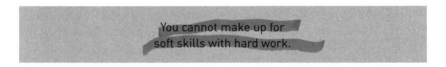

You cannot make up for soft skills with hard work.

To advance as a PM requires understanding and mastery of emotional intelligence concepts. Yes, mastery of emotional intelligence. PMs who master emotional intelligence can develop their careers by delivering more consistently and by taking on larger and more important projects. In fact, success with large and complex projects depends largely on the level of emotional intelligence of the PM.

PMs who master emotional intelligence will set themselves apart from other PMs. They will be able to achieve more with the same team. They will excel in their careers. And they will feel more satisfied with themselves and their relationships with others.

> PMs that master emotional intelligence will set themselves apart from other PMs.

■ Project Management Is Competitive

Most project managers feel the need to set themselves apart from other project managers. If you feel under pressure to compete, you are not alone. Project management is a very competitive field. As an example, consider the recent

Annual Growth in Certified Project Managers (PMPs)

Figure 1-1: Growth in Certified Project Managers (PMPs).

growth in PMP certification as shown in Figure 1-1. PMs increasingly seek certification as a way to differentiate themselves from other PMs. PMP certification has skyrocketed as a result. When I achieved my PMP certification back in 1995, I was number 4,410. By the end of 2005, the total number of certified PMs had exploded to 184,461. In fact, the number of PMs certified in 2005 alone (59,602) was more than the number certified in the first 10 years of the PMP certification program (52,443).[1]

PMP certification does not in itself make a PM more capable; it simply proves that you have the requisite project management experience and can pass the multiple-choice certification exam. To be truly effective you need to be able to implement projects and work well with your team. Emotional intelligence will help you do that.

Emotional intelligence and certification are two very different things. However, the pursuit of PMP certification demonstrates that PMs are seeking every advantage they can get. Emotional intelligence can be just one more way of setting themselves apart. I believe that this will lead to an increased interest in developing and applying emotional intelligence to project management.

---

[1] Project Management Institute (PMI). *PMI Today.* Project Management Institute, Inc. 1993, 1994, 1995, 1996, 1997, 1998, 1999, 2000, 2001, 2002, 2003, 2004, 2005.

■ What Is Emotional Intelligence?

The term emotional intelligence was actually coined by two psychologists, Peter Salovey and John D. Mayer, in 1990. I am a little surprised they didn't call it the Salomayer Principle or something similar. I bet if they had known that Daniel Goleman would come along in 1995 and use the term for the title of his best-selling book, they would certainly have used their own names. In any case, they simply called it emotional intelligence and gave it the following definition:

> *Emotional Intelligence:* "the ability to monitor one's own and others' feelings and emotions, to discriminate among them and to use this information to guide one's thinking and action."
> —Peter Salovey and John D. Mayer[2]

While Salovey and Mayer continued their research work, in 1995 Goleman wrote *Emotional Intelligence: Why It Can Matter More Than IQ*. This was the right message at the right time and soon Goleman was a best-selling author whose name became synonymous with emotional intelligence. Goleman has since gone on to write several more books on the topic. In one of their recent books, Goleman and co-author Cary Cherniss state that emotional intelligence, at the most general level, refers to:

> "the abilities to recognize and regulate emotions in ourselves and in others"
> —Daniel Goleman and Gary Cherniss[3]

As a PM, I hold a pragmatic view of emotional intelligence, thinking of it as "knowing and managing our own emotions and those of others for improved performance." I am interested in the application of emotional intelligence

---

[2]Peter Salovey and John D. Mayer. *Emotional Intelligence, Imagination Cognition, and Personality,* Volume 9, No. 3. Amityville, NY: Baywood Publishing Co., 1990.

[3]Cary Cherniss and David Goleman. *The Emotionally Intelligent Workplace.* Hoboken, NJ: John Wiley & Sons, Inc., 2001.

to life in general as well as specifically to the field of project management. In a project setting, the understanding and use of emotions helps us to have more enjoyable, predictable, and successful projects. That is what the remainder of this book is about.

■ Measuring Your Emotional Intelligence

Each of us has some level of emotional intelligence. The question is, how do we know what that level is? It would certainly be convenient if emotional intelligence were as easy to measure as height or weight. Unfortunately, that is not the case. There are numerous different assessments of emotional intelligence. The instruments tend to be different in three areas: the person providing the assessment, the mechanism for measurement, and the underlying framework.

In terms of who provides the assessment, most of these emotional intelligence assessments available are self-reported. In other words, the individual being assessed completes the instrument him or herself. For a more objective and complete view, there are also multi-rater instruments that can provide 360-degree reviews.

Emotional intelligence assessments also vary in terms of how they measure emotional intelligence. Some are based on traits and others are based on abilities. Examples of assessments that measure traits include answering questions about how individuals tend to respond in various situations. The instruments that measure abilities might show a photo or a short video followed by a series of related questions.

Finally, assessments vary in terms of the underlying framework of emotional intelligence competencies. As we will see in Chapter 2, numerous researchers have developed their own frameworks for emotional intelligence. Some of the best known are Daniel Goleman, Peter Salovey, John Mayer, and Rueven BarOn.

All of the assessments suffer from a question of validity. By validity, I mean the ability to consistently and reliably measure emotional intelligence in individuals. While the authors of each assessment instrument will tout the validity of what they are measuring, there are no validated instruments for measuring emotional intelligence. See Appendix J for a review of the various instruments available and the claims to validity.

Before we entirely give up the idea of measuring emotional intelligence, we should take a look at what some of the existing tools can tell us about ourselves. It is possible to get an idea of your level of emotional intelligence

Table 1-1: Emotional Intelligence Mini-Assessment

	YES	NO
1. Do you feel like you should be more excited about a special event than you are?	☐	☐
2. Do you find yourself not crying under circumstances when you believe others would cry?	☐	☐
3. Do you pride yourself on never getting angry?	☐	☐
4. Have you ever been told you are abrasive, unfeeling, or uncaring?	☐	☐
5. Are you frequently surprised that your expectations of others differ from what actually happens?	☐	☐
6. Do you feel that the problems others have are largely their own fault?	☐	☐
7. Do you find it difficult to work with people on your team whose background differs from your own?	☐	☐
8. Do you find yourself upset or unable to focus when your spouse or a team member is upset?	☐	☐
9. Do you blow up with your spouse, children, or project team over seemingly innocuous remarks or circumstances?	☐	☐
10. Would your closest friends or spouse say that you had problems managing your emotions?	☐	☐
11. Do you frequently make jokes or use sarcasm?	☐	☐
12. Do you storm out of meetings, send flaming emails, or slam doors?	☐	☐
13. Are your relationships with your project team, managers, or sponsors superficial and limited to the task at hand?	☐	☐
14. Do you find that you have minor skirmishes with specific individuals on an ongoing basis?	☐	☐
15. Do you feel like the victim of others or that you say yes when you really want to say no?	☐	☐
16. Do people leave your project teams because of you?	☐	☐
17. Do you find it difficult to communicate?	☐	☐
18. Are you ever surprised that your team doesn't understand your project objectives?	☐	☐
19. Do you experience conflict on projects that never seems to get resolved?	☐	☐
20. Do you want to do a better job of establishing charisma or presence as a leader?	☐	☐
TOTAL	___	___

Table 1-2: Scoring the Emotional Intelligence Mini Assessment

Score	What it means
17–20	You are doing great; you are in the minority of project managers who understand emotional intelligence. This book may help you to fine tune your approach.
13–16	You are doing well, but could use some improvement in a few key areas.
7–12	You have some strong areas but also have opportunities to improve in others. Some work on emotional intelligence will help you to deliver more consistently.
1–6	You have significant opportunities to improve your emotional intelligence. An investment in this area will provide a great pay-off for you in terms of project outcomes and career success.

using a simple set of questions such as those shown in Table 1-1. Though the outcome will be subjective, it will provide some information about your level of EQ. Take the mini self-assessment by reviewing each item and checking "Yes" or "No" as it applies to you.

To score the mini-assessment, count the total number of no responses and use Table 1-2 above to interpret your results.

■ The Good News About Emotional Intelligence

The good news about emotional intelligence is that no matter where you are now, most experts agree that you can improve your level of emotional intelligence. In fact, experts agree that you can continue to improve your level over the course of your life. I know this to be true because I have done it. Over the last five years I have gone from "village idiot" to being aware of and managing emotions. Maybe "emotional genius" is in reach for me!

Here is more good news. Improvements in your emotional intelligence will help your career as a PM. No matter what your emotional starting point is, if you improve your level of emotional intelligence, you will do a better job of managing projects. The remainder of this book is going to tell you how to do just that. We are going to discuss in detail the various aspects of emotional intelligence; how they apply in the project management environment, and the specific activities and exercises you can use to help you improve your emotional intelligence. This will undoubtedly also help you to succeed as a PM.

■ Applying Emotional Intelligence to Project Management

The February 2006 issue of *PM Network* ran a cover story on emotional intelligence. It was interesting that this article appeared eleven years after Daniel Goleman's first book was published. When I began researching this book I found that there had been a previous *PM network* on emotional intelligence featuring Daniel Goleman in 1999. Other than these two examples and a few others, I have not found many people looking at the linkage between emotional intelligence and success in project management.

Based on my own discussions with PMs and surveys of PMs, I have come to believe that most PMs understand emotional intelligence at a conceptual level. The challenge is that they lack the tools to apply it to projects. After all, how do you apply emotional intelligence to project management? It wasn't immediately apparent to me. In my research I found that it wasn't all that apparent to others either. This book is the first book of its kind to spell out in detail how to apply emotional intelligence to projects.

The starting point for applying emotional intelligence is when we acknowledge that project management is getting work done through others. As PMs, we are dependent on others for our success. To achieve anything significant, we need a team. Big, important projects generally require large, effective project teams as well as an effective PM. As a PM, I personally want to take on larger and more complex projects since I believe that is going to advance my career. That is where the application of emotional intelligence pays off big.

> "Project management is getting work done through others."

Emotional intelligence can help PMs to:

1. develop stakeholder relationships that support the project's success
2. anticipate and avoid emotional breakdowns
3. deal with difficult team members and manage conflict
4. leverage emotional information to make better decisions
5. communicate more effectively
6. create a positive work environment and high team morale
7. cast a vision for shared project objectives that will attract, inspire, and motivate the project team

Let's look at each of these benefits in more detail.

1. Develop Stakeholder Relationships That Support the Project's Success

Relationships are the key to success as a PM. This includes the relationships with our team members as well as with the other project stakeholders. Strong relationships with all project stakeholders will buffer us during difficult times, help us gather more complete information, support us when we need it, and enable us to make better decisions. We will address stakeholder relationships in detail in Chapter 6, on relationship management.

2. Anticipate and Avoid Emotional Breakdowns

Emotional breakdowns happen when we lose it. They are the office equivalent of road rage. Over the life of a project, we can experience significant stress. For some of us, this stress will push us over the edge and cause us to do something undesirable. In Chapter 4, Self-Management, we will discuss underlying causes and triggering events for emotional breakdowns, ways we can recognize when we are at risk of a breakdown, and techniques for avoiding breakdowns.

3. Deal with Difficult Team Members and Manage Conflict

In an ideal project, there are no difficult team members and conflict is manageable. Unfortunately, that is rarely the case in practice. When we seek out high-performing individuals for our teams, we often encounter difficult team members. Emotional intelligence can provide us the tools to work with difficult individuals, help us identify ways in which we contribute to the problem, and help us to work through issues with those parties. It helps us in a similar way to address the inevitable project conflict. Emotional intelligence can help us to recognize or even anticipate conflict and deal with it before it derails the project. After the groundwork for recognizing and anticipating conflict is laid in Chapter 5, Social Awareness, we will address stakeholder relationships in Chapter 6, Relationship Management.

4. Leverage Emotional Information to Make Better Decisions

In their 2004 book titled *The Emotionally Intelligent Manager,*[4] David Caruso and Peter Salovey identified six principles of emotional intelligence. The number one principle cited in their book was Emotion Is Information.

---

[4]David R. Caruso and Peter Salovey. *The Emotionally Intelligent Manager; How to Develop and Use the Four Key Emotional Skills of Leadership.* Hoboken, NJ: John Wiley & Sons, Inc., 2004.

"Emotion Is Information"
—David R. Caruso and Peter Salovey

Our emotions are like our own personal radar. They provide us with a steady stream of information about ourselves, our team members, and our environment. When we are in touch with and able to access our emotions, we can leverage that information to make better decisions. If we are not in touch with our emotions, we are missing out on vital information about our environment (see Figure 1-2).

Emotions provide us with the extra data points that we need to make better decisions. They give us an intuitive or gut sense of what we need to do next. In a world where being right 51 percent of the time is often enough to make the difference, those extra data points may be just what it takes for us

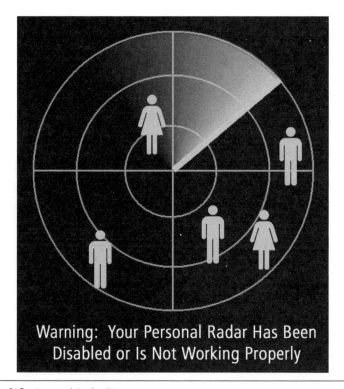

Figure 1-2: Personal Radar Warning.

to be successful. We will discuss emotional data throughout the remainder of this book. We will examine decision making in Chapter 7, Project Team Leadership.

5. Communicate More Effectively

Emotional intelligence helps us to understand ourselves as well as those around us. By understanding the emotions and motivations of our team members and other stakeholders, we can choose the words and messages that will make our point and resonate with the audience. We can anticipate difficult moments and take extra care to send just the right message with the correct emotions, whether we are speaking one-on-one with a stakeholder or addressing a group. We will address communications using emotional intelligence in Chapter 7, Project Team Leadership, as well as in Chapter 8, Creating a Positive Team Environment, and Chapter 9, Excelling with Emotional Intelligence on Large and Complex Projects.

6. Create a Positive Work Environment and High Team Morale

As PMs, we are responsible for the emotional tone of the project. We can approach this in a number of ways. We can leave the emotional tone of the project to chance, or to the various members of our team. The results we get will be unpredictable. Alternatively, we can systematically and proactively manage that project environment to create the positive outcomes we are seeking. The strategic application of emotional intelligence will allow us to create a productive and successful environment with high morale and esprit de corps. We will address this in Chapter 7, Project Team Leadership, as well as in Chapter 8, Creating a Positive Team Environment.

7. Cast a Vision for Shared Project Objectives That Will Attract, Inspire, and Motivate the Project Team

Shared project objectives are important for getting buy-in and commitment from our project team. Unfortunately, this is not always as easy as it sounds. Establishing shared objectives requires understanding the emotions and objectives of those on our project teams and then casting a vision for the project that enables those individuals to fulfill their objectives within the project. One of my first project management mentors always told me that as a PM you are dependent on your resources for success. He used to say:

> "As a PM, you live or die by your resources."

As my career has progressed, I have come to fully appreciate what he meant. The ability to attract and inspire the best project resources is going to make our projects succeed; without this ability, our chances of success are greatly diminished. We will address resources in Chapter 8, Creating a Positive Team Environment.

■ Emotional Intelligence Is Vital to Project Managers

While emotional intelligence is important to managers and leaders of all types, the unique environment of projects makes the application of emotional intelligence critical to PMs for three reasons. First, each project is unique. As PMs move from project to project, we constantly experience a change of teams, sponsors, and other stakeholders. Only rarely do we have the benefit of the same stakeholders and project team. This puts pressure on us to assess, understand, and manage the emotions of our team and stakeholders to build relationships. We need to do this each time we start a new project.

The second reason that emotional intelligence is important to PMs is that projects are temporary. Unlike general management, projects have a beginning and an end. This puts pressure on PMs to move quickly. We don't have the luxury of time to develop strong relationships and create a positive team environment. If we don't work on relationships early in the project life-cycle, our projects can get derailed and never have a chance for success. We cannot afford to get our projects off on the wrong foot.

The third reason that emotional intelligence is important to projects is the limited power and authority of the PM. In most cases, PMs do not have direct authority or power over the project team members. They cannot simply direct others to do what is needed. PMs need to use more sophisticated strategies to get their team members to achieve the desired outcomes. Without an understanding of the application of emotional intelligence, PMs may struggle to get the work of the project completed.

Given the importance to PMs, it may surprise you to find that emotional intelligence is not directly addressed in the *Guide to the Project Management Body of Knowledge (PMBOK® Guide)*, which addresses the technical aspects of Project Management in detail. The closest the *PMBOK® Guide*

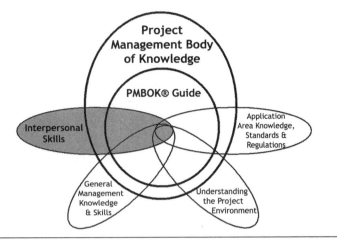

Figure 1-3: Project Management Areas of Expertise.

comes is in the area of interpersonal skills. In Figure 1-3 from the *PMBOK®
Guide,* interpersonal skills are one of the areas of expertise needed by PMs.
Not just an area of familiarity, but an area of *expertise.* Interpersonal skills are
further defined in the *PMBOK® Guide* by the following:

- effective communications
- influencing the organization
- leadership
- motivation
- negotiation and conflict management
- problem solving[5]

You can see that there is quite a bit of overlap between the *PMBOK®
Guide* and the emotional intelligence topics. I believe that our ability to leverage these interpersonal skills is dependent on our level of emotional intelligence. Unfortunately, the *PMBOK® Guide* falls short of providing steps on
how to develop and apply the interpersonal skills listed above. This book will
provide the detailed guide to developing and applying those interpersonal
skills.

---

[5]Project Management Institute (PMI). *A Guide to the Project Management Body of Knowledge (PMBOK® Guide)
Third Edition,* Project Management Institute, Inc., 2004.

If this emotional intelligence business seems a little daunting, take heart. Improving your awareness of emotional intelligence and applying it to projects is not difficult. It has the potential to provide rich rewards for you. Even small steps can make a large difference in your life and in your projects. All it takes is the desire to learn and grow and the courage to step out of your comfort zone. It may even require change.

Change is difficult for all of us. In fact, we resist change because it is easier to let inertia keep us on our current course. Staying the course was familiar to me, yet on some level I knew that it wasn't giving me the results I wanted. Once I realized how much danger was involved in staying on my previous course, I became very motivated to try something new. One definition of insanity is trying the same thing and expecting different results. If you want to get different results or different project outcomes, consider trying something different by learning about and applying emotional intelligence techniques.

2

■ A Brief Primer on Emotional Intelligence

Before we discuss the details of applying emotional intelligence to projects, it will be helpful to explore the background of emotional intelligence. This chapter provides more detail on the concept of emotional intelligence and how the writings of Daniel Goleman and other emotional intelligence researchers have contributed to the field. Using Goleman's generic model of emotional intelligence as a starting point, we will discuss an adaptation of that framework which is applicable to projects and PMs. We also provide some useful definitions for emotions, families of emotions, and emotional intelligence. Finally, we will conclude this chapter with some resources on where to go for additional information on emotional intelligence.

■ The Popularity of Emotional Intelligence

Emotional intelligence is a popular though often misunderstood term. It would be hard to have missed the buzz about it since Daniel Goleman's 1995 book *Emotional Intelligence: Why It Can Matter More Than IQ* became a national bestseller. What made Goleman's book so popular were two claims: 1) that emotional intelligence may be more important than intelligence quotient (IQ) and 2) that you can improve your emotional intelligence. Those claims are what made headlines and got emotional intelligence noticed. And while I believe those claims are true, it is not as simple as that to be successful with emotional intelligence.

I suspect that the PMs who bought Goleman's first book hoping to improve their performance and project success rates were sadly disappointed. The book was interesting and even entertaining in some places, but it fell short of providing the practical means of applying emotional intelligence to project management or to life in general. The PMs who I know are interested in learning things that will help them become better PMs and leaders. They want to understand how to apply techniques to improve their projects.

This chapter will help you to understand the basic concepts of emotions and emotional intelligence and how important these concepts are to project managers.

■ Some Useful Definitions

Emotions

> *Emotion:* "A mental state that arises spontaneously rather than through conscious effort and is often accompanied by physiological changes; a feeling: the emotions of joy, sorrow, reverence, hate, and love."
> —The American Heritage Dictionary

There is a little bit of controversy between researchers over exactly what are emotions. While most researchers agree on a core set of emotions, they differ on including less well-known emotions such as ecstasy, vigilance, adoration, and disgust.

I have learned to use a simple approach to understand a wide range of emotions. This approach uses six primary feeling words to represent groups of emotions as described by David E. Carlson in his book *Counseling and Self-Esteem*. The primary feeling words can be summed up in the acronym SASHET: sad, angry, scared, happy, excited, and tender.[1]

Figure 2-1 shows these 6 primary feeling words as well as the range of emotions each of these words represents. Notice that the figure shows an increasing intensity of each emotion as you move from the center of the wheel to the outside.

---

[1]David Carlson. *Counseling and Self-Esteem.* Nashville, TN: Thomas Nelson, Inc., 1995.

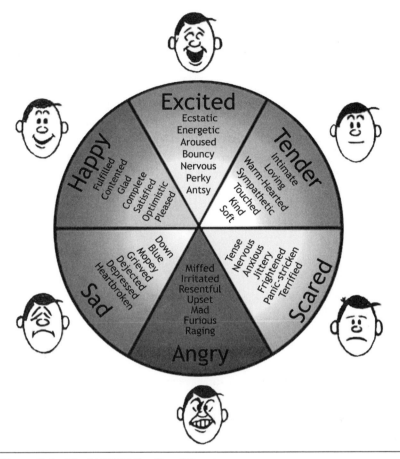

Figure 2-1: The SASHET Families of Emotions.

As you can see, the SASHET framework includes three "negative" families of emotions: sad, angry, and scared. These emotions are negative only in the sense that they are perceived as negative. As we will see, all emotions provide us with data about ourselves and our environment. Just because we experience negative emotions doesn't mean that we feel negative.

The SASHET framework also includes the three "positive" families of emotions, including happy, excited, and tender and all the subtle variations of those emotions.

Using the SASHET framework, we learn to distinguish between the various groups of emotions. It is not critical that we pinpoint the exact emotions we are feeling. However, it is important to know which of the feeling families we are experiencing.

Emotional Intelligence

We briefly introduced emotional intelligence in Chapter 1 and provided some of the definitions used by various researchers. Emotional intelligence is sometimes called emotional quotient, or EQ, to show the relationship to IQ or intelligence quotient. Some researchers use emotional intelligence, EI, and EQ interchangeably. For the remainder of this book, we will use the term EQ to mean emotional intelligence.

As previously noted, Daniel Goleman is the most recognized of the emotional intelligence researchers and journalists. He gets credit for the popularity of emotional intelligence. However, he wasn't the first to study EQ. As noted in Chapter 1, the first emotional intelligence researchers included Peter Salovey and John Mayer. Some would also credit Harvard education professor Howard Gardner as the initiator of the original research work on emotional intelligence.

While some of the research work on emotional intelligence is common, each researcher used a slightly different approach. This is not unexpected for a field that is relatively immature. But there are other factors at work. There is a great deal of prestige and financial reward at stake and that has led to controversy between the researchers. For example, there is disagreement over something as simple as exactly how to define an emotion, as we noted above. There is even disagreement over some of the claims made in the popular press about the value of emotional intelligence.

We briefly mentioned emotional intelligence assessments in Chapter 1; this is another area of disagreement for the research community. Can we objectively measure emotional intelligence? If objective and accurate emotional intelligence tests were available, they would be at least as valuable as IQ testing and perhaps even more valuable. Unfortunately, this has led to a proliferation of various emotional intelligence instruments (as evidence, my brother and I developed the simple tool found in Chapter 1.) It has also fostered a great deal of criticism among the various authors of emotional intelligence instruments. At this stage, my recommendation is to use the assessment that provides you the information you need. I have included information about some of the most popular emotional intelligence assessments in Appendix J.

The good news is that there is some level of agreement over the framework to be used for applying emotional intelligence. This has not always been the case. Mayer and Salovey published one of the first frameworks for applying emotional intelligence in their article titled "Emotional Intelligence," published in 1990. Daniel Goleman first published a framework for emotional intelligence in his 1998 book *Working with Emotional Intelligence.* Figure 2-2[2] shows the Mayer and Salovey framework and highlights the areas where Goleman's work overlapped that of Mayer and Salovey.

The various frameworks have evolved and converged a little in the years since they were first introduced. In particular, the Goleman framework has become better organized and easier to understand and apply. Perhaps because of this or because of the popularity of his books, Goleman's framework has become the *de facto* standard for applying emotional intelligence. This framework is shown in Figure 2-3.[3]

This framework is made up of four quadrants. Two of the quadrants represent personal competence or a focus on self. The other two quadrants represent social competence or a focus on others.

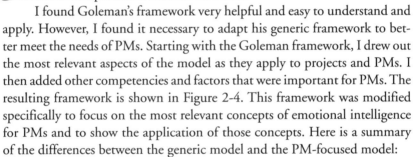

I found Goleman's framework very helpful and easy to understand and apply. However, I found it necessary to adapt his generic framework to better meet the needs of PMs. Starting with the Goleman framework, I drew out the most relevant aspects of the model as they apply to projects and PMs. I then added other competencies and factors that were important for PMs. The resulting framework is shown in Figure 2-4. This framework was modified specifically to focus on the most relevant concepts of emotional intelligence for PMs and to show the application of those concepts. Here is a summary of the differences between the generic model and the PM-focused model:

1. The structure has been changed. I put the first competencies to be mastered at the bottom, to show upward progression. I also added a fifth category called Team Leadership as an overarching group of competencies to be mastered after the first 4 emotional intelligence domains.
2. Some competencies were de-emphasized, including self-confidence and self-assessment.
3. Some competencies have been dropped altogether to allow a focus on the most important competencies for PMs. They include trustworthiness, conscientiousness, adaptability, achievement drive, initiative, service

---

[2]Peter Salovey and John D. Mayer. *Emotional Intelligence, Imagination Cognition, and Personality,* Volume 9, No. 3. Amityville, NY: Baywood Publishing Co., Inc., 1990.

[3]Daniel Goleman, Richard Boyatzis, and Annie McKeel. *Primal Leadership.* Boston: Harvard Business School Press, 2002, p. 39.

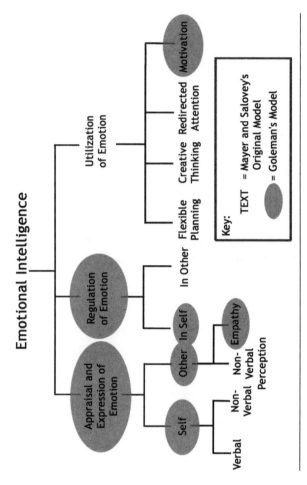

Figure 2-2: Comparison of Early Emotional Intelligence Frameworks.

	Self (Personal Competence)	Other (Social Competence)
Recognition	**Self-Awareness** - Emotional self-awareness - Accurate self-assessment - Self-confidence	**Social Awareness** - Empathy - Organizational awareness - Service
Regulation	**Self-Management** - Emotional self-control - Transparency - Adaptability - Achievement - Initiative - Optimism	**Relationship Management** - Inspirational leadership - Influence - Developing others - Change Catalyst - Conflict management - Building bonds - Teamwork and collaboration

Figure 2-3: Goleman's Framework of Emotional Competencies.

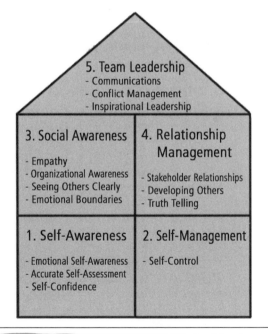

Figure 2-4: Emotional Intelligence Framework for Project Management.

orientation, influence, change catalyst, building bonds, and teamwork and collaboration.

4. I added the social awareness competency of emotional boundaries, and the relationship management competency of truth telling.

This is the framework we will use throughout this book. Let's take a brief look at this framework and the five domains.

Self-Awareness

The first domain of the framework is self-awareness, which means understanding ourselves and our emotions. It involves the competencies of emotional self-awareness, accurate self-assessment, and self-confidence. Self-awareness is the first building block of emotional intelligence. Until we understand how we feel and can accurately assess our emotional state, we will understand emotions from only an intellectual point of view. We need to be able to understand emotions at a gut level—what is going on with us.

Accurate self-assessment includes understanding our own strengths and weaknesses and being willing to explore them both on our own and with others. Self-confidence is the ability to be grounded, secure, and self-assured in whatever situation we find ourselves.

Self-Management

Building on the emotional understanding we gain with self-awareness, we use self-management to manage and guide our emotional state. Self-management is the ability to control our emotions so they don't control us. In fact, the domain of self-management includes just one competency—self-control.

Self-control is a critical competency important for everyone. We have all experienced people and situations that have pushed our buttons and tried our patience. Self-control is what helps us to maintain our cool and not "lose it."

Social Awareness

Social awareness occurs when we expand our awareness to include the emotions of those around us. The domain of social awareness includes empathy, organizational awareness, seeing others clearly, and emotional boundaries.

Empathy is a critical skill for project managers and leaders of all types. Empathy is the ability to understand and relate to the feelings of others; to put ourselves in their shoes. Organizational awareness is the ability to interpret the context for emotions in an organization. It includes the spoken and unspoken rules and values that guide each organization.

Seeing others clearly is the ability to accurately assess and understand others. As PMs, it is important that we are able to understand and interpret the emotions of our team members and other stakeholders. We all have this skill in varying degrees.

Emotional boundaries help us to understand where we end and where others begin. If we have a solid command of emotional boundaries, we are more likely to speak up and say no when we should, we will have more realistic expectations of others, and we will take responsibility for our own emotions and actions and let others be responsible for theirs.

Relationship Management

Relationship management means using the awareness of our own emotions and those of others to build strong relationships. Those strong relationships will serve us on our projects. After all, projects are nearly always team efforts. The domain of relationship management includes the competencies of stakeholder relationships, developing others, and truth telling.

Stakeholder relationship includes the systematic identification, analysis, and management of the relationships with our project stakeholders. Developing others is making an investment in the growth and development of those we work with through feedback and coaching. Finally, truth telling looks at responsible ways in which we can be direct and honest.

Team Leadership

Team leadership is focused on the emotional skills needed to effectively lead project teams. This includes communications, conflict management, and inspirational leadership.

Project managers need to be great communicators. There is no way around that fact. The larger the team, the more important communications become. The communications competency includes the ability to understand and manage the emotional tone of the project team through communications, as well as the ability to be congruent between actions, one-on-one communications, and communications in groups.

An important part of project management is conflict management. The conflict management competency is not new, rather, the focus is on ways to resolve project conflict using emotional intelligence.

Inspirational leadership looks at how project team leaders need to cast a vision that will engage, motivate, and inspire the team.

■ How to Improve Your Understanding of Emotional Intelligence Concepts

The good news is that after reading these first two chapters, you probably already know more about applying emotional intelligence than most of your fellow PMs. I highly encourage you to continue reading and learning more about emotional intelligence through a variety of sources.

During my survey conducted in November 2005, I asked PMs how they learned about emotional intelligence. (See Appendix K for more details about my 2005 Survey of Emotional Intelligence in Project Managers.) The highest responses were through discussions, magazines/journals, books, classes, and blogs or web sites (Figure 2-5). Let's look at each of these sources in detail.

Magazines and Journals on Emotional Intelligence

Magazines were cited most commonly as the source of information about emotional intelligence. Appendix F contains a list of magazines and journals where articles on this topic may be found.

Books on Emotional Intelligence

Appendix G contains a list of emotional intelligence books with a quick summary of each. For those interested in just one or two books, you will find my favorites for PMs listed here.

Take a Course

Several organizations (including the author's) provide training in emotional intelligence. See Appendix H for courses offered in the United States.

Blogs and Web Sites Related to Emotional Intelligence

Appendix I contains a list of emotional intelligence blogs and web sites. There is an overwhelming amount of online information and wading through it can often prove challenging and time-consuming. I have provided some comments here on those sites that I have found the most useful and have categorized the materials to save you time and effort.

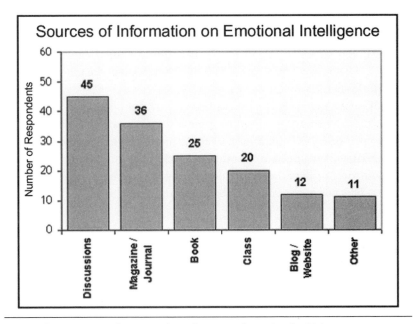

Figure 2-5: Sources of Emotional Intelligence Information for PMs.

Coaches and Mentors

I highly recommend working with a mentor or coach. Working with my personal coach, Rich Blue, was essential for me in learning emotional intelligence techniques and improving my effectiveness. A staggering number of emotional intelligence coaches can be found on the Internet using Google or other search tools.

Assessments

Emotional intelligence assessments can also provide some information for us. Despite the limitations already mentioned, any information is better than no information. More information on available assessments can be found in Appendix J.

■ Learning About Emotional Intelligence Is Only the First Step

While it is important to learn about emotional intelligence, that is only the first step. I personally learned about emotional intelligence through a combination of coaching, study, and ongoing application. I won't downplay the importance of coaching and study but I truly believe that people learn best by doing. There is a big difference between studying a concept and applying it. That is why I have focused on the application of the topics and concepts in this book.

To make the most of what we learn about emotional intelligence and to retain what we learn, we need to apply it to our lives and to our projects. This book is heavy on application. Each chapter will provide a series of techniques that will be summarized at the end of the unit. I highly encourage you to choose some or all of the techniques and put them to use after reading each chapter. This will help you to get the most out of this book.

PART 2

Project Management Begins with Self-Management

As leaders, we must focus on ourselves before we can try to manage or lead others. Without mastery of our own emotions, we will never be in a position to lead others.

Self-awareness and self-management are the two key aspects of self-leadership. With self-awareness, we identify our own emotional states and the sources of our emotions. Self-management means handling or directing our emotions with skill. This is not possible without awareness.

3

Self-Awareness

■ Introduction to Self-Awareness

The first building block of emotional intelligence is self-awareness. Self-awareness is our ability to recognize our own emotions and their effects on us and others. Without being aware of and understanding our own emotions, it will be difficult to move into the other emotional competencies like self-management, social awareness, or team leadership.

In her book *Traveling Mercies,* Anne Lamott writes "you must be present to win" in reference to the way one of her friends was living his life.[1] That book has nothing whatsoever to do with project management or emotional intelligence. However, the phrase "you must be present to win" is very relevant to self-awareness. Present, as in, in the moment. Self-awareness is about the here and now. With self-awareness, we are striving to get in touch with exactly what we are feeling right now. It is about knowing ourselves in this moment.

Self-awareness is not about what happened yesterday or what will happen tomorrow. The only time that what happened yesterday is relevant is if it is impacting how we are feeling right now. Otherwise, we should leave the past in the past. The key to self-awareness is to focus on what we are feeling now.

---

[1] Anne Lamott. *Traveling Mercies; Some Thoughts on Faith.* NY: Anchor Books, 1999.

33

Self-Awareness Is the Starting Point for Emotional Intelligence

Understanding what we feel and what is going on with us is the basic skill we need for self-awareness and for all emotional intelligence. Recall from Chapter 2 the SASHET families of emotions as shown in Figure 3-1. To be self-aware means that we need to know which of these feelings we have at that moment. Are we feeling sad, happy, excited, or some combination of all of these?

As shown in Figure 3-2, the Emotional Intelligence Model for Project Management includes the following competencies under the domain of self-awareness: emotional self-awareness, accurate self-assessment, and self-confidence. We are going to talk about each of these in the following sections.

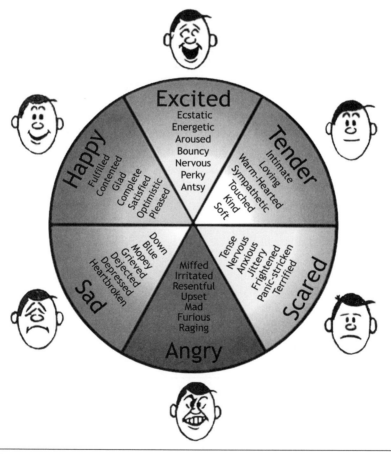

Figure 3-1: SASHET Families of Emotions.

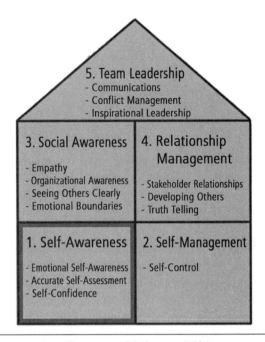

Figure 3-2: Emotional Intelligence Model Showing Self-Awareness.

■ Emotional Self-Awareness

Self-awareness is the ability to understand our own emotions. It is about being conscious or mindful of our own emotional state. Self-awareness may be challenging for us for a number of reasons. First, our emotions can be as volatile as the weather in Chicago. They mix, morph, and evolve, often in a short span of time. One minute we might feel excited and happy about a friend's plan to visit us. A moment later, we might be scared or angry about the same event.

Second, we may actually experience a mix of emotions at any one time. We can be excited, happy, scared, and angry all at once. More commonly, we have one emotion at the surface that masks another emotion. This second emotion is often the more important of the two. Consider a parent who waits up for a teenager with a curfew of 10:00 P.M. If the teenager shows up at home at 1:00 A.M., the parent will often express anger. The parent is likely feeling scared, which is the more important secondary emotion.

A third reason that self-awareness may be difficult is due to childhood wounds that inhibit our ability to access our feelings. For most of my life I suppressed many of my emotions. This was partly a result of growing up in an alcoholic family where everyone (except my dad) was denied the opportunity to show or express emotions. My siblings and I quickly learned that it was safer to mute, ignore, or hide what we were really feeling.

As an adult I found that all my emotions were dampened. In particular, though, I found it difficult to feel happy, angry, or sad. When my brother Marty killed himself in 1996, I remember feeling numb. It was a long time before I actually felt sad and angry about his death.

What I lacked in happiness, anger and sadness, I made up for in fear. I was afraid most of the time. I was scared about how I was performing at work, scared about money, scared about how I was being perceived, and scared about nearly everything. I still deal with a lot of fear in my life though not nearly as much as I did when I was younger.

It took a lot of hard work over the course of nearly five years before I was able to access my emotions directly. This included working with a coach and as well as with two support groups. I learned various techniques for getting in touch with my emotions. I learned to recognize the physical sensations that lead to emotions. I learned to journal. Eventually I was able to feel angry and sad, and to deal with the fear I felt all the time.

We are all different when it comes to being aware of our emotions. For most people, the kind of work that I went through is unnecessary. However, each person may find that some emotions are easier to recognize than others. Some people may be in denial about how they really feel about a situation. Most of us want to believe we are strong and unaffected by various circumstances. It's rare that you can work on a project without experiencing at least one emotion and this emotion directly affects how successful we are in our work. We actually become stronger when we recognize the underlying feelings we're experiencing. Self-awareness is about developing this capacity. It is similar to building a physical muscle in our bodies. Let's look at specific ways that we can begin to train ourselves to recognize our emotions.

Getting Physical with Our Feelings

Emotions have a physical manifestation in our bodies and we can use these sensations to recognize our emotions. What we feel emotionally is reflected in what we feel physically. If you are having trouble feeling an emotion or cannot name what you are feeling, you might be able to use your body as a clue. You can train yourself to recognize what it feels like to be happy or sad.

How do we know which sensations go with each feeling? Figure 3-3 provides a quick guide to the sensations that go with each of the feeling fam-

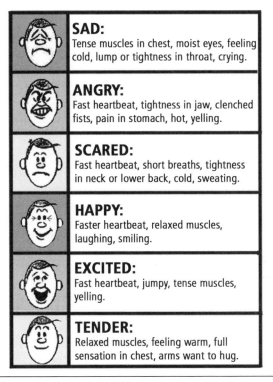

Figure 3-3: Physical Sensations for SASHET Feelings.

ilies. We need to consider things like heart rate, feelings of heat or cold, muscle tightness, and our own eyes. It is important to note that these physical sensations can vary from person to person. As you begin to pay attention to your own body, you may note minor variations from the list provided.

While our physical sensations provide one clue about what we are feeling, there are other ways that our bodies will help us to assess our feelings. Our faces can also provide information about our emotional state. The eyes have been called the window to the soul.

Silvan Tomkins and Paul Ekman were psychologists who first documented the strong link between facial expression and emotions. In the 1960s, Tomkins and Ekman conducted extensive experiments involving human facial expressions and emotions. They found that across all societies, there were a common set of facial expressions caused by underlying emotions. Tomkins and Ekman decoded the facial expressions and catalogued 3,000 unique expressions having emotional meaning. That is, they determined 3,000 different ways for our faces to express emotions. Just as important, Tomkins and Ekman noted that these facial expressions are difficult to fake.

Am I advocating that you learn the 3,000 different facial expressions and the corresponding emotions? No. The face just provides us with additional data to aid in emotional self-awareness. By understanding what emotions look like, you can use your own face to better understand what you are feeling. If other methods fail to tell us how we are feeling, the face is a reliable indicator. In Chapter 5, we will use our understanding of how emotions appear on our faces to understand the faces and emotions of those around us.

By studying our own faces, we can learn about the emotions we are feeling. We can use our own faces as a guide. We don't have to know 3,000 expressions. We have to learn only the various ways in which the 6 families of feelings will show on our faces.

The chart shown in Figure 3-4 contains a quick taxonomy of the faces representing the SASHET families of feelings, including a picture and a brief description of each feeling family.

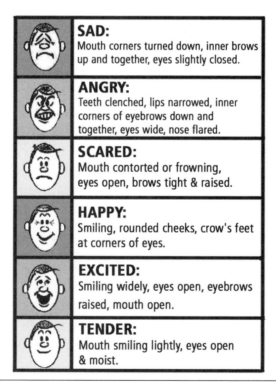

SAD:
Mouth corners turned down, inner brows up and together, eyes slightly closed.

ANGRY:
Teeth clenched, lips narrowed, inner corners of eyebrows down and together, eyes wide, nose flared.

SCARED:
Mouth contorted or frowning, eyes open, brows tight & raised.

HAPPY:
Smiling, rounded cheeks, crow's feet at corners of eyes.

EXCITED:
Smiling widely, eyes open, eyebrows raised, mouth open.

TENDER:
Mouth smiling lightly, eyes open & moist.

Figure 3-4: Facial Expressions for the SASHET Feelings.

If you are skeptical that faces reveal emotions, consider people who make large financial decisions based on emotions. Yes, I am talking about professional poker players. Poker players have long been aware of the fact that faces reveal emotions. The term "poker face" has come to mean a face that reveals no hint of a person's thoughts or emotions.

I like to watch the *World Poker Tour* on television. In fact, for a short time I was a junkie and could not stop watching it. I was fascinated by the various ways in which the different players would hide or camouflage their faces so as not to give away their emotions to their opponents. Each player would try to mislead the other players about what they felt. At the same time, the players were trying to read the emotions of the other players from their faces and body language.

Most players use sunglasses and hats to hide much of their faces. One player named Phil Laak has been dubbed the "Unibomber" for his tendency to wear dark glasses and a hooded sweatshirt to cover much of his head. When he is in a stressful situation (or if he wants others to think he is under stress), Phil will take in the drawstrings on his hood until none of his face is visible to the other players!

Write It Out

A third way to determine what we are feeling is to journal. We can use journaling to explore our feelings in the moment. We may also reflect on something that occurred in the past and re-experience the feelings we previously felt (or should have felt). We can also use journaling to look ahead to the future and explore how we may feel about something we have not yet experienced.

There are many different ways to journal and you may have to experiment to find one that works for you. I have kept a journal for the last five years and I simply use it to jot down what is going on with me emotionally. I sometimes write as if I am praying. You might write as if you are writing to someone else or to yourself.

Emotional Red Flags

Another tool that can help us to be more self-aware is the concept of emotional red flags. As I learned about emotional intelligence and about myself, I became aware of ways in which I acted that were less than helpful. I learned to recognize behaviors that were early symptoms of my own emotional problems. I called these emotional red flags.

The value of these emotional red flags was to help me to understand what was going on with me; increasing my self-awareness. These red flags helped me to identify underlying emotional problems. As I became more self-aware and began to recognize the symptoms of these red flags, I was empowered to make better choices and change the outcomes. The key, and most important part for me, was to recognize these emotional red flags. Here are five emotional red flags:

1. Inappropriate Humor

We would all probably agree that humor is good, especially on projects. I used to consider myself very funny and believed it to be one of my strengths. What I found was that I was using inappropriate humor. My humor was inappropriate because I was using it to be indirect. I was afraid of telling the truth and making my point directly, so I would make a joke instead. As an example, consider when someone showed up late to a project team meeting. Instead of confronting the issue directly, I would make a joke like "looks like the trains didn't wait for you today." I was angry that they did not show up on time. Unfortunately, I wasn't aware of my anger so I did not voice it directly. Or, I was not comfortable expressing my anger so I hid it. In either case, my use of humor was indirect and not effective at addressing the behavior of my team member.

My humor was a way of masking my true feelings of anger or fear. That was a clue that I was not aware of my emotions. Now before I make a joke, I ask myself "Why do I feel the need to make a joke right now? What emotion am I feeling?" Most likely I feel angry, sad, or scared. When angry, I may choose to single someone out and try to make fun of them. Or if I feel sad, I may try to draw attention to myself or get affirmed by others with a cheap laugh. When scared, I may make a joke about someone to shift the attention from me. In each of these cases, I need to look beyond the humor to determine the underlying emotion.

2. Use of Sarcasm

The use of sarcasm is closely related to inappropriate humor. Perhaps sarcasm is just humor taken to an extreme. We use sarcasm for the same reasons as inappropriate humor—we don't want to say something directly. As an example of sarcasm, consider when you say to your boss "everyone thinks the new expense approval policy is a GREAT idea" and then you tack on, "just kidding." The "just kidding" is the exclamation point that makes sarcasm and inappropriate humor easy to spot. When you say "just kidding," you are saying "don't get mad at me for saying what I really feel."

For some excellent examples of sarcasm in the workplace, rent the movie *Tommy Boy*. David Spade plays Richard Hayden opposite Chris Farley as Tommy Callahan III. Spade is naturally very sarcastic and he does not disappoint in this movie.

3. Passive Aggressive Behavior

Another red flag is passive aggressive behavior, which can be very subtle and is often confused with simply being a jerk. Here is the definition of passive aggressive behavior from the *Wikipedia:*

> Passive-aggressive behavior refers to passive, sometimes obstructionist resistance to authoritative instructions in interpersonal or occupational situations. Sometimes a method of dealing with stress or frustration, it results in the person attacking other people in subtle, indirect, and seemingly passive ways. It can manifest itself as resentment, stubbornness, procrastination, sullenness, or intentional failure at doing requested tasks.

Passive aggressive behavior can manifest itself in the project environment in various ways including showing up late for meetings, failure to follow instructions, failure to meet deliverable deadlines, or failing to ask for approval in advance. Let's look at a couple of these in detail.

Being on time for meetings can be challenging. There are a lot of meetings on a project, and it may be difficult to be on time for all of them. If individuals are late, it doesn't necessarily indicate passive-aggressive behavior. As PMs, we need to learn to discern between occasional tardiness and passive-aggressive behavior.

When individuals intentionally show up late for meetings, they are sending a passive message to the other people attending that meeting. That message may be something like "I don't like this project," "I really didn't want to come," or "I have better things to do."

Of course sometimes people are late for reasons other than passive aggressiveness and this is what makes it a bit tricky. We are all late sometimes. It happens to everyone. If an individual is late only once in a great while, that is no big deal. It is also not a big deal if we recognize that we are going to be late and we call to let the others know or provide some sort of advance notice. It is when we have a pattern of showing up late, there may be something else going on.

I once worked for a project director who would lock the conference room doors at the time that the meeting was supposed to start. Anyone who came late would be forced to knock at the door and then would be subjected to ridicule upon entering the conference room. It was his way of trying to force people to be on time. I think this is a bit heavy-handed. I try to communicate directly with the individual, privately, to let them know why I feel it is important to be on time to meetings and to understand any issues they may have.

Another category of passive aggressive behavior is overstepping authority, such as failing to ask for approval in advance. There is a fine line between a go-getter and someone who breaks the rules or rebels against authority figures. All PMs have heard the old adage, "It is better to ask for forgiveness than approval." That saying likely came from a passive-aggressive person. It might very well be true. But that adage can also be construed to mean, "Do whatever you want." Certainly as PMs we need to show initiative. This means that sometimes we are going to need to act in the absence of clear authority. However, we also need to be aware of what is really going on. Is there some underlying reason for acting this way? For example, is it unclear what we are responsible for? If so, we should get clarification from our manager so that our lines of responsibility and authority are clear. If we show a pattern of not getting approval from our leaders, or acting as if it is not required, we may be acting passive-aggressively.

The emotion that underlies all passive-aggressive behavior is anger. It sounds ugly, but it is true. When we act in passive-aggressive ways, we are angry. Perhaps we resent the authority figure in the situation. What ends up happening is that we act in ways that look like we are complying but we really aren't. We show up late. We "misunderstand" instructions from the boss. We turn in deliverables late. We act in the absence of authority.

4. Playing the Victim

Another common red flag is playing the victim. This was something I did frequently. I used to complain about why I was unable to change jobs, or why I lived in a certain part of the country, how I was stuck in the wrong line at the supermarket, and about a host of other situations. I was playing the victim by not going for what it was that I wanted.

Now that I recognize this behavior in myself, I am more sensitive to it in others. Playing the victim instead of completing an activity, changing jobs, staying in a lousy marriage, working for bad bosses, not going for a better position or being a leader, and numerous other outcomes are possible scenarios. The rationalization for victimhood includes all the reasons or the people who "prevented" them from doing what they should have done. It all smacks of victim-hood.

I know a woman who, after divorcing her husband, continues to work at the same company and in the same department as her ex-husband and his new girlfriend. As uncomfortable as that sounds, she claims she can't find a better job and so she is resolved to stay in that position.

Behind the victimlike behavior is a lack of truthfulness about why we don't go for what we say we want. We pile up all the reasons we are not able to pursue our goals or the people who prevented us from getting what we want, instead of going flat out for what we say we want. The truth is that we don't really want it badly enough to really go for it. So we blame other people or circumstances for it instead of just owning that we don't want it enough.

Living life as a victim is not very satisfying. It is also irresponsible and dishonest. We have all been given one life to live and we need to take full responsibility for that life. Being a victim is dishonest because it doesn't address the real reasons for our inaction. A more truthful approach would be to admit we just didn't want it badly enough or we were too damned scared to go for it 100 percent.

We will talk more about playing the victim in Chapter 6 when we discuss the principle of co-creation.

5. Hostility

Hostility is the least subtle of all the red flags. Hostility is in your face. Examples of hostility would include blowing up in a meeting, storming out, using your physical presence to intimidate others, muttering under your breath, and making threats. Hostility is about anger and acting out.

While some may view hostility as a healthy expression of anger, this is not the case. Hostility is not responsible. In Chapter 4 we will explore more constructive and responsible ways of dealing with anger.

Do you recognize any of these red flags in your behavior? Are you sufficiently aware and objective about your own behavior to know if you behave in these ways? If so, what is really going on with you? Are you scared, angry, or sad? Awareness of the red flag behavior and the underlying emotion is the first step toward breaking the cycle. By watching for these red flags, and then exploring the emotional causes, we can begin to act more responsibly. Our teams and stakeholders will definitely appreciate that, and we will be better PMs because of it.

One final thought about the red flags. Another clue about our own feelings and emotions is how we react to others. Do you see any of the red flags in others? Does it bug you? If it does bother you, it is a clue about how you feel. Often, what bothers us the most about others is the very issue that we need to deal with ourselves. So if you have issues with someone else's behavior, ask what that tells you about yourself.

Emotional Self-Awareness Is Important

No doubt you are beginning to wonder why we have spent so much time talking about getting in touch with our feelings. Being aware of our feelings is critical for a couple of reasons. First of all, the reality is that most of us are not good at getting in touch with our feelings. We go through most of our days either too busy to feel or finding ways to numb out so we don't have to feel. As humans, we have learned to use food, TV, shopping, work, drugs, sex, alcohol, more work, hobbies, and anything else we can find so that we don't have to feel. Feelings are often too scary or painful so we have learned to become numb.

The second reason we spent so much time talking about getting in touch with our feelings is that being aware is the single most important EI trait. It is the first building block of emotional intelligence. If we don't know how to interpret our feelings, we will not be good at the other aspects of emotional intelligence. It is our own personal radar, feeding us information about our environment. If you only have time to learn one thing about emotional intelligence, learn about self-awareness.

■ Accurate Self-Assessment

The second competency of self-awareness is accurate self-assessment. This is a lower priority than emotional self-awareness, yet it is still critical for project managers.

Self-assessment is about viewing ourselves accurately and seeking feedback from others to improve our performance. In *Working with Emotional Intelligence,* Daniel Goleman describes accurate self-assessment in terms of people who are:

- Aware of their strengths and weaknesses
- Reflective, learning from experience
- Open to candid feedback, new perspectives, continuous learning, and self-development
- Able to show a sense of humor and perspective about themselves[2]

---

[2]Daniel Goleman. *Working with Emotional Intelligence.* NY: Random House/Bantam Books. 1998.

Learning about our strengths and weaknesses should be an ongoing effort throughout our lifetimes. In Chapter 6 we are going to look at some specific assessment instruments that can help us get to know ourselves better and identify strengths and weaknesses. We can (and should) also leverage those around us to learn more.

As noted earlier, I have been blessed to have several different mentors, coaches, and managers who have invested in me over the course of my career. They have provided me with valuable feedback as well as guidance that I use to improve my performance.

One of the people I am learning to benefit from is my wife, Norma. She knows me better than most people and is one of my best sources of feedback. Learning to view my spouse as my coach has been a positive shift for me. Look for someone in your life who is close to you and feels comfortable giving you feedback. Once you've asked for feedback, make sure you are receptive to it.

■ Self-Confidence

The third competency under self-awareness is self-confidence. Like accurate self-assessment, we would agree that all PMs need self-confidence. No one wants to follow a leader who lacks self-confidence.

In *Working with Emotional Intelligence,* Daniel Goleman describes self-confidence as:

> *Self-Confidence:* "A Strong Sense of One's Self-Worth and Capabilities."
> —Daniel Goleman

He goes on to say that individuals with self-confidence:

- Present themselves with self-assurance; have "presence"
- Can voice views that are unpopular and go out on a limb for what is right
- Are decisive, able to make sound decisions despite uncertainties and pressures[3]

As I have improved my overall level of emotional intelligence over the last five years, my self-confidence has also dramatically improved. I feel more comfortable with myself, with my project teams, and with the other project

---

[3]Ibid.

stakeholders. I am confident when expressing my views and making tough decisions.

■ Techniques to Improve Your Self-Awareness

Now that we understand the first emotional intelligence domain of self-awareness, what can we do to improve our competency in this area? There are many ways we can increase our emotional self-awareness. The following are my favorite techniques:

1. Keep a Feelings Journal

As discussed earlier, journaling can help us to get in touch with our feelings. For best results, we should take notes in our feelings journal throughout the day on what we are experiencing and what feelings result from our experiences. Our notes don't have to be extensive; a journal entry may look like this:

"Talked with Jim this morning and congratulated him on getting his deliverable completed ahead of schedule. I left feeling happy."

The journal can help us track our feelings over the course of the day or week. Once we have journaled for a few days or weeks, we can look for patterns like:

- Balance of negative feelings versus positive feelings
- Same feelings every day at the same time, for example, sad every morning
- Predominant feelings, for example, always scared
- Feelings tied to relationships, for example, angry whenever I talk to my mom
- Dead spots where you are not able to feel anything, for example, numb over a significant loss
- Blind spots, for example, never feeling angry or never feeling happy

I recommend that you keep a feelings journal for a full thirty days. It can be a helpful way to become more aware of what you are feeling and what is triggering those feelings. It may feel awkward at first, but keep doing it. This is an extremely powerful way to gain insight into what's going on with you emotionally.

2. Track Emotions with a Tally Sheet

Another simple way to track our emotions over time is to use an emotional tally sheet. A couple of examples of emotional tally sheets are shown in Appendix A. The first example could be used by an individual to track emotions over the course of the week. At the simplest level, just knowing how often you experience each emotion will aid you in becoming more self-aware.

You can also be more intentional by setting a timer or other reminder so that you record your emotions every thirty minutes or hour. This will give you a more complete view of the range of emotions you experience throughout your day and week. Do this when at work and at play to get the best view of your emotional range and what triggers specific emotions.

3. Conduct a Physical Inventory

Another self-awareness technique is to conduct a physical inventory using the sensations in your body to help determine what you are feeling. Remember the physical signs that we introduced in Figure 3-3. As you go through the course of a normal day, stop periodically and take a physical inventory to help you understand what you are feeling. Check your heartbeat and see if it is fast or slow. Check to see if you feel hot or cold. Look for areas where your muscles are tight. Use these physical indicators to help you determine what is going on with you emotionally.

It is important to remember that we may feel a combination of two or more emotions at any one point in time. While one feeling may dominate, it may be the emotion that is further below the surface that we need to understand and address. For example, if someone does not complete a deliverable on time and does not let us know, we may feel a combination of anger and fear. We might be angry because they did not let us know. We might be scared because we are going to have to slip the schedule or miss other commitment dates. The feeling of anger may dominate in this case. However, it could be the fear underneath that anger that is more important to understand and manage.

4. Checking Your Face in the Mirror

Like the physical inventory in the previous item, you can use the face in the mirror technique to help you become more aware of your emotions. Use the pictures and descriptions of faces that we described in Figure 3-4. Check your face periodically to see what is being shown to others.

You can also train yourself to get better at this by reversing the exercise. As you feel an emotion, check your face in a mirror to see what your expression looks like. With practice, you will be able to recognize what you are feeling without having to rely on your face.

5. Use Paired Sharing

Paired sharing is a technique you can use to better understand what you are feeling at any point in time. It is similar to having a conversation with ourselves except that we have the help of another person. It is almost like thinking out loud, except the focus is on our feelings more than our thoughts.

The way it works is to get together with another person. The two of you each will take turns speaking and listening. The first person will talk for a set period of time; two or three minutes work very well. There is no script. That speaker talks about what they are feeling in that moment, even if they don't know what they are feeling. The speaker just keeps talking about whatever comes to mind. The key is to keep it about emotions and about the here and now.

The person listening has a critical and somewhat difficult task and that is to simply listen. This involves maintaining eye contact throughout and not providing any type of feedback to the other person. This means no verbal clues (e.g., uh-huh) and no non-verbal clues such as nodding or smiling. This may require a little practice for both speaker and listener since giving feedback is such an ingrained part of listening for many of us. To use the paired sharing technique, it is important to simply listen and to let the person doing the talking determine where to go next.

When the allotted time is up, the pair will switch roles; the speaker becomes the listener. The same rules apply for speaker and listener. The second speaker can comment on what the first speaker said earlier; however, the listener should not respond. Their job is to listen with no feedback. It is also OK if there are breaks or silence.

The pair-sharing technique can be used with people we know well or even those we don't know at all. The technique is intended to provide space for the speaker to say what is in their heart. The listener is simply there to provide the space for the speaker. They don't need to know any history or any context; they simply listen to the speaker.

The process continues until the two are able to get down to what they are feeling. Most people will get in touch with their feelings within two or three rounds.

This technique is quite simple and probably sounds more difficult than it is in practice. However, don't let the simplicity fool you; it is a powerful way to get in touch with what is going on with you. Try it a couple of times and see if it helps you to get in touch with your feelings.

6. Backtrack

Backtracking is when we retrace our steps to determine why we are feeling a certain way. I find it most helpful to understand when I am feeling negative emotions like sad, angry, or scared. I will sometimes feel a vague sense of unease, like there is a dark cloud hanging over my head. By using the backtracking technique, I can often connect the dots on what I am feeling and why.

This is similar to the process you follow when you lose something. What would you do if you lost your keys? You would stop and retrace your steps leading up to the point where you lost them. Usually, you find that there is a logical place for the keys based on the steps you took.

The process of backtracking works the same for our feelings, as shown in Figure 3-5. In a recent case where I used this technique, I was at the end of my work day. I was on my way home and I felt disturbed. I had a sense of unease that I could not attribute to anything specific. I then reflected back on the day and the exchanges I had experienced with various people on my project. I thought about all the meetings and the conversations I had throughout the day. And then it struck me very clearly. In my meeting with my manager, he was critical of one of my team members. That criticism hurt.

The criticism hurt on several levels. First, it hurt because I knew it was true. My manager was right in his assessment of my team member and I knew it. I felt personally criticized, as if I should have done a better job. I felt like I should have acted sooner to address this performance issue. I even felt scared that I was perceived as not performing at my highest level. Second, it hurt

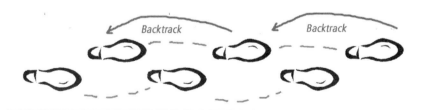

Figure 3-5: Backtracking Process.

because I liked this particular team member. I felt defensive because there were so many positive things he was doing. Third, it hurt because I knew I needed to act on the situation and I was reluctant to do that. I knew that it would mean taking this person off the team. That made me feel sad.

When I backtracked over the day and identified this exchange, it was easy to understand how I felt. There was a mix of negative feelings at that moment. After the meeting with my manager that day, I moved on with other meetings and discussions and those negative feelings moved to the background. It was as if my subconscious didn't want me to dwell on those thoughts. That worked to insulate me from my feelings until I slowed down at the end of the day and I was unable to keep the negative feelings at bay any longer.

My wife sometimes helps me to backtrack. If I come home from work in a less than positive state, she may say something like "so what is going on with you?" She will force me to think back over the day and why I am sad, angry, or scared. It works. By backtracking through my day, I can identify what happened to cause me to feel the way I do.

Whether you do it alone or with the help of another, the backtracking technique can be helpful to understand what you are feeling in the moment. When you feel some discomfort or unease and are unable to pinpoint the cause, review your day and the interactions you had with others. This will often help you to identify the source and the specific feeling you are experiencing. That will put you in a position to do something about it.

7. Use Quiet Time

The sixth and final self-awareness technique I would like to talk about is quiet time. It could also be called reflection or meditation time. You could use prayer, meditation, reflection, yoga, breathing exercises, or any other technique that helps you to relax and tune in to yourself. It is all about ways of getting in touch with what you are feeling right now. As with all the awareness techniques, it is about focusing on the here and now.

The quiet time technique is about getting in touch with ourselves. It can be difficult to find quiet time in the course of our full and busy lives. The fullness and busyness can be the way we avoid getting in touch with ourselves. The antidote to this busyness is to slow down, be quiet, and get in touch with our emotions.

If you already know how to use prayer, meditation, or breathing exercises, then use whatever technique works for you. If you don't use a technique, there are tons of resources available to you on the web and in your community. But you really don't need anything other than yourself for this. You can simply sit quietly and breathe deeply. Try to put the noise of the day out of your mind and get in touch with what you are feeling.

It sounds simple but please give it a try before you dismiss it. When I take the time to do this, I am often surprised by the results. It has helped me to recognize a pattern of feelings that I experience around travel. Every month I make one or two trips to teach courses out of town. It is typical for me to fly out on Sunday afternoon for a class that starts on Monday morning. Invariably, I get scared and anxious as the weekend approaches until I peak sometime Sunday afternoon when I am frantically packing the materials I need for my class while the taxi waits in the driveway to take me to the airport. By then, I have myself in a complete tizzy running around frazzled instead of taking a quiet moment to say goodbye to my wife and children.

I don't mind traveling and I enjoy teaching classes. But both require a certain level of effort and attention. Travel can always bring unwanted developments. Classes can bring surprises and a level of performance anxiety because of the importance of doing a good job. As a result, I feel anxious about going out of town for these classes.

It wasn't until I took the time to get quiet with myself that I recognized this pattern. I prayed about the weekend and realized how scared I was about traveling. Then I recognized that I always feel scared leading up to these trips. That gave me the power to do something about my feelings.

Whether you pray, meditate, use breathing techniques, or simply reflect quietly, use quiet time to get more in touch with yourself. Focus on what you are feeling now, in the moment.

4

■ Self-Management

Self-management happens when we begin to use our awareness of our feelings to manage ourselves. Building on the base of self-awareness, we use that information to control and manage our emotions. Self-management is the ability to control our emotions so that they don't control us. That is the simple but powerful truth about self-management. We need to use what we know about our emotions to control and manage those emotions and our behavior. This includes techniques that help us to regulate our emotions, to identify and prevent emotional triggers, and to identify and prevent thinking that can lead to emotional breakdowns.

Why is it important to manage our emotions? The alternative is not very attractive. Individuals who don't manage their emotions in the business world are called rage-aholics and drama queens. They cause others to sigh, roll their eyes, or even leave the room in fright. It should go without saying that if you cannot manage yourself you cannot manage others. No one wants to follow someone who is not in control of themselves. The stereotypical boss who is valued because they use whatever means necessary to get the results from their teams is a relic of the past.

I had a caveman manager like that for several years. He was a loose cannon; a rage-aholic who survived only because he achieved results. I worked for him on a couple of large projects and he had the same modus operandi—to berate people, run roughshod over them, and intimidate them into performing as he wanted. And it didn't matter if you were on his team or somehow in the way of his success. He treated everyone the same.

52

In fairness to this manager, the stakes were high and it was a high pressure job. We were involved in recovering red projects, that is, projects that were failing. It was our job to go in and recover the project. The environment was very stressful. That said, the end did not justify the means. There were other, better ways of achieving the results. The manager simply was not able to use any other means because he did not have control over his emotions.

When I worked for this manager years ago, he was valued by the organization for the results he was able to achieve. These days, I don't think that organizations tolerate or want that kind of behavior. They want positive results, of course, but are unwilling to sanction caveman-like methods that reflect a lack of emotional self-control. PMs and leaders today are expected to be in control of themselves and their emotions.

We all probably know managers who have reputations for kicking butt and then taking names. You might recall the controversy over John Bolton, the U.S. ambassador to the United Nations. When John Bolton was identified as a candidate for the ambassadorship, news reports surfaced about his alleged negative behavior at previous government positions. Mr. Bolton was called the "quintessential kiss up kick down manager," which clearly is not a compliment. Bolton's nomination was nearly derailed because of that criticism.

That is not to say that anger doesn't have a place in business or in project management. Channeled productively, anger can move us and our project team members better than any other emotion. The key is to have control over anger, just as we need to control all of our emotions. That is all part of self-management.

Project managers and leaders of all types need to control themselves and manage their emotions. They cannot afford to let their emotions overtake them and dictate their behavior or they will find they aren't leading anyone for very long.

◼ The Emotional Intelligence Model for Project Management

In Figure 4-1, we show the emotional intelligence model for project management and the domain of self-management. As shown in the diagram, self-management includes the single competency of self-control. Self-control is the ability to be in control of our emotions so that they do not control us.

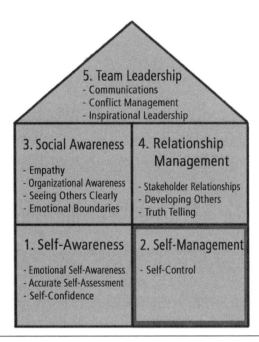

Figure 4-1: Emotional Intelligence Framework Showing Self-Management.

Self-Awareness Precedes Self-Management

Self-awareness is a necessary predecessor to self-management and self-control as shown in Figure 4-2. After all, if we don't know what we are feeling it can be difficult to do anything about it. Awareness can be a big help when it comes to managing negative emotions. When we are feeling a negative emotion, we can often disarm or control the impact of that feeling just by being aware of what it is and why we are feeling it.

For example, if I feel scared before a meeting with an important client, I can often calm myself simply by naming the feeling and acknowledging the reasons for it. Once I realize that I am scared, I can do something about it. Almost anytime I am doing something important, I am going to feel scared. So when I feel scared, I simply remind myself that this means it is important.

Figure 4-2: Self-Awareness Precedes Self-Management.

Meetings make me scared because they are important. Recognizing that I am scared because the meeting is important is usually enough to calm me and remind me that my feelings (fear in this case) are serving me.

■ Self-Control

What Is Self-Control?

Self-control is the ability to remain composed in spite of our emotional state. This does not mean forcing a smile when we are sad or angry. It does mean registering sad and angry feelings as well as controlling our reaction to those feelings. For most PMs, managing the negative feelings is going to be the biggest priority.

Negative Feelings Can Cripple a Team

In a team environment, negative emotions can be crippling, especially when they stem from the leader. This environment provides plenty of opportunities to practice self-management. Emotions can run rampant on projects where the stakes are high for both individuals and organizations.

Projects can be stressful due to the constraints placed on them. Deadlines are usually aggressive if not downright unrealistic. Budgets are often set without regard to the work required. The scope of work can be unrealistic or subject to interpretation or negotiation. They often involve doing things for the first time. Many project managers take the success or failure of the project as a personal success or failure. These factors can place a lot of pressure on the project manager. PMs need to learn to manage their own stress and calm others by their example.

All of this can cause negative emotions in the project team and the PM. Negative emotions can poison the project environment, especially those emanating from the leader. Anger, disappointment, rage, sadness, and fear all need to be monitored and managed so that they don't impact the rest of the team. That doesn't mean stuffing these emotions, dismissing them, or pretending they don't exist. It does mean managing those emotions.

There is nothing like the pressure of an intense project to bring out the best and the worst in us. Any tiny crack in our emotional foundation is brought to light and often, when exposed to heat and pressure, it will result in unpleasant side effects. Tough times tend to reveal our true emotional nature.

If we don't manage our emotions in the project environment, very bad things can happen. In addition to poisoning the atmosphere of the team, we can get a reputation for being out of control. Others may avoid working with us and our team. We may have a difficult time retaining the best resources, and we will tend to attract team members who are comfortable working in negative environments. Our team members might quietly try to sabotage the project. Our relationships with stakeholders will suffer.

I have been there myself. Sadly, I have lost control of my emotions on a project more than once. Sometimes the consequences were no big deal and the project moved on. Other times, my lack of emotional control hurt me and my team.

In one particularly painful example, I was managing a large international project. I had a poor relationship with one of the team leads working for me. The relationship had deteriorated to the point where it was adversarial. There was an ongoing battle of wills about this team lead's travel to the client site. It culminated one day when my team lead sent me another travel request via e-mail. I was incensed and had reached my breaking point. I was also feeling under pressure due to some criticism from the client about the project team's performance. Without thinking about my reaction or waiting to calm down, I replied to the e-mail in a terse and critical way. The team member was angry about my response and escalated it to my manager, who called me to ask, "what gives?" It was embarrassing. Worse, it led to a painful, formal investigation that dragged on for 2 months.

Of the many mistakes that I made in this situation, the main one was that I responded inappropriately out of anger. I should have calmed down, evaluated alternative courses of action, and then chose an appropriate response. I also should have been addressing the underlying relationship breakdown that was the undercurrent for the issue. As it was, I responded too quickly, using emotions and without thinking. I was not managing myself. The e-mail response was the single event that I wish I could have taken back.

In this particular situation, the e-mail and the formal investigation showed that I needed to manage myself better. When the investigation had run its course, the individual felt he could no longer work for me and left the project. That turned out to be very helpful to me and to the overall project. It was something I wish I had addressed sooner and directly.

Self-Control Is for All Emotions

As noted, self-control is critical for negative emotions because they can poison the atmosphere in a team. But we also need to exercise control over our expression of positive emotions.

Consider a situation where you are happy and excited over the achievement of a significant milestone just prior to a meeting with a team member who is upset about a conflict. Exhibiting your positive emotions would be inappropriate in this discussion, just as they would be in a situation when someone has just received bad news such as a death in the family. As the PM, you may need to dampen your excitement or happiness in situations like this.

There are lots of opportunities for emotional self-control on a long project. In fact, being on a prolonged project can be like riding an emotional roller coaster. The longest project I ever managed was three years. During that time, the team went through a lot of emotions. We reached six major client milestones and numerous minor milestones. We kicked off new years, new phases of the engagement, and new initiatives. As a team of nearly 100 people, we experienced promotions, demotions, firings, resignations, the birth of babies, marriages, and deaths in our families.

Over the course of that project, it was important that I managed my emotions. I shared the excitement of reaching important milestones with one part of the team while sharing sadness over the loss of a key resource in another part of the team. I also had a team lead who lost his father and his father-in-law within six months. It was critical that I managed both the highs and the lows during this time.

The larger the team and the longer the project, the more likely it is that you will have a wide range of emotions at any one time. As the PM and leader of the team, you have to be balanced and not go to extremes. This requires a high degree of emotional self-control.

Self-Control Helps Us Avoid Emotional Breakdowns

An emotional breakdown is an involuntary response to an emotional situation. We are "losing it" when we have an emotional breakdown. Road rage is an extreme form of emotional breakdown. Individuals who experience road rage become unpredictable and out of control. Unfortunately, we don't see a physical sign like the one in Figure 4-3 warning us of impending emotional breakdowns.

While road rage may be unheard of in a project environment, emotional breakdowns are not. The stress and strain of everyday life can cause emotional breakdowns. Add to that a challenging project environment and the likelihood of emotional breakdowns is very high.

In *Emotional Intelligence,* Daniel Goleman uses the term "emotional hijacking" for these breakdowns. He contends that our emotions are hijacked

Figure 4-3: Warning of Emotional Breakdown Ahead.

by our primitive neurological systems. These systems were designed for our survival. Most of us are familiar with the fight or flight responses. Emotional hijacking is an involuntary and extreme form of the fight or flight response mechanism.[1]

Whether we call it emotional hijacking or emotional breakdown, the end result is the same; our emotions have been taken over by something else and we are not in control. Emotional breakdowns are involuntary. We are reacting to an event without control of our behavior.

I once hired a project leader based on his stated ability not to lose it. I knew that I felt under pressure on this particular project and I needed someone who would not lose their cool. In the interview, he said that he prided himself on "staying one degree cooler than everyone else in the room." That was critical for us on this particular project and his statement got him the job. We worked well together for two years and during that time, true to his word, he was usually one degree cooler than everyone else.

Not everyone is able to stay cooler than everyone else. In fact, many people experience some sort of emotional breakdown during work. Each person may have one breakdown that is more likely to occur than any other. Here

---

[1]Daniel Goleman. *Emotional Intelligence: Why It Can Matter More Than IQ.* NY: Random House/Bantam Books, 1995.

are some examples of emotional breakdowns that you might see in a project environment:

1. Angry Tirades

Whether at work, in public, or in private, we have all seen someone explode with anger and blast someone else. We may know individuals who are likely to explode. Perhaps we even avoid certain people for fear they will blow up on us.

2. Door Slamming

Not able to take any more, a person leaves the room and slams the door behind them.

3. E-mail Letter Bomb

Our modern office tools make sending an angry e-mail easier than ever. This is a common way for people to vent anger on a project. Most of us have probably sent something we wish we hadn't.

4. Withdrawal and Isolation

This is when people pull away, avoid meetings, and perhaps even dodge specific people on the project.

5. Holding Grudges and Getting Even

Holding grudges often comes in response to unfavorable decisions being made, criticism received, or some other perceived slight. This type of breakdown often results in a secret vow to get even. A score may even be kept of who is winning and who is losing. This breakdown is especially harmful because it may be secret and it can go on for a long time.

6. Criticizing

This breakdown results in criticism intended to hurt another. Unwarranted criticism often comes from individuals who are feeling insecure, threatened, or emotionally vulnerable. Criticism is often the response to the hurt we feel. Criticism may be buried in helpful sounding remarks or it may be out in the open. Either way, the impact is the same.

7. Sarcasm and Inappropriate Humor

Sarcasm is a red flag for emotional breakdowns as discussed in Chapter 3. Both sarcasm and inappropriate humor are learned responses to situations where we don't want to address the truth directly.

8. Playing the Victim

Playing the victim is also one of the red flags for emotional breakdowns that we discussed in Chapter 3. When someone plays the victim, they act as if they are powerless and not responsible for their actions. They will blame someone (or perhaps the entire world) for their situation and their actions. This is disempowering to the individual and unacceptable to the team.

How many of these emotional breakdowns do you experience? Look at the list and reflect on the last week, month, and year. Have you had more than one of these? Do you experience all of these or have one or two preferred breakdowns?

My own common breakdowns include e-mail letter bombs, criticizing, sarcasm, and inappropriate humor. I have become aware enough to eliminate many of these responses from my repertoire and I have the grace and peace of mind to not go down on myself if I have a relapse. I just say, "there I go again" and try to determine what caused the emotional breakdown.

If you are having trouble identifying your emotional breakdowns, try getting some input from others. Take the time to ask your peers, team members, or your spouse how they see you. They will be glad you are investing in yourself and you might be surprised to learn more about yourself from them.

Emotional Breakdowns May Be Preceded by Emotional Triggers

Specific emotional breakdowns may be traced back to emotional triggers. An emotional trigger is a situation, external stimulus, or activating event that leaves us vulnerable to emotional breakdown. Triggers are not necessarily the cause of the breakdown, but they serve as a catalyst, or provide fertile ground for a breakdown.

One way we can protect ourselves against emotional breakdowns is to identify the emotional triggers that immediately precede breakdowns. By sensitizing ourselves to what leads to the breakdown, we can break the cycle.

Adele Lynn identified the following ten emotional triggers in her book *The EQ Difference; A Powerful Plan for Putting Emotional Intelligence to Work.*

- moods and attitudes of others
- prethinking or foreshadowing
- dwelling
- personality
- hot words/hot buttons
- perceived criticism

- physical environment
- illness or physical conditions
- situations[2]

You may recognize many of these emotional triggers at work in the project environment.

Moods and Attitudes of Others

Most of us are vulnerable to the moods and attitudes of others. When others are feeling down or angry, this can have a negative impact on us, leaving us open to an emotional breakdown.

This has been the case for me due to growing up with an alcoholic father. In my childhood, I was acutely attuned to the moods of my dad. It was one of the ways I tried (unsuccessfully) to control my chaotic home environment. If my dad was in a good mood, I could let up and relax a little. If he wasn't, well, then I was on edge and always on the lookout for some kind of trouble.

Do you take your cue on how to feel from how those around you feel? Do you get bummed out when your boss is angry or sad? Do you ever say, "Well, I was in a good mood until you called me" or something like that? If this applies to you, consider taking the following actions to understand and begin to protect yourself from emotional breakdown:

1. Who Is It?

Try to evaluate whose moods make you feel the most vulnerable. It could be your spouse or your parents. Perhaps, like me, you are vulnerable to your boss or other authority figures. Determine who it is that causes this trigger for you.

2. Why Is It?

If possible, try to understand why you feel vulnerable. Is it because you grew up with a parent with addiction or boundary issues? Or is it because you want so much to please your spouse or fear the loss of their love? The cause may be easy to understand, or it could require some help from a trained therapist.

3. Cut the Cord

Try to desensitize yourself to the moods of others as much as you can. Envision yourself with this key person who is in a bad mood. Practice laughing

---

[2]Adele B. Lynn. *EQ Difference; A Powerful Plan for Putting Emotional Intelligence to Work.* NY: AMACOM, 2005.

a little and saying, "Wow, you sure are in a bad mood today" or something similar.

4. Don't Take It Personally

Don't personalize or try to control how the other person feels. They are responsible for their feelings, just as you are responsible for your own. If they are reacting to something you said or did, let them have their reaction. Don't walk on eggshells when you are around them or try to cushion the blow of what you say.

For some people, just becoming aware of the connection between the breakdown and the moods of others can be enlightening. It is the first step toward choosing different, healthier responses.

Prethinking or Foreshadowing

Foreshadowing is when we predict negative outcomes or events in the future. For example, when we experience some critical issue that threatens to delay our project, we may predict that our client is going to be upset or worse, that the project will be cancelled.

Some of us, myself included, have a tendency to anticipate the worst. We may even pride ourselves on being able to see the worst in every future situation. But in the project environment, this can be both a deadly poison to the team morale as well as a trigger for emotional breakdown.

Chicken Little was one of those who anticipated negative future events. Chicken Little interpreted a small piece of evidence (a falling acorn, I think) to mean that the entire sky was falling. Of course, the sky was not falling and eventually Chicken Little learned a valuable lesson—learn more about emotional intelligence.

Before you e-mail me about proper risk management for a project, let me distinguish between unhealthy foreshadowing and proper risk planning. Project managers need to address risks as well as to have a healthy skepticism about potential outcomes of tasks and projects. They need to be able to challenge overly optimistic estimates and outcomes and help the team plan for risks and the unexpected. That is all a part of being a good PM. That is not the type of negative foreshadowing I am discussing.

Behind foreshadowing is fear, which leads to irrational thoughts. For me, it became apparent as I worked with a coach that I was predicting negativity in the future. I began to see that I frequently talked as if I was about to be fired or cut from the project team. I often tied this to some negative vibes

I was picking up or news that I heard. My coach helped me to see that it was irrational, unhealthy, and could even become a self-fulfilling prophecy. When I lacked self-confidence and acted out of fear, I was short and critical of others. This in turn reduced productivity and caused others to question my leadership. Fortunately I was able to break the cycle and avoid being fired.

Here are some steps you can take if you find yourself foreshadowing:

1. Identify the Pattern

The first step is to identify the pattern of negative thinking. First, keep a journal of your negative predictions and track the outcomes. Second, check it out with your boss. This will only be possible to the extent you have an open relationship with your superior and trust it will not backfire. Third, develop a trust relationship with a friend or coworker and use them as a sounding board. Check out your thoughts and negative predictions and ask what they think. The more objective that other person can be, the better. Someone that works for you is less likely to be objective than a spouse or a peer.

2. Interrupt the Foreshadowing with Logic

Once you see the pattern, try to interrupt it with logic. Be patient; this can involve some level of internal strife. When my coach began to point out my negative thinking to me, I resisted. I was vested in seeing the negative and I wanted to continue as I always had. I was mired in it and it was comfortable. It took time to recognize that after two and a half years on a stressful project engagement, I wasn't on the verge of being fired.

It also helps sometimes to say, "there I go again" when you catch yourself predicting negativity. Laugh aloud and say, "whew, glad that isn't really going to happen."

Breaking a pattern like foreshadowing can be difficult; in particular if you have done it for as long as you can remember. Remember that change is possible and with change comes a tremendous payoff.

Dwelling

Dwelling occurs when we become fixated on one particular thought, remark, event, injury, or outcome. Our minds obsess and that incident becomes the focus of all our attention. We become stuck. This dramatically impacts our performance and leaves us vulnerable to emotional breakdown.

Have you ever found yourself dwelling or obsessing over something? If you have, you know that you cannot perform well as a PM. It reminds me of the behavior of my computer when it is busy doing something else in the background when I am trying to use it. Even the most simple task can be slow. The program may say it is "not responding" and will sometimes even crash. That is probably how you appear to your stakeholders when you are dwelling and obsessing and they need something from you.

I have fallen prey to dwelling and obsessing on a minor scale. My mind got stuck on something and then just churned away. It was not enough to prevent me from being effective, but it did keep me awake at night on several occasions.

I have also had people who worked for me become so obsessed and stuck on things that they were unable to perform at acceptable levels. In one particular case, it began to affect his interpretation of events. He began to misinterpret things that were said, to take every comment as a personal attack, and to become overwhelmed. No matter what was said, the team member seemed to hear "you are not good enough." This was not actually the case and it caused him to become ineffective.

Let's hope that you do not suffer from dwelling and obsessing on that same scale. As a PM, we can easily become obsessed with our performance and that of our team, as well as on the success of the project. Here are some ideas for dealing with this behavior if you find yourself falling into that trap on your project:

Become Aware
First, be aware of the behavior and see it for what it is. Sometimes it is enough to simply acknowledge it in order to break the cycle. If you have a tendency to dwell and obsess, become alert to signs that you are getting sucked in.

Get Clear
Take action to be clear or to get over it. Whatever the hurt, it probably tracks back to some injury caused by someone else. What do you need to do or say that would help you feel OK? This might mean having a difficult conversation with someone about their behavior. It is amazing how often taking a simple but courageous step can relieve us from the obsession.

Recharge
If you find yourself dwelling or obsessing, evaluate whether you are getting enough rest and downtime away from the project. Some time away may help to keep your emotions in check. Also, invest in hobbies; in particular those that involve other people. Try also taking regular vacations that are long enough to allow full relaxation.

Break the Link
If a particular person is the root of your obsessions, try to get as far away from that person as possible. While not as effective as getting clear, it may help to eliminate the obsessive behavior.

Don't Try NOT to Think About It
Sometimes, if we are consciously trying not to think about something we find we cannot stop. Instead, dedicate a specific time to dwell, obsess and worry about it. Limit this time to something reasonable like ten to twenty minutes at the end of the day. You might find that having a specific time set aside for dwelling allows you to get it out of your system and then put your mind back on what is important.

Relax
Try relaxation techniques such as breathing, prayer, or meditation. These can often break the cycle.

Tease Yourself
If we take ourselves too seriously we often set up conditions that lead to obsession. Try teasing yourself about how silly you are being. Sometimes you can acknowledge the behavior and poke a little light-hearted fun at yourself.

Seek Professional Help
If you are unable to break the cycle on your own, it might be helpful to enlist the help of a professional. Your mental health and professional performance is worth whatever it costs to eliminate dwelling and obsessing from your life.

If your mind is dwelling and obsessing, you will not be open and available to work on your project, and you won't be much of a PM or a leader. Do what you need to do to remove obsessions; this will also protect you against emotional breakdowns.

Hot Words and Hot Buttons

The focus of the following section is on triggers that affect many of us: hot words and hot buttons (see Figure 4-4). A hot word or hot button is a word or issue that triggers a specific and undesirable behavior in us, leaving us open to threats.

I recently had a team member whose hot button was failure. He was acutely attuned to feelings of failure and was on the lookout for that condition. This stemmed from the fact that he perceived himself as a failure. There

Figure 4-4: Hot Button.

was no data to support his feelings of failure about himself. Those feelings came from an internal sense of inadequacy that no amount of striving would overcome.

Whether it was rational or true, the individual had this sense of failure about himself. He also projected on me that I was saying he was a failure. I did not feel this way about the man and valued him as part of the team. However, the words I used triggered him to feel like a failure. When I told him that I did not believe "the team would succeed" using a particular process, he heard "you are a failure." My style of challenging people to perform at a higher level backfired; all he heard was criticism. It would have been more effective to congratulate, acknowledge, and give recognition. This very capable team lead eventually had an emotional breakdown.

Give Yourself a Checkup

Think for a moment about the hot buttons or hot issues that trigger you. Are there any specific concerns that you tend to react to or that cause you to blow up? Do you think that others avoid bringing up issues to sidestep an argument with you?

Here are some things you can do if you want to understand your own hot buttons.

Get a Second Opinion

One quick way to get more input on your hot words or hot buttons is to check with someone you trust. There is no substitute for including others in our analysis and getting honest and accurate insights. More often than not, when we suffer from issues it is because we are trying to work it out on our own. As noted before, this input could come from a spouse or significant other, a trusted co-worker, or a coach or mentor. Ask them if there are issues that they feel they cannot discuss with you.

Go Beyond the Hot Button

Once you know you have a hot button, take steps to determine the underlying issue and feelings (e.g., feeling like a failure, lack of self confidence). What is really going on for you? If you are struggling with self-confidence or inadequacy, perhaps you need to focus on that issue rather than the actual hot button or hot word.

As with the other emotional triggers, it may help to laugh at ourselves when we find that a hot button has set us off. We may also need to seek professional help.

Criticism and Blame

Criticism and blame can often be triggers for emotional breakdown. In particular this can be the case when the criticism is unwarranted, if we feel we have not been fairly treated, or if we were not given a chance to explain or defend ourselves. The criticism doesn't even have to be real; perceived criticism can also trigger an undesired response from us.

Criticism and feeling blamed have been a problem for me in the past. If I thought someone else was being critical of me, I would feel deflated and depressed. The criticism hurt because it resonated with what I already felt about myself. I was my own worst critic. My discussions with others leads me to believe that this is very common and that many people are their own worst critics.

Unfortunately for me, my past response to criticism or blame was to freak out and to immediately turn around and blame someone else. When problems occurred, I was often short with people, I lacked tact and empathy, and I immediately would dig in to figure out exactly who was responsible for the problem. This led to some ugly confrontations on past projects. This has been one of my most common emotional breakdowns.

The good news is that over the last few years I have learned to deal with criticism in healthier ways. Here are some of the ways I now deal with criticism and blame:

My Own Worst Enemy

With some work I have learned to recognize when I am being my own worst critic. Only rarely do I find that others are criticizing me; more often it is just me. If I can eliminate the voice in my head that criticizes my work, I can overcome the feeling of being criticized.

Look Ahead

Anticipate situations where I will feel or be criticized by others. Often, I know ahead of time when I am vulnerable to feeling criticized. If I do, I can visualize criticism coming from others and then practice healthy reactions. One healthy reaction is to calmly turn around and ask the critic what is going on with them or why they feel the need to criticize.

Check It Out

In some situations, we perceive criticism that is actually not criticism. Check it out to determine first if it is actually criticism and second, if that criticism is meant for you. Sometimes we may be reacting to comments or feedback from others that is meant to be helpful and not critical. Instead of personalizing someone's comments as criticism or blame, check it out. Ask the other person what they meant by their remark. If you receive true criticism, evaluate what part of that criticism you can use. Discard the rest.

The New Wheaties

When I was a kid, Wheaties was called the breakfast of champions. A former co-worker taught me that feedback is actually the breakfast of champions. If we want to be champions, we need to be open to feedback. We may even need to go so far as to seek it out.

Could Be Just Them

Sometimes we need to be reminded that other people have their own opinions and that doesn't make them right. Also, many people, myself included, are not that good at providing constructive feedback. So before we overreact to some comment from someone else, we need to consider the source. More often than not, criticism says more about the person who criticizes than the one receiving the criticism. Sometimes we need to ignore or discount the feedback from others.

Doesn't Change Anything

Remember that even if true, criticism and blame do not make you a bad person.

Set a Mistake Quota

Mistakes are part of being human and we all should expect to make them if we are growing. If you are not making mistakes, you are not trying hard enough. You may want to consider setting a quota of mistakes each day or week. I used to joke with a recent project team that we would strive to make only new and very creative mistakes. We certainly should not make the same mistakes, of course, but our focus should be more on success than on not making mistakes. If your goal is to not make a mistake, you will be too cautious to be effective at anything.

Finally, I would like to refer to the words of Theodore Roosevelt and his view of critics. Though these words of his are often quoted, they are worth repeating.

> "It is not the critic who counts, not the man who points out how the strong man stumbled, or where the doer of deeds could have done better. The credit belongs to the man who is actually in the arena; whose face is marred by the dust and sweat and blood; who strives valiantly; who errs and comes short again and again; who knows the great enthusiasms, the great devotions and spends himself in a worthy cause; who at the best, knows in the end the triumph of high achievement, and who, at worst, if he fails, at least fails while daring greatly; so that his place shall never be with those cold and timid souls who know neither victory or defeat."
> —Theodore Roosevelt

Physical Environment

Our physical work environment and specific situations can leave us vulnerable to emotional breakdowns. This should not be surprising. Imagine how you feel when you are in environments that are hot, cold, noisy, cluttered, filthy, or isolated. If we are not physically comfortable, we may be vulnerable to an emotional breakdown.

There also may be specific situations that leave us emotionally vulnerable. For example, I feel vulnerable when I am in a large crowd of people. I also find that the winters in Chicago cause me to feel vulnerable to breakdowns. Chicago in the summer is a tremendous playground. However, in the winter it is more like Gotham City. The days often seem cold, gray, and so dreary that they suck the life out of you. It can really make you appreciate the few sunny days we experience during the winter!

Illness and Fatigue

Illness and fatigue can also leave us vulnerable to an emotional breakdown. Like our environment, they can leave us feeling less than our best. When we don't feel well or are extremely tired, we let down our guard and become vulnerable to emotional breakdowns. An extreme example of this would be individuals experiencing some type of chronic pain. It is hard to show grace and not react emotionally when you are experiencing chronic pain. In a similar way, fatigue can leave us vulnerable to a breakdown. I know that if I don't get enough sleep and let myself get run down, I risk making emotional mistakes.

Reduce Your Vulnerability to Emotional Triggers

What can we do to reduce our vulnerability to these emotional triggers? Here are some specific ways to reduce the impact of these triggers.

Know Thyself
The first step is to know yourself. Make it a point to understand what your specific emotional triggers are.

Evaluate Your Physical Environment
Are you as comfortable as you can make yourself? What needs to change to make you comfortable? If you are isolated, what can you do to feel more connected? If you are a work-at-home professional, try staying connected with Instant Messaging or go to work in a public space, like a Starbucks, rather than stay at home in isolation. Is your work area continually cold? Get a small space heater.

Take Care of Yourself and Stay Healthy
If you don't take care of yourself, it will be hard for you to care for others. Taking care of yourself includes eating healthy foods, exercising, and getting enough sleep.

Keep yourself healthy to prevent illness and fatigue. Take basic preventive care to avoid getting sick by washing your hands frequently and avoiding direct contact with those who are sick. If you do get sick, don't try to be a hero. Some people think it is important to come to work even when they are sick. They mistakenly believe that the team is better off with them there. Unfortunately, illness can spread and cripple an entire team. Set a good example for everyone else by staying home and getting better. Even if you believe you are indispensable, the team is better off without you while you recuperate.

Sharpen the Saw
Stephen Covey talks about the importance of sharpening the saw in *The Seven Habits of Highly Effective People*. In essence he is talking about self-renewal. This means taking your vacations as well as investing in training and development. Are you too busy on your project for vacation or training? That is a common refrain and one that is easily debunked. First of all, no one person is that critical to a project. Second, there will never be a perfect time on

your project to take vacation or go to training. The busier your project, the more you will benefit from downtime away from it.[3]

Avoid Long Work Weeks

We all have to stretch once in a while and we all have a different level of stamina. However, if you are working more than forty-five, fifty, or sixty hours every week, you are likely setting yourself up for fatigue and illness.

Get Support

When feeling sick, tired, or worn out, you need to seek support from others. This support could be from your manager, a trusted co-worker, friends, a spouse, or a mentor. Reach out to others and engage them on an emotional level. Get the help you need to stay on top of your game.

Stinking Thinking Can Cause Emotional Breakdowns

There is one more type of emotional breakdown and it is caused by the way we think. As strange as it sounds, we can affect the way we are feeling based on our thoughts. It is through distorted thinking that we set ourselves up for an emotional breakdown.

This distorted thinking is also called stinking thinking. We can literally think ourselves into feeling bad and that can leave us vulnerable to an emotional breakdown. Just when things seem to be going well our mind convinces us that things are falling apart. It seems that we self-sabotage. Negativity, despair, and global thinking are the keys themes that I notice. See if you can relate to any of these or if they are causing emotional breakdowns for you.

1. All or Nothing Thinking

With all or nothing thinking, we see things as a total failure if they fall short of perfect. We see no good in an imperfect situation.

As an example, consider what happened to me recently on a return trip from Washington, D.C. to Chicago. My class in D.C. finished early and I sprinted to the airport with the hopes of getting on an earlier flight. As it turned out, I was able to leave on a flight that was one hour earlier. However, I had to give up my first class upgrade and sit in a middle seat in economy class. I felt a sense of loss and was angry as I flew from Washington to Chicago in that center seat in economy class.

---

[3]Stephen R. Covey. *The Seven Habits of Highly Effective People: Powerful Lessons in Personal Change.* Salt Lake City, UT: Franklin Covey, 1989.

When I arrived at home that evening and my wife asked me about the trip, I said it was awful. Though I did get home earlier than planned, I considered it a bad trip because I did not get everything I wanted. I was unable to see beyond the fact that I gave up my first-class seat. Beware of all-or-nothing thinking. If you find yourself doing this, try to turn it around and affirm what went right. Try to recognize that things (and people) will never be perfect.

2. Always and Never

Another form of stinking thinking is when we see one negative event as a never-ending series of defeat or failure. The clue to this type of thinking is when we use words like always and never. This sounds like my daughter when she says, "we never get to do anything fun."

Do you use words like always and never? When you and your project team need to work through a weekend, do you find yourself thinking "we always have to work on our weekends," or "I never get any time to myself?" If someone else gets promoted, do you think "I never get considered for better jobs?" When we use the terms all or never, we are choosing to be a victim to circumstances and viewing life as beyond our control.

The key to breaking this type of thinking is to be alert to the use of the words "always" and "never." Rarely is it true that things are always or never a certain way. Instead of using always or never, look for and acknowledge the exceptions. More important, empower yourself by thinking through the ways that you can create different outcomes for yourself. If you feel like you never have enough time for yourself or you want a better job, determine what steps you can take now to have more time or get that better job. Remind yourself that you have a say in the outcome of your life.

3. Being Negative

Being negative is when we choose to focus only on the disagreeable things that happen. If we dwell on the negative, that becomes our reality.

I did this recently after teaching a class. In this case there were twenty-six students. As I went through the students' evaluations of the course, there was one in particular that was harsh. The student felt there were "too many irrelevant stories" and that I should have "kept the class moving." While the other twenty-five evaluations were all very positive, I focused only on the one negative evaluation.

Another situation was on a large, long-term project I was managing. At the end of the first year, we solicited feedback from our clients on how we were doing. There was a mix of positive and constructive feedback. I chose to focus on one negative statement. The client stated that the delivery of "software was often late and of poor quality." To this day, that is the only piece of feedback that I remember from the meeting and the client feedback.

In both of these cases, I vividly remember the negative comments and little if anything else. I chose to focus on the negative only.

We can also be negative by ignoring or discounting the positives. Instead of focusing on the negative, we choose to discount or reject examples where we did well or were successful. We find a reason for the positive not to count because it wasn't good enough or because anyone would have done the same thing if they were in our shoes. This type of thinking really strips us of the happiness and satisfaction we should experience.

I sometimes do this to myself by hiding behind my project team. When there is a success on a project, I say to myself "this was the result of having a strong team," or "any PM could have succeeded in this situation."

Negative thinking and behavior can be so ingrained that you are unable to see it without the help of others. If you are a person who focuses on the negative, you may not be aware of it. You can start by asking your friends and family if they see you as a negative person.

Breaking the habit of being negative can be tough. If you do find out that you are negative, ask others for support. Practice finding the positive in every situation, in yourself and your performance, and in every other person.

4. Filling in the Blanks

We fill in the blanks when we interpret things a certain way, usually negatively, without any facts to support our interpretation. We attribute a negative interpretation to a person or situation without any justification.

For example, consider a situation where you've submitted a project proposal to a client. If the client does not get back to you immediately, you may jump to the conclusion that they did not like you or your proposal. You may start to think things like "that was a waste of time, I shouldn't have spent my time working on that." A more accurate interpretation is that you simply expected the client to respond faster than they actually did.

5. Should Statements

The word "should" is a red flag. It has many negative connotations and where possible I advise you to strike it from your vocabulary. When someone tells you that you should do something or should have done something, they are meddling, controlling, or shaming you. Should is a word that makes the hair on the back of my neck stand up.

You may direct should statements at yourself with the intent to motivate. You might say something like, "I should have known better than to trust Jeremy" or "I shouldn't have told them they could take until Monday on the deliverable." Should statements can lead to guilt and frustration. If you use should on yourself or on others, stop. It is unhealthy.

One way to overcome use of the word should is to use "I want" statements. Instead of saying, "you should turn in your status report by Friday" (or worse, "you should have turned in your status report last Friday"), say "I want you to turn in your status report by Friday." The expression "I want" is a more direct and clean way of stating your expectations for the desired behavior.

6. Personalization and Blame

Personalization is when we take responsibility for events that are not entirely within our control. We take personally what could be simply a random event. We might combine personalization with a should statement and say something like "I should never have said that to Jonathan; he quit the team because of me."

Personalization can be tricky for PMs and leaders. Sometimes it is entirely appropriate to take responsibility for the results or outcomes of the team we are leading. Sometimes we need to step up and say, "That was my fault." However, it is not always healthy to take responsibility for everything that happens.

Blame is the opposite of personalization. This is when we are quick to affix the blame for an event or incident. Blame is when we put the responsibility for ourselves and our situation on others.

A more balanced approach is to think of the principle of co-creation. We co-create everything that happens to us. We are partly responsible and others are partly responsible. We will talk more about co-creation in Chapter 6, Relationship Management.

Identifying Your Own Patterns of Stinking Thinking

The common theme with all stinking thinking is its negative connotation. We are choosing to be negative instead of positive. This thinking often represents our own fears and dark thoughts.

The first step toward overcoming stinking thinking is to recognize what you are experiencing. This type of thinking is a habit and perhaps one that we have had for our whole lives. We need to be able to see and recognize the habit before we are able to change or eliminate it. As with the other self-management concepts we have talked about, we can use some of the following techniques to overcome distorted thinking:

Journal

Keep a journal of what has occurred, your thoughts, and your feelings. You can use this to track back and understand how your negative thoughts are impacting you.

Get Help from a Friend

Get input from a trusted friend, spouse, co-worker, boss, or mentor. Use their feedback to see where your thinking is distorted.

Seek Professional Help

As noted earlier, you may need to seek professional help if you get stuck and cannot get to the next level without it.

Good News About Emotional Breakdowns

There is some good news about emotional breakdowns. First, they are predictable. If we can identify the triggers that set us off, we can begin to predict when we are vulnerable and are likely to experience a breakdown. That predictability is good because it can help us to avoid or reduce the severity of the breakdown.

Second, breakdowns often escalate slowly. We don't normally go from a calm and peaceful state directly into a breakdown. Rather, there is more likely a series of steps we go through that builds until we are primed for a breakdown. That slow escalation can provide time for us to interrupt the process and prevent the breakdown. Knowing that breakdowns are predictable and escalate slowly gives us motivation to interrupt the breakdown before it occurs.

■ Techniques to Improve Our Self-Management

A Three-Step Process for Self-Management

We have talked about the need for PMs to use self-management and self-control when it comes to emotions. Before we move from a focus on self-management in this chapter to a focus on others in Chapter 5, I would like to introduce a three-step process that can be used for self-management. This process will help us to improve our self-control and avoid emotional breakdowns.

As we have discussed, emotional breakdowns are often predictable and escalate slowly. Leveraging our self-awareness, we can take steps to understand the emotions and underlying cause. As shown in Figure 4-5, the three-step process includes identifying the feeling, determining the underlying cause, and taking action to get clear.

Step 1—Identify the Feeling

The management of emotions starts with awareness of emotions. This awareness might simply be strong anger over a missed deliverable, unease about a

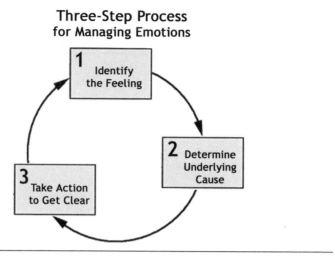

Figure 4-5: Three-Step Process for Managing Our Emotions.

meeting, or simply a nagging awareness of something that is not quite right. Whatever our starting point, we need to use the self-awareness techniques to identify the feeling. Once we are aware of the specific feeling or emotion, we can start to do something about it.

Step 2—Determine the Underlying Cause

Once aware of our feeling or emotion, we need to trace back and understand the source or cause of that emotion. In the previous example of the anger over a missed deliverable, we can trace our anger back to the deliverable. But we need to look further than the simple act of missing the deliverable. We need to ask what else is leading to our anger. Are we angry because we don't tolerate mistakes? Or, are we scared because we should have monitored the progress more closely or because it will make us look bad as a PM?

In the case of the unease over an important client meeting, we can trace the cause to the importance of the meeting. We are scared because the meeting is important to us. Our bodies automatically use fear to generate adrenaline that helps us prepare for the meeting and carries us through that stressful time. So it may be appropriate to feel scared.

Step 3—Take Action to Get Clear

Once we understand the cause of the feeling or emotion, we can take action to get clear. This is critical. If we take action to get at the cause of the negative feelings, we can establish new ways of thinking and behaving. This doesn't necessarily mean we must take radical action. The appropriate action could be to simply recognize that our reaction was out of line or that our interpretation of the situation caused us unnecessary anger.

The Do-Over

Taking action to get clear could involve a do-over. A do-over is when you repeat the situation but you change your behavior to achieve a different emotional outcome. A do-over may not even involve the other person in the conflict. It might be more appropriate to scream in your car on the way home (with the windows up, of course) or punch out your pillow or mattress.

Sometimes we can role-play the event and choose to handle the situation in a more responsible or appropriate way. You might role-play with someone besides the person involved in the conflict, for example, a confidant, peer, or coach.

How would we get clear in the previous situations? We can get clear with our anger over the deliverable by meeting with the team resource responsible for delivering. We can explain that we are angry because of their behavior and then let them know why (it causes the client to lose confidence or some other reason). We might conclude with what we would want them to do differently in the future. By telling them we were angry, we are able to get clear.

■ Additional Techniques for Self-Control and Self-Management

The basic three-step process for self-management is helpful for most situations. Here are some additional techniques you can use to manage yourself and your emotions:

1. Reduce Your Stress Level

PMs should be familiar with the need to reduce stress and have at least one method that they employ. There are a multitude of stress reduction methods starting with easy things like exercise and self-care all the way through more radical approaches like getting a new job or leaving an abusive relationship. Previously discussed techniques include prayer and meditation. My coach is a big believer in using breathing techniques. The point is that there are a lot of different ways to reduce stress and I encourage you to experiment until you find one that works for you. On the other hand, if you are one of those people who thrive on stress and intentionally create it in your life, what I write here won't matter much to you anyway.

2. Conduct an Inner Dialog of Self-Parenting

You may find that you benefit by speaking to yourself as if you were parenting a small child. Replace any harsh self-talk with kind and gentle words. Just don't do this out loud in front of your project team or they may think you are losing it.

3. Talk It Out with Someone

Besides having several different mentors and coaches outside work, I have had the luxury over the last 2 years of having a good friend and member of my program management team who is always willing to be a sounding board for my ideas. I have found this invaluable. If you don't have someone in your professional life whom you can bounce ideas off, find someone. It is a bonus if you can also ask them to hold you accountable to make changes or follow through on your commitments.

4. Give Yourself a Time Out

If you find yourself heading toward a breakdown, give yourself a time out. Leave the building, go to lunch early, quit for the day, or just head out to the nearest coffee shop for a snack. If you are at home, you can punch a pillow or hit a bed with a tennis racquet. Some people find exercise helpful.

5. Write a Letter or E-Mail You Will Not Send

A technique that Abraham Lincoln reportedly practiced was to write letters he did not plan to send. The idea is that through expressing your emotions in writing, you are able to release any emotional charge. This worked well for Abe when he used paper and pencil but may not work as well today with our modern office tools. For example, we may type an e-mail that we don't plan to send and then actually end up sending it inadvertently. Some organizations monitor all e-mails, even unsent ones. Other organizations use keystroke logging software to record everything typed at a keyboard including documents, unsent e-mail, and instant messages.

6. Use Appropriate Humor

There is nothing like laughter to remind us to not take ourselves too seriously. You can crack a joke, watch a sitcom, read something funny, or find someone amusing to hang out with. Scott Adams is great at skewering PMs in the Dilbert cartoon; check out his collection online. If you can afford it, add a really funny person to your project team. Of course they would need to have an official role and work assigned to them or your project sponsors might not find it all that funny.

7. Take Care of Yourself

As noted in the chapter, we need to take care of ourselves to help prevent emotional breakdowns. This includes taking vacations, getting enough sleep, resting when sick, and getting support from others. Evaluate how you are doing at self-care and select one or more of these areas to make an investment in yourself.

Building Project Stakeholder Relationships

In Part 3, we are going to shift from focusing on ourselves to focusing on others. In particular, we will explore the emotional and social skills that support relationships.

Leading others is all about relationships. If we build solid relationships with team members and other project stakeholders, we improve our ability to lead. Without relationships, leadership is difficult or impossible.

Relationships build on the foundations of emotional self-mastery that we established in Chapters 3 and 4. Our ability to build relationships comes from our emotional self-awareness and self-management. We cannot skip over those steps. It is tough to build strong relationships with others if we are struggling with our own issues.

We will start with Chapter 5, Social Awareness. Social awareness involves our ability to read people and situations. Part 3 concludes with Chapter 6, Relationship Management, which deals with developing strong relationships with others.

Social Awareness

An Introduction to Social Awareness

Social awareness is the ability to understand the emotions of others. It is one of the five building blocks of our project management framework for emotional intelligence as shown in Figure 5-1. It includes the competencies of empathy, organizational awareness, seeing others clearly, and emotional boundaries.

Simply put, social awareness is the ability to accurately read situations and people, and to understand and empathize with the emotions of others. I believe that most PMs have at least some level of social awareness. It is impossible to progress very far as a PM without social awareness for the following reasons.

First, as we said in Chapter 2, project management is about getting work done through others. If you cannot understand and relate to others, it will be difficult to get work done through them.

Second, all projects are temporary (or at least they are supposed to be). As PMs, we don't usually have the luxury of gradually building long-term relationships with our teams. Rather, we need to work with new teams and new stakeholders on a regular basis, maybe as often as every six or nine months. Each new project brings with it the potential for different faces and relationships and the urgency to move quickly to develop productive relationships. Our ability to quickly and accurately read and understand others is critical to our success.

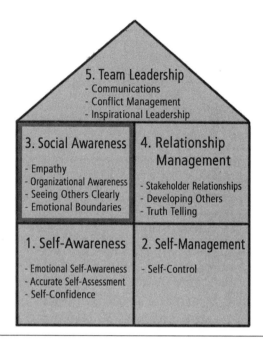

Figure 5-1: Emotional Intelligence Model for PM Showing Social Awareness.

Finally, projects are risky and successful delivery is never guaranteed. PMs need all the help they can get to succeed. Being adept at reading situations and people is one way that project managers can improve their chances for success.

So how do PMs use social awareness? It comes into play whenever we are working with others; that is, all the time for project managers. Here are some typical situations where social awareness is at work:

1. Understanding the verbal and nonverbal communications of different stakeholders.
2. Understanding the motivations of our team members so that we can align them with the objectives of the project.
3. Improving your understanding of stakeholders and politics.
4. Providing feedback and constructive criticism to team members.
5. Recognizing and addressing hostility, conflict, and other negative behaviors.

Social awareness is part of our own personal radar, which provides us a rich source of information about our environment. Recall how David Caruso and Peter Salovey made the point in their book *The Emotionally Intelligent*

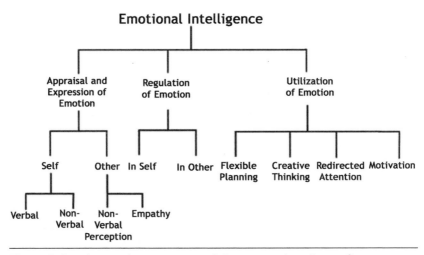

Figure 5-2: Salovey and Mayer Framework for Emotional Intelligence.[2]

Manager that emotion is information.[1] Now think about that for a moment. Emotions provide us information about our environment. Social awareness is specific information about the people we are interacting with on our teams.

Unfortunately, not everyone is able to leverage this radar or the information it provides. Self-awareness is the precursor to social awareness. We understand others through awareness of our own emotions. Individuals who have a difficult time recognizing their own emotions will struggle to recognize emotions in others. In the next section, we are going to dive into the topic of social awareness and provide some tools and examples on how we can improve our skills in this area.

What the Experts Say About Social Awareness

Mayer and Salovey were the first emotional intelligence researchers to address the concept of Social Awareness in their 1990 paper titled "Emotional Intelligence." That paper contained one of the first Emotional Intelligence Frameworks. Though they did not call it Social Awareness, that is essentially what Mayer and Salovey described in the section of their framework called "Appraisal and Expression of Emotion" in others, as shown in Figure 5-2.

[1]David R. Caruso and Peter Salovey. *The Emotionally Intelligent Manager; How to Develop and Use the Four Key Emotional Skills of Leadership.* Hoboken, NJ: John Wiley & Sons, Inc., 2004.

[2]Peter Salovey and John D. Mayer. *Emotional Intelligence: Imagination Cognition, and Personality,* Volume 9, No. 3. Amityville, NY: Baywood Publishing Co., Inc., 1990.

Mayer and Salovey introduced two sub-components of that domain of appraisal and expression of emotion in others: non-verbal perception and empathy. Nonverbal perception is the ability to recognize the unspoken emotions of others. Non-verbal cues include facial expressions and body language.

The second sub-component, empathy, is the ability to comprehend another's feelings and re-experience those feelings. Mayer and Salovey were the first to link empathy back to self-awareness. That is, you cannot feel what others feel without first being aware of what *you* feel. As previously discussed, Daniel Goleman's research came after and built on the work of Mayer and Salovey. Goleman first called this domain "social competence" and later changed it to "social awareness" in the framework included in *Primal Leadership*. That framework included the three social awareness competencies of empathy, service orientation, and organizational awareness. Goleman's use of empathy is consistent with Salovey and Mayer. However, service orientation and organizational awareness were new with the Goleman framework.[3]

Service orientation and organizational awareness are both relevant to project managers. Service orientation is about understanding the unstated emotional needs of a customer. Organizational awareness is the ability to interpret the emotions and politics of groups. Think of organizational awareness as the expansion of social awareness from individuals to groups of people. It is about the ability to accurately understand situations in spite of our own distortions.

A good question right now is what does all this mean to you as a PM? That is exactly the question we are going to address in this chapter. We will look at the specific aspects of social awareness that are most important to PMs. This includes a few social awareness competencies that are not part of Goleman's framework. For project management purposes, I extended the basic framework to include seeing others clearly and emotional boundaries.

■ Empathy

Empathy is one of the most important parts of social awareness and perhaps one of the most critical people skills for PMs and other leaders. Empathy is the ability to understand and relate to the emotions of others. It helps us to walk in the shoes of another or to see things from another's point of view. This

---

[3]Daniel Goleman, Richard Boyatzis, and Annie McKee. *Primal Leadership.* Boston: Harvard Business School Press, 2002, p. 39.

section introduces the following facets of empathy and how they play out in the project environment:

1. Ability to read the spoken and unspoken thoughts and feelings of others
2. Ability to appreciate the thoughts and feelings of others and why they have them
3. Capacity to respect and value people from diverse backgrounds and cultures

Empathy is not a new concept by any stretch of the imagination. Most people have probably heard the following quote:

> "Don't criticize someone until you have walked a mile in their shoes."
> —Unknown

Or perhaps you have heard the twisted adaptation of that idea as reflected in this quote:

> "Before you criticize someone, you should walk a mile in their shoes.
> That way, when you criticize them, you're a mile away
> and you have their shoes."
> —Unknown

That second quote is funny only because it highlights one of the biggest challenges to empathy; our own self-centeredness. The truth is that we are all primarily selfish, self-absorbed, self-obsessed and self-interested. We will take a closer look at that in a moment.

The importance of empathy was explained very well in Stephen Covey's book *The Seven Habits of Highly Effective People.* Covey's fifth habit was empathy: Seek first to understand, then to be understood.

Embedded in that phrase is the simple wisdom of orienting first to the other person. A great deal of conflict that we experience on projects could be reduced or eliminated if we simply tried first to understand the other person's point of view before we tried to convince them with our own message. We need to listen to them with the purpose of understanding what it is they are trying to say.[4]

---

[4]Stephen R. Covey. *The Seven Habits of Highly Effective People: Powerful Lessons in Personal Change.* Salt Lake City, UT: Franklin Covey, 1989.

Seeking first to understand is a simple premise that is often difficult to execute. Granted, many PMs excel at empathy. But for the rest of us, empathy can be difficult. Why do we find empathy difficult as PMs? Here are some possible reasons:

1. Self-Orientation

As noted above, as humans we are selfish and self-oriented. It is unnatural to think of others first. Further, we are anxious to impose our worldview on others. We expect others to think like us and act like us. After all, ours is the correct way. Covey called this our own "rightness" and putting our "autobiography" on others.

A good example is when as parents we are talking with our children and we say things that start with, "When I was a kid. . . ." Don't think this only applies to our child rearing; we do the same thing to our teams. Our feedback and coaching is often based on what worked for us in similar projects or situations.

2. Results First

As PMs, we are focused on getting results and achieving the end goals of the project. The Nike slogan "Just Do It" was likely created by a PM. (Perhaps the PM could have enhanced it by saying "Just Do It Now!"). Spending time understanding others can be viewed as in direct conflict with the need and urgency to complete the work on the project.

One way to overcome this thinking is to see the development of others (the project team, our peers, and our leaders) as one of the goals of the project. People learn best by doing and the project is a great environment for that learning.

Paradoxically, the approach of viewing the development of the team as a goal will often speed the achievement of the other project goals. Rather than taking away from the work on the project, this approach provides energy, inspires people, and builds the capacity to do more. We will explore the competency of developing others in Chapter 6.

3. Tough Stuff

Empathy requires communicating in difficult ways. For example, many of us never developed effective listening skills. We often approach conversation as simply taking turns talking. Listening for most of us is being poised, waiting for the other person to take a breath. Then we quickly jump in, like a Chicago taxi driver waiting for enough space between the cars in the lane beside them so they can barge on over. We are often less invested in listening to others than we are about getting our own point across.

4. We Are Smarter Than Others

As the PM, we are smarter than everyone else or at least the rest of the project team, right? Otherwise, why would the project sponsor put us in charge? Because we are smarter, everyone else should hear what we have to say and do things the way we want things done. Obviously I am kidding to make a point. To the extent we buy into that theory or act like that, we are not being empathetic.

These are probably only a few of the reasons that empathy is so hard for PMs. In the next section, we are going to explore empathy more and then turn our attention to ways to improve our empathy toward others.

Empathetic Listening

One of the key applications of empathy is empathetic listening, listening without judgment. When we listen empathetically we: 1) focus on the words and behavior of another without judgment and 2) periodically summarize what they think, feel, and need in the moment. That seems like a pretty tall order and one that requires a little more explanation.

Empathetic listening is considerably different than just regular listening. Many of us listen half-heartedly, attempt to multi-task, or view listening as a pause that allows us to gather our thoughts before we can continue with our own monologue. We might consider that pathetic listening.

Empathetic listening is when we give ourselves over to the other person and listen with their best interest in mind. Project managers that master empathetic listening benefit by:

1. Making the speaker feel valued and important.
2. Improving the depth of the communication.
3. Understanding the underlying emotions, which adds richness to the conversation.
4. Building trust and the relationship with the other.

So what do we do as PMs to improve our empathetic listening? Consider applying the following techniques to enhance your empathetic listening skills:

1. Let Others Speak

When we listen empathetically, we simply let the other person speak. We avoid "helping" the speaker by providing verbal or nonverbal clues, or by finishing sentences. When we jump in and help others with what they are trying to say, we unintentionally inject our own agenda. We may unknowingly steer the speaker toward what we want or expect them to say instead of simply letting them take the conversation where it needs to go.

2. Maintain Eye Contact

When we listen empathetically, we should maintain eye contact with the speaker. This provides the speaker the space to say what they need to say. Note that this doesn't mean we should be staring them down or boring in with our best "Dirty Harry" scowl. It does mean looking at the speaker with a neutral expression, providing minimal feedback, and breaking eye contact periodically if it becomes uncomfortable.

3. Give the Speaker Your Full Attention

As PMs, we are often trying to accomplish several things at once. In our efforts to be productive, we might be trying to multi-task while we are listening. Empathetic listening is a single thread activity. It doesn't work if you multi-task.

You probably know how it feels to have someone multi-task while they are listening to you. Whether that person is reading their PC screen or looking over your shoulder to see someone else, it feels dismissive. Have you ever been speaking to someone when their cell phone rang or their Black-Berry buzzed and they immediately turned away from you to see who was calling? This kind of behavior says to the speaker that the listener does not value them.

4. Playback and Summarize

When we listen empathetically, we should periodically repeat back what we heard to make sure that we understood what was being said. This provides the speaker an opportunity to restate or clarify anything that was misunderstood.

As an example, consider a team member who comes to you with a concern. They tell you that they are hurt by the actions of Bob, their co-worker. You might say "Let me see if I have this straight. You feel dismissed by Bob when he doesn't say positive things about your contribution to the deliverable." In this way, they have the opportunity to either agree or clarify the concern.

5. Orient to Emotions

Empathetic listening involves interpreting the thoughts and feelings of another. In addition to playing back what we hear and summarizing it, we should also add feeling words to what we say. "That sounds frustrating," or "you seem angry" might be appropriate to the team member in the previous example.

6. Try on Their Shoes

Trying on someone's shoes requires us to imagine ourselves in their situation as we listen. We need to do this in a compassionate way and not come at it from a superior "Boy, are you screwed" point of view. We need to be thinking, what would it be like to be that person right now? What would I be feeling in that situation? This sounds more difficult than it really is; we just need to use our imagination or perhaps think back to a similar situation that we were involved in.

7. Suspend Our Judgment

Empathetic listening requires us to suspend our own judgments, needs, and priorities and focus on the other person. This is a skill that requires some practice. Listening without regard for our own agenda is very generous and self-less.

What we do with what we hear during our empathetic listening is also important. I personally find it easy to jump in and problem-solve or to use this as an opportunity to apply my own autobiography on others by telling them how I solved the same problem. The temptation is to simply tell them to be like me and solve it the way I did. This method is not terribly empathetic or effective. It doesn't work with my wife and it doesn't work in the project environment.

A more effective approach is to simply say, "that sounds tough," "how can I help?" or "what support do you need from me right now?" This puts the focus on the speaker, where it belongs. Many times you will find that the speaker is not asking for us to solve the problem. They may realize during the course of the discussion what they need to do next. They often don't need (or want) us to do anything—they simply needed to be heard. If we proceed to tell them what to do to solve the problem when they simply want to be heard, we risk alienating them. They will probably come away thinking that we are superior, uncaring, and unsupportive. In addition, we take on the work of that person instead of empowering them to solve their own problems.

One of the best and most memorable comments I received from a team member came a few years ago. This guy had worked for me for about six months when he said, "You are not like other project managers I have worked with. You always ask me what you can do to support me." Frankly, I wish I were more consistent with this behavior. If you are asking a lot from people, it helps to show them that you care and are willing to help them to get it done. In the case of this particular team member, he rarely asked me for help but apparently appreciated the fact that I was willing to help if he needed it.

■ Seeing Others Clearly

We can also use our knowledge of emotions, emotional triggers, and emotional breakdowns to better understand and even predict the behaviors of others. I think of this as our ability to see others clearly. As PMs, it is important that we are able to understand others and their emotional state. This includes our project team, executive sponsor, and all the other project stakeholders.

How do we see others clearly? How do we understand and interpret emotions in others? Actually, it is something that we already do to some extent or another. We were probably never taught a step-by-step method for doing it, but we all read people and their emotions all the time.

That said, I believe that it can be more difficult to read others in the workplace than in other settings. The workplace has become an arena where people are not expected or allowed to show emotions. People mask, cover-up, or attempt to hide their true emotions. Many just don't believe it proper to display emotions.

Consider this example from an organization I recently worked with. The president of the company was comfortable expressing his emotions. In fact, he was known for getting choked up and crying during presentations or heartfelt discussions. While some in the organization simply ignored it, others felt uncomfortable and thought it was inappropriate. Some even believed it was contrived. Those people were uncomfortable with that level of emotional display in the workplace.

How Do We See Others Clearly?

When someone is crying, it is easy to see they are experiencing a lot of emotion. What if they aren't as direct about what they are feeling? Here are some techniques we can use to determine what others are feeling.

1. We can start by asking ourselves what we are feeling. Awareness of the emotions of others starts with our awareness of our own emotions. What we are feeling when we are with someone is a great clue as to what they are feeling. If we feel scared, it is likely the other person feels scared. Or, it could

be that they are angry and we are responding to that anger. If we feel happy, it is likely the other person feels happy or excited. Our emotions are a guide to the emotions of others.

2. Listen for emotion words. Another clue to what people are feeling is the words that they use. They may not always say it clearly, but if they use emotion words, we can use that as information to the underlying emotion.

When someone uses the words "disappointed," "hurt," or "ticked off," they are talking about levels of anger. If they mention "nervous," "concerned," or "worried," they are talking about being scared.

When we listen with empathy, we may want to say the emotion words back to them. For example, we might say "you sound angry" or, "you sound worried." This can often prompt someone to open up and share what they are feeling.

3. Another way to determine what others are feeling is to look at their face. Look into their eyes. As discussed previously, the eyes are the window to the soul. It is difficult to fake the emotions on our faces. Figure 5-3 shows the 6 emotional families and how they will appear on our faces.

Look for congruence between what people say, what their faces show, and their body language. I remember an incident with a project team member who was clearly upset. When I said that she sounded angry, she sat with her arms crossed and said in a defiant tone, "I am not angry!" The inconsistency between her stated emotions and her body language was a tip-off that her emotional rules said that anger was not appropriate. Even though she was very angry, she was not going to express it.

Seeing others clearly is a critical skill for a PM who is striving to be emotionally intelligent. However, it is not always easy to do. There are three main obstacles to seeing others clearly: our own filters and biases, our autobiography that we impose on others, and the shortcuts we take to put others into categories.

1. Filters and Biases

We view the world through our filters. We all have a set of prejudices, biases, rules, and distortions that affect the way we see the world and the people in it. These prejudices and distortions are ingrained in us. They have been part of us for so long that it is nearly impossible to be conscious of them without significant work. Like the fish in a fish tank, we cannot see or appreciate the water around us.

One of the biggest filters is our own family of origin, or the family we grew up in. How we see others is impacted by the interactions we had with our parents and siblings growing up. A common example is that our view of

SAD:
Mouth corners turned down, inner brows up and together, eyes slightly closed.

ANGRY:
Teeth clenched, lips narrowed, inner corners of eyebrows down and together, eyes wide, nose flared.

SCARED:
Mouth contorted or frowning, eyes open, brows tight & raised.

HAPPY:
Smiling, rounded cheeks, crow's feet at corners of eyes.

EXCITED:
Smiling widely, eyes open, eyebrows raised, mouth open.

TENDER:
Mouth smiling lightly, eyes open & moist.

Figure 5-3: Faces of the 6 Families of Emotions.

authority figures is impacted by our relationship with our fathers. Any unresolved conflicts we have with our family of origin will create conflict in other relationships throughout our life.

Our family of origin is just one type of filter; there are others. The 2005 movie *Crash* was a big hit because it exposed the various biases and prejudices that different groups of people had toward each other. Whether the biases and prejudices are based on race, gender, appearance, social status, or ethnic background, they all have the same end result. They highlight the differences between us and others and cause unnecessary separation. The net result is that we are not able to see the members of our project teams for who they are and are unable to recognize their individual strengths and weaknesses.

2. Imposing Our Own Autobiography

The second obstacle to seeing others clearly is our own autobiography. We cannot see others clearly when we put our own story on them. We do this when we believe that others should do things the way that we did them, or that ours is the right way to approach things.

I often find that I do this when people on my teams ask me about career advancement. A frequent question that I get is "should I go for my PMP certification or go back to school for my MBA?" Instead of focusing on them and trying to help them think through the decision criteria, I often find myself referring to my situation and what worked for me. This doesn't serve others well.

3. We Take Shortcuts for Efficiency

The third obstacle to seeing others clearly is the shortcuts we take. Project managers are generally pretty busy individuals. We take shortcuts to be as efficient as possible. One shortcut we take is pigeonholing people. We pigeonhole others when we try to quickly sort out what they are about so that we can put them into a category or group.

The benefit of the shortcut is that we think we understand or know all about them because of who they are, how they appear, or where they are from. We don't have to learn everything about them.

Not all shortcuts are bad, but you should be very careful when you use them. In the following section, we will look at a shortcut that will help us to identify the emotional behaviors of others.

Identifying the Modus Operandi (MO) of Those You Work With

When we work closely together with the same people, we can identify a predictable emotional modus operandi (MO) or profile for each of them. Once we understand the MO of others, we can better understand and begin to predict their actions, emotions, and thoughts.

How do we determine the MO of the people who work with us on projects? We can extend the tools we learned earlier for self-awareness to social awareness. This includes determining their emotional state and seeing emotional triggers and stinking thinking in others. We can also use our understanding of emotional triggers and stinking thinking to better understand and even predict the behaviors of others.

The Emotional Intelligence Assessment Checklist shown in Appendix B includes the aspects of emotional self-awareness. You can use this checklist as a tool to understand the emotional intelligence of one of your team members, a sponsor, your manager, or some other stakeholder. The checklist includes the following sections:

- automatic or default emotion
- self-awareness
- expressiveness
- self-management
- emotional breakdowns
- stinking thinking
- changes and surprises
- stress
- social awareness

This checklist can help us to see others clearly and to understand their emotional state. This is the key to social awareness.

Techniques to Improve on Seeing Others Clearly

For those of us who want to improve our abilities to see others clearly, here are some steps we can take.

1. Recognize Our Own Biases
We can start by recognizing that we all have biases and prejudices. Just admitting that we have biases is a good first step. Then we can start to explore what those prejudices and biases might be.

2. Practice Studying Others
We can expand our understanding of others by viewing life as a game of exploration. We can strive to learn as much as possible about each person and be empathetic toward others.

Are you taking advantage of the opportunities around you to get to know people on a one-to-one basis? The key to improving our social awareness and ability to see others clearly is to practice. Like a muscle, we need to use our social awareness or we will lose it. Start today with the interactions you have with your project stakeholders. In your one-on-one meetings, take the time to reflect back what you think the other person is feeling. In meetings with groups, keep a tally of what people are feeling. You can use the Emotional Tally Sheet shown in Appendix A. Check it out with the individuals later to see if your observations were correct.

3. Use the Emotional Assessment Checklist
Try assessing yourself and others using the emotional awareness checklist. Be aware of the areas that you feel comfortable with as well as those areas where you feel less secure.

■ Organizational Awareness

The third competency of social awareness is organizational awareness. What exactly is organizational awareness? In *The Emotionally Intelligent Workplace,* Cherniss and Goleman define organizational awareness as:

> "the ability to read the currents of emotions
> and political realities in groups"
> —Cary Cherniss and Daniel Goleman[5]

Hmmm . . . "read the currents" sounds a little like reading the tea leaves and that reminds me of astrology or fortune telling. I hope organizational awareness is a little more grounded than that.

Interestingly enough, organizational awareness was not even part of Goleman's original framework for emotional intelligence. Instead, he included competencies like political awareness and team capabilities. In his 2002 book, *Primal Leadership,* which he co-authored with Richard Boyatzis and Annie McKee, Goleman simplified the framework and included organizational awareness as follows:

> A leader with a keen social awareness can be politically astute,
> able to detect crucial social networks and read key power
> relationships. Such leaders can understand the political forces
> at work in an organization, as well as the guiding values and
> unspoken rules that operate among people there.
> —Daniel Goleman, Richard Boyatzis, Annie McKee[6]

That description sounds very relevant, perhaps critical, to our success as project or program managers. I believe that the more we progress as PMs, the more our success is linked to organizational awareness. As we will see, this awareness includes not just the project, but also the company, customers, and vendors that are related to the project.

---

[5]Cary Cherniss and David Goleman. *The Emotionally Intelligent Workplace.* Hoboken, NJ: John Wiley & Sons, Inc., 2001.

[6]Daniel Goleman, Richard Boyatzis, and Annie McKee. *Primal Leadership.* Boston: Harvard Business School Press, 2002, p. 255.

Table 5-1: PM Assessment for Organizational Awareness

Level 1: Understands the structure and organization of the company and the client and uses that to manage effectively.

Level 2: Is familiar with the inner workings of the company and how to get things done informally. Is able to leverage the organizational capabilities for the client's benefit.

Level 3: Understands and leverages not only the company but the client and vendor organizations. Recognizes key decision makers in the environment.

Level 4: Understands the client's business as well or better than the client; consistently acts with the client's best interest in mind.

I first heard of organizational awareness back in 1993 before emotional intelligence was popular. Back then I was a senior project manager at a consulting firm. Our annual performance review was based on an instrument that measured 11 different dimensions of project management, including organizational awareness. Table 5-1 is a summary of the 4 levels of capability of organizational awareness. Read the description and then take a moment to see where you would place yourself on this progressive scale:

The focus of that assessment tool was to gauge a project manager's understanding of the people, climate, and culture of all the players in the project environment. It was an assessment of exactly what Goleman describes as organizational awareness.

The thing I liked about that tool was that it specifically called out the PM's understanding of the entire project environment. That included the company of course, as well as customers and vendors. I also liked that it provided me a vision of what it meant to excel in this particular area. I strove to master all the different levels.

You can also use this as a guide to mastering organizational awareness. How aware are you of all the players or stakeholders in your project environment, including customers, clients, subcontractors, and vendors? Are you aware of whom to call to get things done? Do you know how to influence the decision makers?

The two main aspects of organizational awareness that Goleman and Boyatzis discuss are identifying key power relationships and understanding the values and culture of the organization.

Key Power Relationships

Identifying key power relationships is about accurately recognizing the individuals who have power and political influence on our projects.

How well do you think you understand the power relationships for your project and organization? Here are some questions you can ask to help you sort out the power relationships

1. Who are the real decision makers on your project and in your organization? Are there any decision makers who are outside the official project chart or organizational chart?
2. Who has influence on the decisions made? Who has the power to say yes? Who has the power to say no?
3. Who gets advice from whom?
4. Who in this organization or team worked together before at another company? Have team members always worked together, even when they moved from organization to organization?

Questions like these can remind us to be systematic in evaluating the power relationships in our environment. For many of us, this is an ad hoc or even a missing process. Recognizing the decision makers for a project or organization is a critical first step to managing stakeholders, which is part of the domain of relationship management.

Understanding the Values and Culture of the Organization

Understanding the values and culture of the organization is also important. For project managers, this analysis must be done at both the project level and the broader organization level. The values and culture may be the same at the project and organization levels, or they might be quite different.

The most straightforward way to understand the value and culture of the organization is to read what the organization says the values are. Organizations declare their values in public ways in their mission or vision statements, by their slogans, or by the posters on the wall. While there could be a disconnect between what organizations say and what employees actually feel, the published version is a starting point for the analysis.

I was recently visiting one of the many Motorola facilities in Schaumburg, Illinois. The walls of the building were plastered with posters. It would be impossible for any employee in the building not to see the posters. The Motorola posters had the theme "My Moto," and they featured employees pictured with their various projects. Each of the posters showed a different facet of serving customers. The message seems to be "we're not the paternal organization we used to be; start acting like an entrepreneur."

Some organizations use symbols instead of posters. Consider the picture of loaner bikes shown in Figure 5-4. What does this picture say to you?

Figure 5-4: Loaner Bikes at Hewlett Packard in Roseville, CA.

I saw these loaner bikes at the Hewlett Packard Training Center in Roseville, CA. The bikes are scattered around the grounds of the facility to allow employees to move from building to building without using a car. When I saw them I immediately felt an emotional connection. I felt tradition, a sense of family, trust, independence, as well as stewardship. Were they intended to send an emotional message about the culture of the organization?

Take a moment to evaluate the posters and symbols in your work environment. What is the point that is being made? What do you think is the unstated messages of those posters and symbols?

A second place to look for the values of the organization is the annual report. What does this document say about the organization? Which projects, initiatives, and successes are bragged about in the report? Which are not mentioned?

I once led a large and long-term IT project for a big company. Each year when their annual report came out, I would scan it to see what was said about my project. When the project was prominently featured in the annual report the first year, I felt elated. The following year, when the project was not even mentioned, I felt sad. I felt like the message was that this project was no longer deemed to be important.

A third way to evaluate the culture and values of the organization is to look at the recognitions and rewards. Here are some questions you can use to evaluate them in a particular organization.

1. Who gets promoted and why?
2. What behavior gets rewarded?
3. What type of behavior gets punished?
4. How does the organization react to problems or challenges?
5. What happens when mistakes are made?
6. Are there written or unwritten rules about starting early or working late?
5. Are there rules around telling the truth or not telling the truth?
6. What does it take to succeed in your organization?
7. Who gets the largest bonus and why?
8. Who has been fired and why?

I have worked for several consulting organizations where there was a practice of laying off any individuals who were not working on any specific projects and were non-billable for any length of time. The value in those organizations was likely, "What have you done for me lately?" It is clear that this type of behavior affects project teams and the project managers who are trying to get work completed.

Consider also those organizations that reward hero-like efforts to meet deadlines. By hero-like, I don't mean people working hard. I am talking specifically about those last-minute efforts to rescue projects that are not doing well.

I once worked for an organization where individual hero-like behavior had actually become the norm because it was rewarded. Instead of planning ahead and managing to a reasonable schedule, the teams learned to stall, delay, and set up emergency situations where it was nearly impossible to succeed. Then the teams would work a long weekend or two (or overnight) to meet the deadline or milestone. These teams were regaled as heroes and rewarded accordingly. And as the stories about these successes were retold, it became clear to all parties that to succeed meant to narrowly avert a crisis.

A friend of mine likened this process to a bus driver "driving the bus close to the cliff" in order to instill appropriate fear in the passengers. The idea is that if the bus driver doesn't make it look dangerous once in a while, the passengers are not able to appreciate the job he is doing. It would be equivalent to a firefighter who sets fires so that he and his fellow firefighters can rush in, put out the fire, and be heroes.

Obviously, if the organization values crises and hero-like behavior, they are not likely to value your well-planned and effectively run projects that quietly move toward completion. And if that is the culture of the organization, it is good to recognize it up front so that you are not surprised when your well-run projects don't get much attention.

Finally, we can look at the stories told by the individuals in the organization to understand culture and values. The stories we tell about our past successes will provide a lot of information about the organization's values. Pay attention to the themes of those stories. They will tell you about the culture and values that are important in that organization.

I recommend that you systematically evaluate your project and organization. Determine the playing field for your project and for the organization. Try to determine the values and culture. If you don't understand it, you just might become a victim to it.

■ Emotional Boundaries

The next facet of social awareness for project managers is the competency of emotional boundaries. An emotional boundary is where one person's emotions leave off and another's begin. Think about the following quote for a moment:

> "Good fences make good neighbors."
> —Robert Frost, "Mending Wall"

It is pretty easy for us to understand the concept of a physical boundary like a fence. What about those boundaries that are less visible? For example, how close can you comfortably stand next to another person? Three feet apart? Two feet apart? What about in an elevator? A really crowded elevator? Have you ever noticed how people in a crowded elevator will continually try to adjust their position so that they maximize their own personal space? They will automatically moving closer together or farther apart as people enter and exit the elevator.

Emotional boundaries are even more difficult to discern, and that makes them harder to navigate. We previously discussed empathy and the need for project managers to be able to recognize and feel the emotions of others. However, empathy does not mean we should take on the emotions of others. As project managers, we need to recognize that we are separate and distinct from others. We need to be responsible for our own emotions and let others be responsible for theirs.

How do you know when there are issues with emotional boundaries? Have you ever heard anyone say that "I was in a good mood until you ruined it?" They are implying that they are powerless to control their own moods, that you have power over how they feel. Or consider a situation where you are in a meeting and someone gathers their stuff and walks out abruptly. As you glance around the room to gauge the responses of others someone invariably says, "was that me or was that him?" Here are some warning signs of individuals with emotional boundary issues.

Warning Signs of Emotional Boundary Issues

Moods and Feelings of Others

Individuals with boundary issues may take on the moods and feelings of others. This is different from empathy, which is the ability to understand the moods and feelings of others as noted above. Individuals with boundary issues will become more vested in the moods and feelings of others and lose track of their own feelings. As my mentor says, they need to "take someone else's temperature to see how they are feeling." They may also become so bothered by the moods and feelings of others that they try to "fix" the other so that they can feel better."

Pleasing Others

Those with boundary issues will often sacrifice themselves to please others. This often results in them forgoing their own choices or needs. As an example, consider when you have a small group going out to lunch or making some other group choice. Some individuals will go along with a choice they do not want (and may even hate) just to fit in and please others or not rock the boat.

Victim-Like Behavior

Pleasing others can be taken to the extreme of becoming a victim. Individuals with boundary issues often find that to please others they feel that they cannot say no. They end up feeling victimized by others. The reality is that they allow others to take advantage of them. This allows them to resent others and feel anger toward them. We will look more at saying no in Chapter 6.

Cannot Express Wants and Needs

Individuals with boundary issues often are unable to express their own wants and needs. They either are totally unaware of what they want or need, or they are afraid or reluctant to share what they need. Ironically, though they cannot (or will not) express themselves, they often mistakenly believe others should anticipate those unstated wants and needs and fulfill them.

Recognizing individuals with boundary issues is necessary for project managers. Otherwise, our efforts to be more emotional in the work environment can be risky. Individuals with boundary issues will play the victim, expect you to act in certain unstated ways based on how a parent or sibling treated them, or create other problems for you. Recognizing these individuals is the first step in protecting yourself against them playing victim to your strong emotional leadership.

Respect Emotional Boundaries

A key concept of emotional boundaries is that we are responsible only for our own emotions. It is unhealthy for us to become too concerned with the emotions of others. This can be a fine line for project managers (and other leaders) looking to understand and affect the emotions of those around them. It can be difficult to discern between healthy and unhealthy concern for the emotions of others. Here are some ways that we can respect our own emotional boundaries as well as the boundaries of others.

Respond Appropriately
How we respond to the emotions of others is a key to our own emotional sanity. While we want to use empathy to understand the feelings of others, we need to be careful not to become "hooked in" to the emotions they are experiencing. We need to exercise our own self-control in emotional and stressful situations. We need to choose our responses carefully. For example, if we can remain calm and steadfast when others are angry, we can help to defuse that anger. We don't need to ramp it up and get just as angry as the other person. Instead, we can remain centered and unemotional and help them to deal with their own feelings.

Take Responsibility
Our own response should include taking responsibility for our feelings. When I take responsibility for my own feelings, I acknowledge that they are my feelings alone and that I have a choice about them. Before we can take responsibility we have to be self-aware enough to know what it is we are feeling.

This could be as simple as saying "I feel angry when you come late to the weekly status meeting." Do you see how this is subtly different from saying "you made me angry?" That is the difference between being responsible for our feelings and being a victim of others. That feeling of anger is a choice that we made based on the circumstances.

Let Them Be

The flip-side of our responsibility is letting others be responsible for their feelings. We cannot control others. Often we need to simply let them have their reaction to our words or actions. If they are going to be angry or sad, let that happen.

This can be tricky for project managers. We want to understand the impact of our actions, emotions, and decisions on the individuals on our teams. But we should not necessarily change just because someone is going to get angry or sad. We need to let them have their reaction.

A few years ago one of my team members thought he should be promoted to a team lead. I remember the angst that I felt since I knew he wasn't the best person for the job. I put off the decision because I knew he was going to be angry. Instead of simply making the announcement and letting that person have his reaction, I tiptoed around it for nearly a month. I lacked sufficient courage to simply let that person be, and let him react to the decision. I was afraid of his anger.

If you can learn to simply let others have their reaction to what you say and do, you will free yourself. Otherwise, you will be at the mercy of other people's emotions. You will be continually looking outside yourself and playing it safe. Others will quickly pick up on your lack of courage and may use it to their own advantage.

You Cannot Fix Other People

An important lesson that I learned with regards to emotional boundaries is that I could not fix other people. While we want to strive to be as aware of the people on our team or in our environment as possible, becoming aware of others is very different from fixing them.

> Trying to fix other people is an exercise in futility.

Better Communications Around Boundaries

One way to improve our emotional communications and keep clear boundaries is to communicate with feeling words. Tell the other person what they did, how you felt about it and why, and what you want them to do differently in the future. There are four distinct parts to this communication:

"when you do . . . _____" (some behavior or action)
"I feel . . . _____" (an emotion, such as sad or angry)
"because . . . _____" (the reason)
"I want . . . _____" (here is what I want in the future).

In the abstract, this may sound somewhat, well, formulaic. Let's look at how you might apply this strategy in the project environment. Consider a situation when you have someone on your team doing something that makes you angry. I once had a team lead named Tom reporting to me who drank alcohol at lunch and then returned to work. I didn't like it and felt it was inappropriate but I never said anything. I was scared of Tom's reaction. Here is a better way for me to have handled the situation.

"Tom, when you drink at lunch, I feel angry because I think it affects your performance and lowers the standards for our entire team. I want you to drink responsibly and not come to work under the influence of alcohol." Had I said something like that I would probably have gained agreement and buy-in from Tom.

In Chapter 6 we will explore further the concept of truth telling and we will see how important it is for our stakeholder relationships.

Seek Professional Help

If you are struggling to deal with individuals on your team who have boundary issues, you might benefit from professional help. A trained therapist, counselor, or psychiatrist might help you to prepare better for dealing with those people.

Please don't interpret this to mean that you should recommend psychiatric help for others. It is generally *never* wise to suggest professional help for the members of your team unless you have a high trust relationship. "You ought to see a shrink" is likely to land you in the HR department attempting to defend all your good intentions.

■ Techniques for Improving Our Social Awareness

Now that we have a solid understanding of what social awareness is all about, what can we do to improve our competency in this area? Here are fifteen different techniques you can use to improve your social awareness.

1. Improve Your Empathetic Listening Skills

Improving your empathetic listening skills is one of the single most important steps you can take to improve your social awareness. Practice listening with empathy, reminding yourself of the following key aspects of empathetic listening:

- Let others speak without helping them
- Maintain eye contact
- Give them your full attention
- Use playback and summarizing
- Orient to emotions
- Put yourselves in their shoes
- Suspend your agenda while listening.

2. Take a Class on Listening Skills

Listening skills are important enough to warrant a class. Find a class on active or empathetic listening techniques and learn all that you can. Practice the skills at work, at home, and in every social situation that you can.

3. Track Emotions During Team Meetings

Becoming aware of the emotions of others is a skill we can learn if we practice. Use the emotional tally sheet shown in Appendix A to track your own feelings as well as those with whom you interact. Try it and see if you start to become more attuned to the thoughts and emotions of others.

　　If you are using this tally sheet during a meeting, don't worry that you won't be ready to talk when the time comes. Social awareness is about being aware of others and not simply waiting for our own turn to talk. By the way, this technique is especially helpful to stay engaged during those interminable teleconferences where you cannot see everyone's face.

4. Identify Emotional Red Flags in Others

In Chapter 3 we discussed the importance of recognizing emotional red flags in ourselves and in others including:

- inappropriate humor
- use of sarcasm
- passive-aggressive behavior

- playing the victim
- hostility

Watch for these emotional red flags in others. When you see them, look beyond that behavior to understand what is really going on. Beneath these red flags is most likely a great deal of sadness, fear, or anger.

5. Mirror Emotions

Mirroring is when we reflect back what we believe others are feeling. For example, when someone is describing a conflict they are having, you might sense their anger and say something like "that sounds frustrating" or "you sound angry." This helps to get the emotions out in the open, helps us to understand others, and even helps others to understand themselves.

6. Go to School

My mentor often tells me to "go to school" on people who are effective at a particular skill. He means that I should study them and learn how they do things. Are there any potential teachers in your project environment that you could learn empathy and social awareness from? You can either study them from afar or ask them directly to help you learn or master what it is that they do.

7. Track Your Own Emotions

Practice seeing others clearly by tracking your own emotions during conversations, listening for them to use emotion words, and watching their faces and bodies for non-verbal clues to emotions.

8. Keep a Journal

One way we can track our emotions is to keep a journal. Journaling is a great way to formalize our learning about ourselves and the individuals in our project environment. Try to approach it with discipline and write a little bit every day about what you are learning about your own emotions and those of others.

9. Explore and Learn About People

As the PM, we have the opportunity to interact with a number of stakeholders on our projects. Take the time to really explore each individual. Find the things that you have in common with them including where they grew up, went to school, and worked. What type of jobs did they have in college (if any)? What sports teams do they like? Do they have a family of their own? What is their ethnic or cultural background?

Learn about and appreciate both the differences and the things you have in common. Great PMs and leaders are always looking for areas of commonality and using them to connect with others.

10. Systematically Dissect the Organizational Culture

Treat the study of your organization as a research project. Talk to people, document the written rules and what you believe to be the unwritten rules. Take an inventory of the posters, slogans, and symbols of the organization. What messages are those posters and symbols trying to convey? Determine which behaviors are recognized and rewarded and which are not.

11. Assess Your Project Team

Use the EI Assessment checklist shown in Appendix B to assess the team members and stakeholders in your project environment. See what you can learn about each person to enable you to see them more clearly and understand them better.

12. Assess Yourself on Organizational Awareness

Use the following mini self-assessment to understand your level of organizational awareness. What steps would you need to take to improve your social awareness? Enlist the help of a mentor or accountability person.

- Level 1: Understands the structure and organization of the company and the client and uses that understanding to manage effectively.
- Level 2: Is familiar with the inner workings of the company and how to get things done informally. Is able to leverage the organizational capabilities for the client's benefit.
- Level 3: Understands and leverages not only the company but also the client and vendor organizations. Recognizes key decision makers in the environment.
- Level 4: Understands the client's business as well or better than the client; consistently acts with the client's best interest in mind.

13. Practice Social Awareness During Movies

You can make a game of developing your social awareness using movies. The entire movie experience is designed to create emotional responses using images, words, and music. The next time you watch a movie, focus on one or two of the key actors and see if you can track their emotions throughout the film. You can do this informally or you can use the emotional tally sheet found in Appendix A. Use your own emotions as a guide to what you believe the actor is feeling. Take a friend along and compare notes afterward. Alternatively, you can rent a movie from the list shown in Appendix E: Movies and Scenes for Emotional Intelligence. You may find it easier to track emotions in the comfort of your home when you can pause and rewind if necessary.

Relationship Management

■ An Introduction to Relationship Management

Chapter 6 is about relationship management, using our emotional understanding of others to build relationships with them. The relationship management domain builds on the first three emotional intelligence domains. In other words, our success in relationship management is going to be a function of our success in self-awareness, self-management, and social awareness.

What does relationship management have to do with project managers? Most people would agree that relationships are the bedrock of life, business, and even projects. They are especially critical to PMs for the following reasons.

Projects Are a Team Effort

Remember that project management is getting work done through others. Getting work done generally requires a team. The success of the team is going to be largely a result of the strength of the relationships.

I don't want to disparage those "working project managers" who work by themselves as a team of one. Teams of one can be difficult; I don't recommend them. A team of one can accomplish some things, but little of significance can be accomplished alone.

111

PMs Often Lack Direct Authority

As compared to most functional managers and leaders, project managers are often in the position of having to lead without direct authority. To be effective, they have to rely on more than positional power and authority to get others to accomplish what is needed. This is difficult to do without a relationship with the team members.

PMs Compete for Resources

In many organizations, resources are shared or spread across multiple project teams. This is common in organizations that use a matrix management approach. These days though, I find more and more companies trying to "do more with less." As a result, there are often severe constraints on key resources, which may be spread across three, four, or even five projects. In these types of environments, PMs will be competing against each other for the resources they need at the time that they need them.

Relationships are the key to success in matrix organizations and those organizations that are resource constrained. This includes both relationships with the individual team members and relationships with the functional or resource managers responsible for allocating resources to teams. Building solid relationships in this environment is the key to getting the resources you need.

PMs Need to Negotiate

PMs often need to negotiate to get what they need or to help parties reach agreement. PMs who use relationship management to understand the emotions and objectives of others will become more effective negotiators.

PMs Are Communicators

In the project environment, the PM is often the center of communications. They will typically have the most information about the project and will usually get the big picture. The PM is the center hub in a hub-and-spoke communication network as shown in Figure 6-1. They are often the one person who connects all of the members of the project team. Having critical information is a function of the relationships that the project manager has with the team members.

That is not to say that relationship management is easy for PMs. In fact, the temporary nature of projects makes relationship building a challenge. Why should we invest in relationships on the team if the project is temporary?

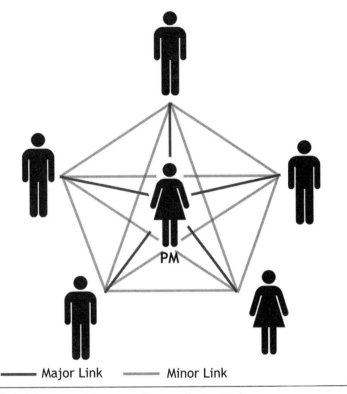

Figure 6-1: The Project Manager as Communications Hub.

In this chapter, we will look at several aspects of relationship management. We will start with what the emotional intelligence experts say on the topic. Then we will examine the project management framework for emotional intelligence. That framework includes the following competencies in the domain of relationship management: stakeholder relationships, developing others, and telling the truth. We will explore each of these, provide examples, and discuss tools and techniques we can apply in the project environment.

What the Experts Say About Relationship Management

As we begin to explore the emotional intelligence domain of relationship management, it might be helpful to see what the experts have to say about it. Daniel Goleman's most recent framework includes the following 6 competencies: inspiration, influence, developing others, change catalyst, conflict management, and teamwork and collaboration.

Table 6-1: Evolution of Daniel Goleman's Relationship Management

Working with Emotional Intelligence (1998)	The Emotionally Intelligent Workplace (2001)	Primal Leadership (2002)
	Visionary Leadership	Inspirational Leadership
Influence	Influence	Influence
	Developing Others	Developing Others
Change Catalyst	Catalyzing Change	Change Catalyst
Conflict Management	Conflict Management	Conflict Management
Building Bonds	Building Bonds	Building Bonds
Collaboration and Cooperation	Teamwork and Collaboration	Teamwork and Collaboration
Communication	Communication	
Team Capabilities		

Hmmm, that is strange. I distinctly remember communication as part of Goleman's framework. Has this changed since his book *Working with Emotional Intelligence?* Yes, indeed it has. In fact, it seems to have evolved over the last few years as reflected in Goleman's *Primal Leadership* (see Table 6-1).

Confusing? Perhaps. Surprising? Not really. I would expect some evolution in the framework due to the immaturity of the entire field of emotional intelligence. Based on this progression, I would not be surprised to see additional evolution in Goleman's framework.

Here is a quick summary of the items in Goleman's emotional intelligence framework from *Primal Leadership* (p. 39):

- inspirational leadership—guiding and motivating with a compelling vision
- influence—wielding a range of tactics for persuasion
- developing others—bolstering others' abilities through feedback and guidance
- conflict management—resolving disagreements
- building bonds—cultivating and maintaining a web of relationships
- teamwork and collaboration—cooperation and teambuilding[1]

---

[1] Daniel Goleman, Richard Boyatzis, and Annie McKee. *Primal Leadership*. Boston: Harvard Business School Press, 2002, p. 39.

The PM Framework for Emotional Intelligence

The PM Framework for emotional intelligence includes the following three competencies for the domain of relationship management: stakeholder relationships, developing others, and truth telling.

You might be wondering why the PM Framework has only three competencies for relationship management in comparison to Goleman's six competencies. For the PM framework for emotional intelligence, I chose to make a distinction between PMs dealing with one-on-one relationships and PMs dealing with teams. This division provides a more manageable breakdown of the concepts. In the framework for project managers, I included stakeholder relationships, developing others, and truth telling in the relationship management domain. These competencies primarily involve dealing one on one with individuals. What remains, then, are those areas where we are primarily dealing with groups or project teams. These include communications, conflict management, and inspirational leadership. Though communications is at both the individual and the team level, we will address it at the team level. I have included these competencies in the team leadership domain as shown in Figure 6-2.

Figure 6-2: Emotional Intelligence for PMs Showing Relationship Management.

■ Stakeholder Relationships

The first competency we are going to look at under Relationship Management is stakeholder relationships. The goal of the stakeholder relationships competency is to strategically establish meaningful one-on-one relationships that are going to do the following:

• increase our likelihood of success on the project
• provide cushioning to weather the inevitable storms that occur on every project
• provide an environment that is personally satisfying

Stakeholder relationship management is the process of systematically developing stakeholder relationships that help us with the project. We can break it down into the following 4 steps:

1. identify our project stakeholders
2. collect and analyze information about the stakeholders
3. develop relationship strategies
4. manage the ongoing relationships with the stakeholder

Let's tackle each one of these starting with identifying our project stakeholders.

Identify Project Stakeholders

Most PMs are familiar with project stakeholders and the importance of those stakeholders to the project. For those new to the concept of stakeholders, the simplest way to think of them is that they are the individuals or organizations that can make or break the project. This is an area where the *PMBOK® Guide* provides some guidance:

> Project stakeholders are individuals and organizations that are actively involved in the project, or whose interests may be affected as a result of project execution or project completion.

The *PMBOK® Guide* goes on to identify and define the following groups of stakeholders present on every project:

- project manager
- customer/user
- performing organization
- project team members
- project management team
- sponsor
- influencers

It is important to cast a wide net when trying to identify stakeholders. It has been said that the stakeholder that can hurt you the most is that one you failed to identify. Don't overlook those stakeholders who are opposed to the project.

In addition to the categories above, the *PMBOK® Guide* also mentions other stakeholders such as owners and investors, sellers and contractors, team members and their families, government agencies and media outlets, individual citizens, lobbying organizations, and society at large.[2] Which makes me think that this exercise will quickly reach a point of diminishing returns. If you were to include society at large, pretty soon you'd have all earth dwellers as your set of stakeholders and that is a lot of people to worry about. You don't need to go to that extreme. That said, I would try to cast a very wide net initially to make sure that no significant stakeholders are overlooked. For example, here are some additional categories the *PMBOK® Guide* should have included:

- senior management of the customer and performing organizations (if different)
- the program management office of the customer and performing organizations (if different)
- functional management or resource management of the performing organization
- vendors (break into subcategories as appropriate)
- suppliers
- end users of the project deliverables

Figure 6-3 shows the main categories of stakeholders and the relationship to the PM.

---

[2]Project Management Institute (PMI). *A Guide to the Project Management Body of Knowledge (PMBOK® Guide)— Third Edition,* Newton Square, PA 19073-3299. Project Management Institute, Inc., 2004.

Figure 6-3: Project Stakeholders.

Using the diagram and descriptions above, think through the various stakeholders for your current or recent project. Start by listing the categories of stakeholders and then detail out the specific names for each category. It will be important to have the specific name of each stakeholder in order to effectively manage the relationships. Of course with some stakeholders, like end users, there may be too many to manage individually.

Collect and Analyze Information About the Stakeholders

Armed with an understanding of who the stakeholders are, we can begin to collect and analyze information about them. The collected data and analysis become the basis for managing the relationship effectively.

Fans of the TV show "24" are familiar with Jack Bauer and the approach he took whenever he encountered some new threat on the show. Jack would immediately call Chloe, one of the security analysts on his team, and say, "Chloe, give me everything you've got on Dr. Evil. Just do it, Chloe!"

You don't need to be so dramatic. You do need to find out what you can about each stakeholder. The more you know, the better you will be able to manage the relationship.

Much of the information is going to require an interview or conversation with the stakeholder. As a general rule, you should always meet one-on-one with key stakeholders before meeting them in a group. It is better to discuss their needs and objectives individually rather than in a large group.

I recommend that you start gathering information even before you meet with each stakeholder. Ask around the organization to see what you can learn. Search the Internet or other public information sources. I have used the Google search tool to gather information about new executives. Google will turn up press releases, evidence of books authored by the stakeholder, and even information about hobbies like running.

You will show a lot of initiative by gathering some information prior to meeting with the individuals. When they see your interest, they may be flattered. They may respect or trust you more because of your initiative. They may also be more open and less guarded about sharing information with you.

One of the techniques that I like to use early in the project life cycle is to start meetings with icebreakers. In addition to helping to build the team, icebreakers are an excellent way to begin to collect information about the project team and stakeholders. These can be used during the initial stages of the project, such as during kickoff meetings. We will explore icebreakers further in Chapter 7, Team Leadership.

Here are some suggested categories of information to collect for each stakeholder. This list starts out with easy-to-obtain or known information and ends with information that is more difficult to obtain. See Appendix C: Stakeholder Management Tool, for a template that can be used to collect this information.

Stakeholder Priority

You will want to identify the relative priority of this stakeholder to the project. This should be based on the ability of the stakeholder to affect the outcome of the project. You can use a simple high, medium, and low or you could use a scale of 1 to 5. A stakeholder who can bring the project to a halt, like a funding sponsor, would be given a high priority. On the other hand, an end user responsible for using the project deliverables might be a medium or low priority.

The value of the priority is to help us to focus our stakeholder relationship efforts. We usually have limited time and we need to focus our efforts on the high priority stakeholders without completely ignoring lower priority stakeholders.

Role on the Project

The role on the project is somewhat self-explanatory. The stakeholder categories that we previously described may be a good starting point for role identification (e.g., vendor, end user, senior management).

Position Relative to the Project

The position relative to the project is a judgment call on how the stakeholder views the project. You could use a simple scale such as positive, negative, and neutral. Of course you can use a more elaborate scale that would include both direction and strength, such as strong positive or weak negative. You could also use a positive and negative numeric scale such as −5 to +5. The idea is to understand where the stakeholder stands in relationship to the project outcomes. If you don't know what the stakeholder's position is relative to the project, that could be a problem. Make it a priority to find out.

Stakeholder Objectives

In the stakeholder objectives section, we want to describe as succinctly as possible what it is that the stakeholder wants the project to achieve for them. This may not be something that is readily apparent to you. If necessary, you might need to guess at first. Follow up with the stakeholders and ask them "what is in it for you?" Examples of stakeholder objectives include reaching their personal or professional goals, getting promoted, reducing costs, increasing market share, and providing productivity tools to their staff. Each stakeholder has some objective for the project. You stand a better chance of connecting with that stakeholder when you speak their language, that is, when you understand their objectives and how the project relates to those objectives.

Facts, Passions, and Areas of Interest

This is an area where we do a somewhat subjective analysis of the person. Examples of the types of information to include in this section are: background on the individual, their previous jobs, conflict style, membership in certain clubs or professional organizations, sports teams they follow, or other personal information. The idea is to get as rounded a picture of the stakeholder as possible.

A word of caution is appropriate here. Anything written in this section must be factual and written as accurately as possible without being in any way offensive. Further, there are several categories of information that you should avoid documenting. This would include things like drinking habits, ethnic/racial/religious background, political tendencies, and sexual orientation. For example, the fact that a major stakeholder is having an affair with one of the project team members may be important to know; I just don't recommend documenting it. This type of information has the potential to cause a lot of harm; proceed with extreme caution.

Communication Style

In the communications style section, we want to outline the preferred forms of communications for this stakeholder. Do they prefer e-mail, voice mail or phone, or one-on-one communications? Do they want to hear from you regularly or only when there are problems?

This can sometimes be a tricky balance for a project manager dealing with senior managers. There is often a tension between our need to meet and spend time with stakeholders and the stakeholders' desire to protect their time. Some stakeholders will want to minimize time spent in meetings and may ask for e-mail or other forms of written communications. The stakeholder may also be protected by a gatekeeper who is protective of their time. Or, the stakeholder may ask that you work with a designated person in their organization.

For project managers, regular and direct communications with our key stakeholders will be to our advantage. We need to strike a balance between our need for face time and a senior manager's desire to protect their time.

Emotional Intelligence Assessment Checklist

In Chapter 5, Social Awareness, we introduced an Emotional Intelligence Assessment Checklist (see Appendix B). We can use that checklist on stakeholders just as we did with individuals. Going through the analysis steps for each stakeholder will provide additional insights about their level of emotional intelligence.

Emotional Connections

An emotional connection is an opportunity for us to make a heart-to-heart bond with the other person. What are the topics, objectives, and common interests where we are likely to connect with this stakeholder? These connections could be on a personal or a professional level. Examples of personal interests include having children of about the same age, sharing a passion for golf, following the same sports team, or even a love of mystery novels.

As an example, I was doing quite a bit of running during a recent project and was in the process of training for my first marathon. The CEO of my client company was one of my major stakeholders. When the normally quiet gentleman learned that I was preparing to run my first marathon, he instantly perked up and became quite animated. He was anxious to share his own marathon stories and his tips for me as a new marathon runner. Over lunch with other members of the program management team, he went into gory detail on some of the hygiene issues that marathon runners suffer from. It was amazing to me that a senior manager who was normally quite shy and reserved could become so animated and excited about a topic that we shared. From that point forward, he would ask about my running whenever we saw each other and that would be the start of a friendly discussion.

In some cases, you might find it easier to connect on professional interests than on personal topics. Examples of professional interests include excelling in the profession, membership in a professional organization, advancement in the current position, desire to network, and a myriad of others. Once you understand a little more about the individual, it greatly expands the potential for connecting with them emotionally.

Information Overload?

You might be overwhelmed by the list that I have suggested. How can anyone collect all this information? The short answer is that you don't try to collect it all at once. You start with the highest priority stakeholders and gather what information you can. Then, use every meeting with a stakeholder to gather a little more information about them. View this as an ongoing activity throughout the life of the project. As you learn, you can apply that information to building the relationship. Pretty soon you will find that the relationship building has momentum; it will take less work to maintain the relationship.

Collecting this information requires that you learn to ask the right questions and then listen a lot, applying the empathetic listening techniques we discussed in Chapter 5. Where possible, take notes.

A mentor that I had early in my career knew the value of building relationships with a stakeholder. His strategy was to get out of the office for stakeholder meetings. He used his lunchtime as well as his dinnertime for opportunities to meet either one-on-one or in groups. Though he was a hard worker, he was adamant about setting personal boundaries and taking care of himself. For example, though he always started his workday as early as 6:00 or 7:00 A.M., he always took lunch every day. These were sit-down meals in a restaurant; not a quick sandwich at his desk. He was also disciplined about ending his workday at 5:00 or so and then heading off for drinks and dinner.

This flew in the face of my own work style at that time, which was to get to work early, work as hard as possible all day (including through lunch), and leave when I felt I had completed all or most of my work. With coaching from my mentor, I was able to start leveraging lunch as a critical time for relationship building. Now I consistently use lunch to build relationships. I try to ask questions and listen a lot more than I talk. I ask each stakeholder about themselves as well as what they know about the other stakeholders. People are usually willing to talk about themselves and will readily open up once they feel comfortable.

I made good use of lunchtime to build stakeholder relationships with the members of a large and diverse team on a recent project. I created an award for the team player of the week. As part of winning the award, another project manager and I would take the weekly winner out to lunch. This became a great time to get to know the team members in a low-threat environment. We were able to talk about the project and each individual's objectives and ideas. We were also able to go beyond the project to learn more about each person, their background, their hobbies, and even their family.

Develop Relationships Strategies

The analysis from the previous step provides the basis for us to develop strategies for the relationship. This includes identifying areas where we have emotional connections to the stakeholder, exploring relationship strategies, and then developing action steps to help us to achieve those strategies.

Given everything that we know about the stakeholder, what strategies should we pursue to build the relationship? How can we systematically develop a relationship that serves the project and the two of you? How can we show that we understand the stakeholder's interests and objectives for the project and that we will treat those objectives with importance? Here are some aspects of relationship strategy to consider:

1. The Direct Approach

Often the best strategy is the most direct one. This requires us to consider how to work closely with the stakeholder to build the relationship. We determine what types of meetings we should have and how frequently. We evaluate ways of having both formal and informal updates and reasons to stay in touch with them. Finally, we consider ways of directly influencing the stakeholder.

2. The Indirect Approach

The indirect approach is something to consider for those informal or impromptu meetings with stakeholders. I was once a project manager for a large IT project at the headquarters of my company. I found that even when I didn't plan to meet with my stakeholders, I would often bump into them in the hallways. The stakeholders would often ask how things were going. Unfortunately, when this first happened I was unprepared. I would blurt out something like "not good, our lead developer just left the team."

With time, I learned a better approach. I began to keep a 3″ × 5″ card in my back pocket that contained a few talking points about the project. These talking points were positive items or conversation starters. With that card in my pocket, I was prepared for these impromptu discussions. I didn't actually pull that card out of my pocket. Just going through the process of preparing my message helped me when I needed it.

3. Talk to My People

In some cases, we will have to develop strategies to reach hard-to-get stakeholders. This applies to those senior managers who have an administrator or staff or who serve as the gatekeeper to the stakeholder. The gatekeeper may have implicit or explicit instructions about your level of access to the stakeholder. If your stakeholder is protected by one or more administrators, your strategy will need to include how to handle the gatekeeper. Otherwise, you might have good intentions for building relationships but little success in actually making it happen. Your stakeholder may simply be "too busy" to meet with you.

A related situation is when your key stakeholder has designated someone on their staff to work with you. The stakeholder may make it quite clear that they will be happy if their staff member or key manager is happy. In this situation, we need to treat this key manager or staff person with the same care we would show the stakeholder. We need to add them to our stakeholder list, collect information about them and analyze it, and develop relationship strategies as we do for the other stakeholders.

4. Keep Your Friends Close

In the movie *The Godfather,* Don Corleone advises his son to "keep your friends close and your enemies closer." This may run counter to your own intuition to distance yourself from individuals who don't like you or who oppose your project. After all, if someone doesn't like us or want our project to succeed, why would we want to be in relationship with them? The reality is, when you have stakeholders who are neutral or negative toward the project, you cannot afford to ignore them or distance yourself from them. They are perhaps more important than those who are friendly to the project. You need to do your best to keep them close. It is important to try to build trust and respect with them especially if they are negative toward the goals of the project. Your goal may be to earn their respect even if they don't agree with your goals and objectives.

5. Delegate Responsibility for the Relationship

Delegation is a relationship strategy that we may need to employ when there are many stakeholders and we are spread thin. There will be times when we cannot nurture stakeholder relationships personally and we need to ask for help. In those cases, we can delegate responsibility for management of specific stakeholder relationships to members of our team, or even upward to our boss.

As an example, I recently led a large project with a client in another country. In addition to being far apart geographically, I was separated from the client culturally and by eight time zones. Since I was unable to get much face time with this client, I delegated responsibility for the relationship to one of the project managers who worked for me in the client's country. He had a better understanding of the culture and language than I did and I trusted him to build the relationship and keep me informed. Though not a perfect strategy, it worked better than my efforts to directly manage the relationship remotely.

Action Steps to Nurture the Relationship

Once we have the strategy for the relationship, we can begin to document the tactics and specific steps we are going to take to build relationships with each of the stakeholders. This could be as simple as planning a series of meetings, writing a single or set of reports, or setting up recurring lunch appointments. It could be as extensive as learning more about the policies and objectives of a particular lobbying group or attending a meeting of a professional organization. Here are some examples of action steps:

1. Regular One-on-One Meetings

As previously mentioned, one of my favorite techniques for managing project team members as well as other stakeholders is the regular one-on-one meeting. By establishing a set time on a regular basis, you can stay in touch with and up to date on your stakeholder. Set a meeting length and frequency appropriate to the relationship. Some will require a monthly meeting of thirty minutes; others could be a weekly one-hour meeting.

2. Customized Project Briefing Reports

Consider drafting project briefings that are targeted status accounts for key stakeholders. You can present the relevant information in a way that minimizes their time investment.

I learned to do this from a mentor earlier in my career. I was having some trouble getting involvement from a key stakeholder. My mentor suggested that each week I draft a very crisp, one-page briefing report that was tailored to that stakeholder. This briefing report contained key status updates, any major issues and what was being done to manage them, and actions needed from the stakeholder. The stakeholder understood that the briefing report was written specifically for him and he valued it. My ability to get his involvement and action on key items increased significantly after preparing the weekly briefing report.

3. After-Hours Meetings

Some stakeholders may be easier to connect with after hours. I once worked for a program manager who frequented a pub every night after work with his key team members. The conversation and information flowed freely. It was as if he was keeping office hours every night. No appointment was needed, I just showed up to connect with him. Whenever there was anything important to discuss, I would make it a point to go and see him at his pub. If he had an issue or wanted to talk, he would ask me to stop by for a pint.

With some relationships, it will be easier to build connections outside the workplace. This could include attendance at professional organizations, attending sporting events together, or golfing together.

4. Maintain an Action Log and Follow Up Regularly

When managing stakeholders, we should not lose sight of the basic tools used to manage other parts of the project. Simple tools like an action log and regular follow-up should be used. Even stakeholders who initially squirm under this level of accountability will often come around to appreciate it. If nothing else, the action log provides us a built-in reason for contacting our stakeholders. Be sure to include owners for each action item and follow-up dates.

5. Lunch Meetings

As mentioned earlier, lunchtime is an excellent opportunity for relationship building. Nearly everyone eats lunch and the environment can be good for informal discussions.

I was reminded of the usefulness of lunch meetings recently by a stakeholder who was a master at effectively using lunch. Over the course of two years I lunched with this stakeholder numerous times and it is something I look back on fondly. He would select a very nice restaurant and sit back and thoroughly enjoy himself. During lunch he was entirely focused on our discussion and relationship. It was as if he had no other cares or responsibilities during that time. This was hard to imagine since he was a senior vice president of the organization. On the other hand, I had to work to relax and enjoy myself. I would be scared that somehow I wasn't working or being productive if I was spending one-on-one time with this key stakeholder.

If it helps, you can use a framework for recording all the information you collect and the strategies you've developed for the stakeholder and the relationship. As previously mentioned, you can start with the template in Appendix C: Stakeholder Management Tool. This can be tailored to your specific needs by adding or subtracting to the sections that address the areas most important to you. However you document it, I recommend that you exercise some caution with the sensitivity of the information. Don't leave the information lying around the office, don't store it on the company's shared drive, and don't leave it on the network printer.

For some people, using templates and processes for managing relationships may sound stiff, unnatural, contrived, or manipulative. It certainly is unnatural to me but then again, I am not naturally a great relationship person. If you are naturally good at building relationships, you will succeed without using templates or a rigid process. Project management is anything but a step-by-step formula. However, I don't think all project managers are naturally good at relationships and I think they are important enough not to be left to chance. An ad hoc approach to managing stakeholders just might work, but who wants to take that risk?

You might also consider tools beyond the template to help you manage information about your stakeholders. You might use a simple database program or a contact management tool such as ACT! MS Outlook could even be used to capture much of this information. Use the tools you are most comfortable with, ones that provide the value you need.

There are a number of parallels between stakeholder relationship management and customer relationship management. An entire category of CRM tools exist today to manage customer relationships. In a project environment, each stakeholder could be thought of as a customer. Just like companies have adopted CRM applications for managing customer relationships, PMs need to treat relationships with stakeholders with the same importance.

Manage Stakeholder Relationships

We use the analysis of our collected data and our strategies to actively manage the stakeholder relationship. Based on the priorities we assigned to each relationship, we strategically and intentionally engage our project stakeholders. We don't leave it up to chance.

The collected information becomes a framework and a basis for managing the relationship on an ongoing basis. We structure the relationship in a way that we can be systematic about the attention we pay to it. The goal is to have deep and satisfying relationships that are going to support the project.

Also consider the use of this information in light of the other emotional intelligence domains we have discussed, like self-awareness, self-management, or social awareness. Knowing what we know about our stakeholders, think about the steps we need to take to make our communications with them more effective. Using our own emotions when we interact with them, we can more easily understand what they are feeling and can relate to them better. We can also consider the importance of the stakeholder's objectives, interests, and needs and use that to relate to them. Finally, when we are self-aware and relating to them on their level, we are more likely to be the kind of people they want to be in a relationship with.

Here are some examples of how I have used these principles to manage stakeholders on previous projects.

The Division Vice President

Some time ago I was in charge of implementing a project accounting package. The executive sponsor for the project was a nice guy but he was not engaged enough at the level we needed him. This sponsor didn't really understand his role on the project and was more comfortable staying out of the details. I needed this sponsor's help with training and roll-out of the accounting package but found him aloof and uninvolved, so I avoided him. I did what I could to accomplish the project objectives without him.

Fortunately, my functional manager intervened and coached me to do better. He told me that I had to get the VP involved, that it wasn't optional. He encouraged me to get on the VP's calendar with a set of regular "executive briefings." Using the executive briefing approach, I was able to get the face time I needed, I learned what I needed to know about the stakeholder, and I was able to build a personal relationship with this important executive. That relationship helped me to get the project buy-in I needed from the division, to get the resources I needed for training and roll out, and to get the VP's help resolving several thorny issues.

I learned some valuable lessons from that experience. First, executive sponsor involvement wasn't optional. Second, I was coached to call the meetings with the sponsor executive "briefings," but they were really about building the relationship. Finally, I learned the importance of ongoing meetings to continue to manage the relationship.

Consulting Firm

On another project I led, there were several outside consultants from one particular firm. These consultants played a key role on our project and we were dependent on them for our success. These consultants were great performers, but like many high achievers, they could be challenging to manage. Since they were critical to our success, it was important to keep them focused on the project's objectives and interested in staying until their work was finished.

I recognized that in this environment, the key stakeholder relationship to be managed was with the resource manager for the consulting firm. He had direct control over the resources and a strong incentive for each team member to perform at a high level. He also had insights about each of the resources that came with knowing these people for many years. I made it a point to meet with the resource manager from that firm every two weeks. We talked about where the project was going and about how each of those key consultants was performing. He was able to share with me any problems, frustrations, or suggested improvements that he heard about from the individual consultants. He was able to do so in a frank and candid way.

In turn, I was able to provide the resource manager with feedback about his consultants. Our personal relationship helped to provide a free flow of information. It also helped the project to thrive even with the inevitable staffing turnovers and transitions.

Technology Vendor

On another project I managed, a key technology vendor was critical to the project's success. The relationship with this stakeholder had been managed by a technical lead who reported to me. When my technical lead left the project, I let the relationship atrophy. This was a near disaster. We were well into the project before I realized that some of the vendor's products were not performing well and that we were not getting the level of technical support that we needed. Due to the near lock that this vendor had on the market, they had grown arrogant about customer support. My technical staff had become dissatisfied with the support from this vendor and stopped calling them to report our problems. My initial calls to them did not address my concerns and left me feeling angry and dissatisfied.

I started by working on the relationship with the vendor's business development manager responsible for our account. I was able to set up a series of face-to-face meetings with him to build the relationship, show him that I understood and cared about his objectives, and then to focus on our problems. He and I worked together to set up meetings with my project team and his help desk and technical support team. While the relationship was never as good as I would have liked, it did improve significantly after those meetings.

Rookie Mistake—Focusing Only on the Project Team

A common mistake made by some PMs is to focus all their energy on managing relationships with the immediate project team at the expense of managing the other project stakeholders. This was a mistake I made early in my career. I focused downward and concentrated my relationship efforts solely on the team. I did not focus outward on the other project stakeholders. This was dangerous and career limiting. While good relationships with the team members are important, it is vital for the PM to manage all the stakeholder relationships. Without the support of your stakeholders, your project will suffer and could possibly fail.

This does not mean you should ignore your project team relationships. You need to strike a balance between the relationships with your team members and the relationships with the other stakeholders.

This mistake was easy for me because I placed a high priority on the relationships with my team. I also think it was because I lacked courage. Relationships with the team were easy; they were the path of least resistance. It was significantly more difficult and scarier to reach out to the stakeholders and manage the relationship with them. PMs may also find it very obvious who the team members are and less obvious who the other stakeholders are on a project. The bottom line is that we need to identify all the stakeholders and manage the relationships with them.

■ Developing Others

The second competency in the relationship management domain is developing others. For PMs, developing others means to invest in and grow the project team. Most PMs would agree that developing their staff is an important component of the job. The *PMBOK® Guide* mentions development of others in section 9.3, Develop Project Team. The objectives in the *PMBOK® Guide* are twofold:

1. Increasing team member capabilities
2. Teambuilding

The *PMBOK® Guide* mentions the following 6 tools and techniques for developing others:

1. a project manager's general management skills, in particular, interpersonal skills
2. formal and informal training of the team members
3. team-building activities
4. ground rules
5. co-location
6. recognition and rewards[3]

As PMs we need to recognize that developing others is making an investment in them. As a result of this investment, we create goodwill and deepen our relationship with our team members. In *Working with Emotional Intelligence,* Daniel Goleman identified the following competencies for individuals skilled at developing others:

- acknowledge and reward people's strengths and accomplishments
- offer useful feedback and identify people's needs for further growth
- mentor, give timely coaching, and offer assignments that challenge and foster a person's skills[4]

This sounds exactly like the type of investment my coaches and mentors have made in me over my career. Let's explore further this concept of developing others to understand what it means for project managers.

---

[3]Project Management Institute (PMI). *A Guide to the Project Management Body of Knowledge (PMBOK® Guide)— Third Edition,* Newton Square, PA 19073-3299. Project Management Institute, Inc., 2004.

[4]Daniel Goleman, *Working with Emotional Intelligence.* NY: Random House/Bantam Books, 1998.

Acknowledge Strengths and Contributions

Acknowledging the strengths and contributions of your project team members is a powerful tool for encouraging them. We must start by being able to clearly see others and to recognize and appreciate the uniqueness of each person. We need to understand their strengths and how they are contributing to the team. Of the two, contributions to the project may be easier to see. Strengths are about potential, and contribution occurs when that potential is realized. If someone on your project team is not able to leverage or apply their strengths, those strengths may not be apparent to you. If we are unable to recognize and utilize the strengths of our team members, we are not leveraging the potential of the team.

Work by the Gallup organization highlights the importance of focusing on strengths when providing feedback. Gallup has developed an online assessment tool called StrengthsFinder (see *www.strengthsfinder.com*) that can be used to identify the top five strengths of an individual out of a universe of forty-five strengths. These forty-five strengths include such straightforward strengths as Focus and Strategic as well as less clear strengths such as Woo and Learner.

I have used the StrengthsFinder tool and found the results helpful and fascinating. My top five strengths are shown in Table 6-2.

Understanding my strengths was an important part of my accurate self-assessment. I am better able to appreciate why I am successful in certain

Table 6-2: The Author's Top Five Strengths

Focus:	People strong in the focus theme can take direction, follow through, and make the corrections necessary to stay on track. They prioritize, then act.
Significance:	People strong in the significance theme want to be very important in the eyes of others. They are independent and want to be recognized.
Strategic:	People strong in the strategic theme create alternative ways to proceed. Faced with any given scenario, they can quickly spot the relevant patterns and issues.
Self-Assurance:	People strong in the self-assurance theme feel confident in their ability to manage their own lives. They possess an inner compass that gives them confidence that their decisions are right.
Learner:	People strong in the learner theme have a great desire to learn and want to continuously improve. In particular, the process of learning, rather than the outcome, excites them.

areas and why others are difficult for me. Since taking the assessment, I have been more intentional about choosing opportunities that leverage my strengths. I am also able to focus on growing in the areas of my strengths.

As PMs we should also be aware of and recognize each individual's contribution to the project. Recognition is one of the most powerful yet underused tools in the PM's arsenal. It takes so little effort and cost to recognize team members, and the payoff can be huge. There are thousands of ways to recognize and acknowledge our team's contributions: in one-on-one meetings, in chance encounters in the hallway, in a team meeting, in an e-mail to the individual or the line manager, in a status report, etc.

Try thanking each person on a regular basis for their appropriate contribution to the project. Hearing a heartfelt thank you for your hard work can be a major motivator for a team member.

> Recognition is one of the most powerful yet underused tools in the PM's arsenal.

Targeted Feedback

The competency of developing others also includes providing feedback. I like to qualify the feedback by calling it "targeted feedback." Remember that we said earlier that feedback is the breakfast of champions. Providing feedback to others is an investment that we make in their growth.

There is certainly an art to providing effective feedback. Positive feedback is usually easy to give and does not require much risk. However, providing constructive feedback can take courage and may involve risks. If we don't take care and use the feedback as an investment, the team member can take offense and become de-motivated. Here are some keys to providing constructive feedback.

Stick to the Facts

Feedback to others should be based on facts. We should not rely on hearsay or jump to conclusions. If we are in doubt about the facts, we should ask the individual in question to clarify them.

Focus on the Positive

Positive feedback is always easier to hear; it is also motivational. Strive to provide feedback that recognizes those things that are going well along with areas in which the employee's work has improved.

My wife is great at focusing on the positive when it comes to giving feedback to our kids. While I tend to react to the negative things they do, she often coaches me to wait until they do something well and compliment them on that.

Be As Clear As Possible

Feedback should not be ambiguous. Individuals should not walk away wondering what you were trying to tell them. Keep in mind that giving and receiving feedback can be stressful and our minds may not be working very clearly. Our fear can cause us to have trouble saying what we want in a clear and concise way.

The recipient of feedback can also get so scared they do not clearly hear what is being said. They may also put their own filter on the message and focus in on only one part.

To get the best results, write out your message in advance. Make notes, even in bullet form, of the message you are striving to get across. Be as clear and specific as possible and use words that are accurate and easy to understand. Use phrases like "here is what I need from you." Don't make it a mystery.

Make It Accurate

If we provide inaccurate or partially inaccurate feedback, the recipient may feel unseen and will dismiss our assessment. For example, if we use the words "always" or "never" in our feedback, we need to make sure that they are true and accurate. Rarely do individuals "always" do the thing that we think they always do. If someone hears "you never show up to my meetings on time," they will likely think of the one or two times that they did show up on time and use that to ignore or dismiss your feedback.

Keep It As Objective As Possible

While we all impose our own subjective voice on feedback, we should strive to be as objective as possible with each individual. Separate the behavior from the person. It is better to say "I don't like it when you don't meet your commitments" than to say "you are lazy." We should also avoid comparisons with others when we provide the feedback.

Invest, Don't Punish

The goal of our feedback should be to help the person to develop. Before you give feedback, explore the feelings and emotions you have toward that person. Determine if you are operating from another agenda or trying to repay some slight that you feel. For example, if you are angry, you should address that anger separately and not punish others. If you are not trustworthy with your feedback, you will not be successful in developing others.

We need to recognize that if we are feeling angry or scared, we may inadvertently make the feedback more negative than appropriate. Conversely, when we feel happy or excited about someone, our feedback may be more positive than appropriate and we may withhold candid feedback that could really help the other person.

Coaching, Mentoring, and Work Assignments

The third area of developing others is coaching, mentoring, and work assignments. This is one of the biggest opportunities for project managers. Whether it is formal or informal, coaching and mentoring can be used to develop the project team. What is the difference between coaching and mentoring?

> *Coach:* A coach is a person who teaches and directs another person via encouragement and advice.
>
> *Mentor:* a trusted friend, counselor, or teacher, usually a more experienced person.
> —(Source: Wikipedia.)

The key elements of these definitions include trust, encouragement, and experience. As PMs, we need to consider coaching and mentoring as a large part of our job. Remember that project management is about getting work done through others. By coaching and mentoring we encourage others and help them to grow and develop, which gives them the potential to contribute more to the team.

I have been fortunate to have had several great coaches and mentors over my career and I recognize the value of their investment in me. In fact, it is hard for me to imagine having grown as a PM without receiving their valuable input over the years. I have worked for a number of managers and project managers in my career and some were great coaches and mentors. As an independent consultant and business owner, I no longer have a formal manager. However, I continue to seek out coaches and mentors. I would not have been able to start and maintain my own company without the encouragement of my mentors. This book was the direct result of the investment of one of my mentors.

The final topic in the area of developing others is the assignment of work. The allocation of work assignments on a project is one of the most important roles of a PM. How the PM executes this will determine if people are given room to grow on the project or whether they feel their role is limited and perhaps the PM doesn't know or care about them.

Consider your own approach to making work assignments. What is your level of intention? Do you think of both the short-term and long-term needs of the project team? Or do you find that when you have a short-term need you simply fill it and ignore the development needs and objectives of the team members?

We must also consider the longer term needs of the project and the individual. Sometimes we need to assign work not based on who can currently do it but who needs to learn it. We need to think about cross training and reducing risks and dependencies on key people on the team. We may also need to consider the savings we can incur in the long run by developing junior people to take on more responsibility within the team.

■ Telling the Truth

The third relationship management competency is telling the truth. Being honest and forthcoming with the people we interact with on our projects sounds quite simple but it is rarely a simple thing to do.

You might think that we should always tell the truth. I am not talking about owning up to "who chopped down the cherry tree" or "who took my lunch from the company refrigerator." I am talking about more than simply not lying. I am talking about telling the truth when it is difficult, when it makes us vulnerable, or when it could create conflict. Let's look at a couple of examples.

If you were out to dinner with your spouse and they had broccoli stuck in their teeth, would you tell them? Of course. We wouldn't want them to look ridiculous. What if instead of your spouse it was the CEO or a key client with broccoli in their teeth? We still would probably want to tell the truth, right? What if we were in a big group? Would we still tell them? What if the CEO or key client was making a presentation and it was clear from everyone in the room that they were embarrassing themself? What if for a man their fly was open, or, if a woman their bra strap or underwear was showing?

Or consider this example. What if your boss told you that you were needed to work on a weekend and you already had other plans with your spouse? Would you simply swallow quietly and then call your spouse to cancel your plans? Or would you stall and try to avoid the inevitable conflict between work needs and your spouse? Or would you speak up to your boss on the spot, saying that you have other plans for the weekend and that your boss will have to find another way to reach the objective?

Here is an even more vulnerable situation. How many of us have had someone say something to us that was dumb, inappropriate, insensitive, or simply politically incorrect? We can often be so stunned by something that another person says that we don't respond. My own reaction was often low in courage; I would pretend not to hear the comment or simply change the subject. A more courageous approach is to stop the discussion immediately and say something like "I don't like your comment," or, "that was rude."

This is the subtlety of truth telling. We all strive to tell the truth all the time. But sometimes it is difficult and we are tempted to not completely tell the truth. We need to be willing to tell the truth with courage and not hold back.

Some of us may have baggage about truth telling, which will make it difficult. I was taught as a child that if I didn't have something nice to say, I shouldn't say anything at all. My mother enforced this rule at our house. It certainly helped us around my dad, who was volatile and punitive. I learned early on not to volunteer to him any more information than was necessary. Some people would consider this behavior as polite or demonstrating good manners; others would consider it withholding. Withholding the truth has the same impact as lying or being manipulative.

One of the many topics addressed in the book *Crucial Conversations: Tools for Talking When Stakes Are High* is the ability to remain focused on what we want out of our conversations. The authors describe the importance of recognizing what is at stake in a crucial conversation. When the stakes are high, we may feel as though our choices are limited to one of two things: either saying nothing at all or venting our feelings and making a mess. When the moment of truth comes, it may seem as if these are our only two choices. *Crucial Conversations* calls these two options a sucker's choice.

You have probably experienced this type of situation before in a meeting where you feel that you must choose between either blowing up or being silent and withholding. The authors of *Crucial Conversations* recommend that we ask ourselves two questions to help us see beyond those initial choices. The first question is, what is our objective? The second question is, what do we not want to have happen? Once we orient back to what we want, and what we don't want, we can then explore alternative approaches.[5]

---

[5]Kerry Patterson, Joseph Grenny, Ron McMillan, and Al Switzler. *Crucial Conversations: Tools for Talking When Stakes Are High.* NY: McGraw-Hill, 2002.

Consider an example from a project I led. We had a serious system problem with our network that was affecting most of my team. I set up a meeting with the infrastructure manager responsible for that system problem to discuss the issue. It was clear from the beginning of the meeting that he was not interested in solving my problem. He only wanted to get me out of his office. He did not provide satisfactory answers to my questions about his action plan, and worse, he had scheduled another meeting at the same time as our meeting. Almost as if on cue, less than 15 minutes into our meeting, one of his staff interrupted us to say it was time for his other meeting. Deflated, my team members and I shuffled out of the room.

The problem with my approach was that I saw my choices in that moment as limited to the sucker's choice. I could either blow up and tell him he was being an ass, or I could withhold and say nothing. Unfortunately, in that moment I did not think about what I wanted. I did not go for my own satisfaction. I was uncomfortable with the way he ushered me out of the office yet I did not say anything.

A better approach would have been to recognize what I wanted (get the action plan to fix the problem) and what I did not want (to blow up and act like a jerk) and try to come up with a third alternative. That could have involved negotiating a follow-up meeting later in the day, a brief meeting just between him and me, or some other action. In order to develop good relationships, we need to be willing to tell the truth. We need to share what we feel, what we like and dislike, and what we need in a particular situation. We also need to be willing to risk upsetting others.

Techniques for Truth Telling

Fortunately there is help for those of us who have a hard time telling the truth with diplomacy. Here are some tools and techniques to provide a framework for telling the truth in the project environment. I have listed them in order from the lowest risk to the highest risk.

Providing Your Reaction

What others do and say affects all of us. It is entirely appropriate to provide your reaction, especially if you are asked. For example, if your boss goes overboard with criticism of a team member, you might say "you probably didn't need to be so harsh to get your point across."

Saying No

Many of us struggle with saying no. When we are asked to do something, most of us like to oblige by saying yes. For some of us, we say yes to show that we are helpful and competent. For others, we say yes to be liked or valued. As a result, we may agree to things that we really should say no to. How many of us have ended up taking home extra work and even disrupting personal plans because we were unwilling to say no? How many of us, when asked, find it impossible to say no even when we we are being asked to do something beyond the limits of reasonableness? When we are asked about it later, we are likely to say something like, "I couldn't say no."

Improving our ability to say no is the subject of a recent publication by Dr. Susan Newman, *The Book of No: 250 Ways to Say It—and Mean It—and Stop People-Pleasing Forever.* Dr. Newman gives us the following reasons for why we say yes when we should say no:

1. most people have been programmed to think saying no is negative
2. our inability to think clearly about what is being asked due to fear or guilt[6]

For some of us, saying no is a muscle we simply have not practiced using. We tend to say yes first without thinking about it, then later we regret having responded that way. We try not to offend or disappoint without realizing that by saying no in the first place, we are less likely to disappoint others.

When we cannot say no, we set ourselves up in a couple of ways. First, we cannot honestly say yes to anything. If we never say no, we always say yes. Our yes might actually be a "yes for now but I am going turn it into a no later." We may say yes but in reality never intend to follow through and deliver whatever it was we agreed to in that moment. We will somehow sabotage that yes and ultimately make it a no.

The second way we set ourselves up is by feeling like a victim. We may say yes now only to be able to resent others and make them pay later. Think about situations where you or someone you know volunteered to do something and then complained and showed resentment afterward. This may be a recurrent pattern in your life or their life. Some people volunteer and then find themselves stewing about others who did not volunteer.

As a project manager, saying yes too much can damage our careers. We cannot always say yes to additional work, client requests for freebies, vacation requests, changes in responsibilities, or requests for individuals to be promoted or take on larger roles on the project. We need to know when to say no. If we don't protect ourselves and our team by saying no, we will alienate our team and perhaps even cause them to leave the project. We need to be able to say

---

[6]Susan Newman. *The Book of No: 250 Ways to Say It—and Mean It and Stop People-Pleasing Forever.* NY: McGraw-Hill, 2005.

no and to say yes with honesty and integrity. We need to remember that we have a choice and that we should exercise that choice. Saying yes when we don't mean it can be far more damaging than saying no when we need to.

Using "I Like / I Dislike" Statements

A very helpful technique for relationship building is to state what you like or dislike. You might say, "I like when you get your deliverables done on time" as a way to encourage your team members. A higher risk version is when you say "I didn't like when you made that disparaging comment about Bob". That type of communication is clear and to the point.

Another example of stating what you like is when you have a group trying to make a decision. Let's say a group of 6 are trying to decide where to go for lunch. If someone suggests a Chinese restaurant, and you really do not like Chinese food, it would be responsible to say something like "I don't care for Chinese food. How about (fill in your choice here)?" That is stating what you like or dislike.

What makes it hard is if we don't want to appear selfish or we don't want to offend others. In that case, we don't say how we feel and we wind up eating at the Chinese restaurant. We feel miserable, angry, and resentful of the others in the group. The reality is that we could have avoided that resentment by speaking up about how we felt.

Using "I Need" and "I Want" Statements

Closely related to the concept of likes and dislikes is the concept of stating our wants and needs. When we state in a clear and direct way what we want or need, we greatly increase our chances of getting it. This simple-sounding technique may often prove difficult in practice.

Many of us have developed erroneous beliefs about expressing our wants and needs. Some common misbeliefs include:

- we won't get what we want by asking for it directly
- asking directly for something is vulnerable and puts us at risk
- if someone really cared about us, then they would know what we wanted without us having to tell them

Many of us learned to manipulate instead of asking for things directly. We might say something like "I knew you liked Chinese food so that is what I ordered" instead of the more truthful "I wanted Chinese food for lunch so that is what I ordered."

One of the most powerful phrases I learned to say in the context of a project was "I need you to do a favor for me." Early in my career, I would have felt very vulnerable saying that. As I grew as a project manager and learned more about emotional intelligence, I found that asking others directly for what I needed was liberating. I could be clear and clean in my communications by just stating what it was that I wanted or needed from others.

Stating Your Beliefs or Judgments

A belief or a judgment is something we feel about others based on our own values. It is the rough equivalent of saying, "If I were you in this situation, I would be feeling angry." It sounds like "my judgment is that you are angry."

As an example, consider when you have a team member who habitually arrives late and leaves early. While they have been productive for you and for the team in the past, lately they seem to have other priorities. You might say "my judgment is that you aren't giving the team your best effort." That clear communication can start a healthy discussion about expectations. You might follow it up with "I want you to arrive by 8:00 every day" or some other request that indicates the specific behavior you expect from them.

Getting Clear

Getting clear with someone means that you are addressing any anger or conflict in the relationship. It is the emotional intelligence of cleaning your windshield of bugs and dirt. Getting clear requires that you voice any issues that you have with another person. You might say something like "that hurt when you didn't show up prepared for the staff meeting the other day. What was going on?"

It helps when we include our own emotions in the process of getting clear. A useful technique is to state the words or actions that the other person does and the emotional impact that this has on you. This technique was introduced back in Chapter 5, Social Awareness.

"when you do . . . _____" (some behavior or action),
"I feel . . . _____" (an emotion, such as sad or angry)
"because . . . _____" (the reason)
"I want . . . _____" (here is what I want in the future).

We might say something like the following: "I felt sad and angry when you made that joke at the staff meeting yesterday during my presentation. I had worked hard on that presentation and I wanted to make the point that everyone could do a better job on quality. In the future I want you to refrain from making comments that take the team off track."

The point of getting clear is that it frees us to move on and focus on other things. Like having a clean windshield, we no longer have issues that bog us down. We don't have to carry any of the emotional baggage of issues or conflict; we can voice them and forget them.

I recently worked for a manager who was great about getting clear and then forgetting about it. In one memorable occasion, he sharply criticized me for an e-mail that I had sent to a wide distribution list. My e-mail was poorly written and sounded critical of him. He told me that he didn't like the e-mail and he wanted me to limit the distribution list on e-mails that were critical of him. Later, when I called him to apologize, he was completely over it. He had made his point and then had moved on and let it go. He felt "clear" and he let me know that the issue wasn't going to affect our relationship.

Keep Short Accounts
A concept closely related to getting clear is the idea of keeping short accounts. Do not let small issues build up into larger ones. This is a trap that many of us fall into.

How do you respond in situations where there are small hurts or issues? Do you address each one? We might feel like it is better to simply let them go or ignore them. We may also feel that we are showing grace if we overlook small hurts or issues. The problem with that approach is that the issues tend to build into larger issues. We need to get clear on those small issues on a regular basis so that we don't end up with overwhelming resentment or anger.

The benefit of keeping short accounts is that we can get a more objective view of what happened. Often we will find when clearing up small issues on a regular basis that we didn't have the complete picture. Others were unaware, or perhaps we actually contributed to the problem. Rarely have I experienced these small hurts as being intentional on the part of the other person. Sometimes it is possible that we caused the hurt. Instead of having a justified complaint about someone else, we might actually be part of the problem. By clearing up these small issues when they occur, we provide an opportunity to better understand exactly what is happening.

What about being on the receiving end of someone who has not kept short accounts? Have you ever had a project team member or other stakeholder blow up and tell you about everything you have done wrong in the last year? Have you been surprised with the level of anger expressed over seemingly small issues or perceived slights? This is the case of holding in those hurts and resentments.

Keeping short accounts as a PM means that we don't let resentments, wounds, or anger build over time. If we have an issue, we address it quickly. Project managers need to lead in relationships and encourage others to keep short accounts with us.

The Importance of Courage

A common theme through all the truth-telling techniques is the willingness to take risk and face our fears. It is not always easy or pleasant to address sensitive topics in a straightforward way. It can be scary for some of us to take risks and tell the truth. Facing that fear requires courage. Courage is not the absence of fear; it is the willingness to act in the face of our fear. Telling the truth requires taking a risk and being vulnerable in order to develop the relationship.

■ Additional Principles of Relationship Building

There are some additional principles that are important to relationship-building. These include trustworthiness, co-creation, and the idea that some people are simply difficult to deal with.

Trustworthiness

Trustworthiness is an important component of honest relationships. Trustworthiness is when you can be counted on, when you are reliable, and when you do what you say you will do. It is when you have earned the trust of others.

Without a doubt, trustworthiness is important for project managers. Project managers who are trustworthy will find it easier to build stakeholder relationships, tell the truth (and hear the truth from others), and attract good resources to their teams. PMs who are not trustworthy will find it difficult to do any of the above.

Trust is earned over time but it can be lost very quickly. It may take only one event or action to cause others to lose trust in you, so I encourage you to do what it takes to be consistent, reliable, and trustworthy in all your relationships.

Co-Creation—Results We Create Together

The principle of co-creation is an important one for relationships. It says that a relationship is created by both of the individuals involved. The quality of the relationship and the results from that relationship are a co-creation of the two individuals. This means that both parties in the relationship are responsible for the outcome; neither is solely responsible.

Co-creation is an important principle because it places responsibility and accountability for relationship outcomes on both people. It means that I share the responsibility for any outcomes from our relationship. I cannot distance myself or blame you for what we create together.

Looking at relationships this way is both sobering and empowering. It means that I cannot sit back and claim to be the victim in the relationship or claim that I didn't play a part in the outcome. If I am not getting what I want or need from the relationship, it is my job to work with the other party to change that.

On the flip side, it means that we have the power to affect relationship outcomes as needed. As project managers, we want to make things happen rather than have things happen to us. We are drivers and we work with others to achieve the results and outcomes we want.

If we do not get the results we want, we need to first examine our own behavior. What was our part in creating the outcome? How did we contribute? This is where it can be tempting to lay the blame completely on the other person for any undesired outcomes. That is extremely unproductive. We must examine our own part.

Instead of making a list of the ways the other person created the negative outcome, make a list of the things you could have done to ensure the outcome you wanted. What could you have done differently? In what ways did your actions (or lack of actions) contribute to the end result? Remember that you are not a victim. You have the power to create the outcome you want. Make a decision now to do things differently in the future.

The attraction to victimhood can be a strong one. At its heart is blaming others for our problems. If you view all outcomes as a co-creation, you can no longer be a victim and blame others. You must acknowledge the part that you played in creating the outcome. There is power in this acknowledgment; you admit that you can change those outcomes. If we perceive the world as a place where things happen to us, we lack power and the ability to impact our outcomes. If, on the other hand, we view the world as a place where we have a hand in everything that happens to us, we have power, the power to make different outcomes possible.

It is not easy to own, or co-own, the results and outcomes from our relationships. We may be more comfortable blaming those around us for the things that happen.

Co-Creation Corollary—I Think I've Been Here Before

A corollary to the principle of co-creation is the idea that we will begin to see patterns in our relationships due to the part that we contribute. This can be especially apparent when we look back over all of our relationships. We may see recurrent patterns of behavior. We experience déjà vu, the feeling that we have been here before.

If a pattern does occur, remember that the common denominator is you. If you have unresolved issues in one relationship, those issues or other very similar ones will repeat themselves in future relationships.

Consider this example of co-creation that is so painful it is almost humorous. My father worked nearly forty-five years as a laborer in different manufacturing companies. Though an early starter and a hard worker, he had a history of moving from job to job and probably worked for over twenty different companies in his working life. As a child, I can remember him telling story after story of the different ignorant bosses he had at each job. He always found that he knew so much more than his bosses, who were all unbelievably stupid. Over time, the issues with the ignorant boss would fester and grow and eventually cause my father to quit the job. He would pack up his toolbox and move on to the next job. "Who needed that kind of BS?" he would ask. That certainly sounds like an unfortunate string of bad luck to have all those stupid bosses.

Let's look a little closer to see if bad luck was the only factor or if there was some way that my father was contributing to the situation. If we look across my father's entire work history, a clear pattern emerges. Any thinking person would have been able to predict this after just knowing my father a short while. As he took a job at a new company, he would pretty much start over at or near the bottom or entry-level position in the company. This was primarily a result of his not going for a more senior position and partly because his previous experience and attitude didn't warrant it. Even as my father grew in experience, he was rarely put in charge of more than a few people. When he started in the bottom-rung position, my father's boss would often be someone who was barely above entry level. These bosses were often younger and less experienced than my father.

My father was perhaps correct in his assessment that he was smarter than his bosses. After all, the boss was often younger and less experienced. But then my father would criticize the boss and make a point to show how much smarter he was than the boss. My father came into each relationship with a chip on his shoulder. He was angry and critical though he was street smart enough to cloak his anger in humor. He was sarcastic and used humor inappropriately. Eventually, my father would find some way to drive a wedge between himself and his boss or "the management." The outcome was usually that my dad would walk out. Sometimes he would be fired. The way my dad told the story was that a string of ignorant bosses forced him to quit good jobs.

Take a moment to consider your own history and see if you have any repetitive relationship patterns. While it may not be as obvious as a string of ignorant bosses, there are likely other situations where your behavior patterns have been consistent over time. For me it was the use of inappropriate humor and how many problems that created for me. Think about your part in any repeating patterns of conflict or issues. What specific steps do you need to take now to prevent those conflicts from happening again?

This may be the type of thing that is hard for us to see on our own. It may be helpful to ask a spouse or close friend to help you assess patterns. Find people who have known you for a long time and ask them if they see patterns of issues.

As a general rule, relationship outcomes are the co-creation of the two individuals involved. Neither individual is solely responsible; both are jointly responsible. But there may be some times when this is not the case. Let's take a look at situations where we experience relationship breakdowns that are directly related to the other person.

Working with Problem People

At some point in our careers as PMs, we are going to work with individuals who are challenging, difficult, or even what I would call problem people. Even project managers who are adept at relationship building need to recognize that some people are so difficult that any unilateral relationship-building efforts will fail. We may even find that the relationship is causing unhealthy stress or putting us in danger. These relationships require strategies far different than what we have described earlier in this chapter.

If we are having a problem with someone else, we should explore the possibility that we are causing that problem. We should try our best to make the relationship work. We should not be too quick to throw in the towel and assume the problem is with that other person.

That said, there will be some cases where we have exhausted all efforts to build a relationship with another person or we recognize that the other person is broken in some fundamental way. The reality is that if we work in projects long enough, there will be individuals who are more than just difficult to work with. We need to recognize that our own relationship-building efforts will be pointless when dealing with certain types of personalities. At the extreme, some people can even be dangerous to you. Here are some general categories of problem people who go beyond the definition of difficult and will thwart our efforts at relationship building.

Micromanagers and Critics

Micromanagers and critics are people who want to control or criticize everything you do. They often have difficulty with trust, control, and delegation. They may be perfectionists and find fault with everything you do. The underlying emotion for micromanagers and critics is fear.

As your boss, a micromanager can be impossible to work with. They will check in on you too often, dictate how to do things, and always seem to know the one best way to complete a task. They may be also perfectionists and constantly pick apart your work or ask you to revise your deliverables. As a team member or peer, a micromanager or critic may focus their energy on telling others what to do. They may get frustrated with others and bring issues to you that relate to how others work or to their inability to control others.

Dishonest Employees

Dishonest employees range from those who occasionally tell little white lies to those who lie compulsively and may even cheat or steal. This category would also include those who act unethically or ask you to act in unethical ways. The underlying emotions for dishonest employees could be anger or fear.

A dishonest boss can misrepresent the truth about you and your efforts. They may take credit for your work or blame you for their own mistakes. They may project dishonesty on you and discount or discredit what you say and do. It is especially dangerous to have a boss who asks you to act in unethical ways.

Dishonest team members and peers can cause conflict by blaming others for problems. They will often assume others operate as they do and attribute malicious intent to otherwise innocuous members of your team.

Cavemen

The category of cavemen includes bullies, powerfreaks, racists, and sexists. They tell off-color jokes or single out individuals and pick on them. They may think they are just having fun with others by teasing when they are simply trying to cloak their aggression in humor. They are usually men but women may also fall into this category.

As your boss, cavemen may make it a point to show you who is boss or get off on treating you like dirt. They may try to make themselves feel more powerful by singling out you or one of your peers and trying to humiliate you in front of a group. Or, they may make unwanted sexual overtures or discriminate against members of the opposite sex. They may label groups of people and use derogatory language toward people who are different from themselves.

As a team member or peer, cavemen may be less threatening than if they were your manager since cavemen are generally too scared to go after powerful individuals. However, you need to monitor the cavemen on your team closely as they can cause conflict with individuals reporting to them or working closely with them. For example, if an individual reporting to you were to tell an off-color or inappropriate joke and you either laughed or failed to take appropriate action, you could be viewed as part of the problem and be disciplined.

Addicts and the Mentally Impaired

Addicts include those who abuse alcohol or other substances. Individuals who are mentally impaired range from those with minor problems to the extreme cases of schizophrenia or manic depression. These individuals can be rare in the project environment but that is not to say you won't run into them.

Problems with addicts and the mentally impaired will have more to do with them than you despite how those individuals will want it to appear. It may be obvious to you that they have a problem if they repeatedly show up to work hungover or return from lunch slightly drunk. I once saw a team member spend their lunch break in the parking lot, sitting in their car drinking beer. Unfortunately, denial and defensiveness may make any type of communication about this behavior unproductive. In the most extreme cases, a confrontation about the behavior could be dangerous to you.

If you find yourself dealing with an individual in one of these categories, proceed with caution. These people are usually not interested in your relationship-building efforts. In fact, you may find that efforts to be vulnerable, tell the truth, or identify your part of co-creation can actually backfire, or worse, create fuel for the other individual to attack you. Here are some general guidelines to apply if you find yourself working with one of these types of at-risk individuals.

1. Stick to Business and Avoid Direct Confrontations

Unlike normal relationships where we want to express our feelings, tell the truth, and get clear, with at-risk individuals we want to avoid situations that would make us more vulnerable. Telling the truth or expressing your feelings may add fuel to the fire or spark an attack. It would be unwise in particular to try to fix them, teach them a lesson, or to suggest that they have problems or to diagnose them in any way. The best approach is to stick to the business at hand and to try to avoid any direct confrontations with the individual.

2. Document Everything

If you believe you are working with an at-risk manager or individual, get everything in writing. Document your understandings, instructions, responsibilities, and obligations. The documentation may help you to defend yourself against attack or to support your case if it comes down to your word versus theirs.

3. Seek Help

This would be a great time to seek help from your manager, other managers, or the Human Resources (HR) Department. If your manager is the problem person, you will need to proceed with a little extra caution. Some people are able to turn the charm on and off and conceal their true identities when necessary. This can make it hard for other managers or HR to recognize these personalities. For example, cavemen types will often power-up around those who are weaker or those who report to them. They may actually play small around those who are more powerful than they.

4. Refocus Your Energies

If you find yourself reaching a dead-end in trying to build relationships with an at-risk individual, shift your focus. Unhealthy relationships can be taxing and draining and provide no payback. Choose to invest in those relationships that are healthy. You will get more support and have more energy that way.

5. Consider a Move

Getting away from an at-risk person may sound drastic but can often be the best way to save yourself from further pain. If the problem is with your manager, you may want to move to a new opportunity with the same company. You may even consider leaving the organization. Your mental health is far more important than your current job.

6. Most Important, Don't Take It Personally

Some people are broken in ways that have nothing to do with you. Try to keep that in mind and do not take on responsibility for relationship breakdowns that you did not create.

■ Techniques for Managing Relationships on Projects

Before we close this chapter on relationship management, let's discuss the various techniques we can use to help us manage relationships on projects.

1. Apply the Emotional Intelligence Basics

To improve our ability to manage relationships, we may have to go back to some of the earlier concepts of emotional intelligence. We may need to start with self-awareness, self-management, and social awareness. When we are in relationships with others, we need to be aware of our feelings and manage our emotions. For example, use the feelings tally sheet provided in Appendix A to track how you feel. Practice sharing your feelings with others in appropriate situations. Or use the EQ Assessment Checklist in Appendix B to analyze a stakeholder and assess their feelings.

2. Stakeholder Management Tool

I recommend that every project manager complete the stakeholder management tool (see Appendix C) for the most important stakeholders on your project. This is an excellent first step toward systematically identifying and managing stakeholder relationships. Adapt the template to your specific project or environment as needed. While collecting the information and managing the relationship may seem artificial or mechanical at first, continue to use the tool to create team relationships that provide value for both parties.

3. Regular One-on-One Meetings

I cannot emphasize enough the importance of regular one-on-one meetings with key stakeholders and members of your project team. By meeting regularly, you will be able to stay current and keep short accounts with your project team members. You will also be able to stay on top of managing the expectations of your stakeholders.

4. Out to Lunch!

If you are the type who eats a quick lunch at your desk in order to save time, you are missing a great opportunity for relationship building. Try to slowly change your existing habit by designating one day a week to go out to lunch with someone. Alternatively, set a goal to have lunch out with all your key stakeholders or project team members within the next month or two.

If going to lunch with just one other person seems too intimate, invite a couple of people to dine with you. Or, invite a key stakeholder and a junior member of your team and use the same time for building relationships with the stakeholder and developing the team member.

An alternative approach is to have an informal lunch for the entire team. If your project budget supports it, have lunch brought in for the whole group.

5. Use Icebreakers and Teambuilding Exercises

As noted above, icebreakers provide a way to learn more about project stakeholders in a low threat way. Are you using icebreakers and teambuilding exercises effectively? Consider the following ways in which you can break the ice for team meetings, kickoffs, and other occasions:

- During the start of a meeting, ask each person for their favorite movie or reality TV show, their favorite musician, or their favorite book. You can also ask about worst summer job or worst permanent job. You can ask virtually anything that reveals something about each person and provides a forum for discussion.
- More complex team-building exercises can also be used including activities that involve team competitions, survival type exercises, or other scenario-based exercises. One of my favorite team-building exercises was a competition to build specific items out of Legos. Teams were graded based on speed and quality, the two factors that were most relevant for that particular project.
- There are a number of team-building activities directly related to improving emotional intelligence. As an example, Adele Lynn has a workbook of 50 EQ activities called *The Emotional Intelligence Activity Book* (see Appendix G: Books on Emotional Intelligence).

In addition to these, there are a number of other resources available on the web that can be easily found with a search tool.

6. Develop Others by Becoming a Coach and Mentor

Make a shift in your approach to managing others by becoming a coach or mentor. Think about ways to become systematic in your efforts to invest in others. Set up regular meetings focused on the development of those who work for you. Consider the work assignments that you could give individuals to help them grow in their areas of strengths.

If you are not sure how you are doing, ask for feedback from the people who work for you. Find out what you can do to improve in this area. You can also get a coach or mentor for yourself and learn how to coach from them.

7. Recognize Others

Evaluate your current performance in terms of recognizing others. Remind yourself that every person craves recognition and affirmation. Are you leveraging recognition as an opportunity to build the relationship?

Consider implementing systems to become more consistent at recognition. You could make a list of the project team members or key stakeholders and use that as a tally sheet to keep track of when you recognize them for their work. Alternatively, you could use weekly or bi-weekly meetings as the forum for recognition. Make it a habit to start every one-on-one meeting by recognizing the contributions the other person has made to the project and why you appreciate having them on the team.

8. Assessment Instruments

The use of assessment instruments can provide information for development of your team members as well as for general team building. There are many assessment tools that can be used for this purpose including general assessments, strengths assessments, and emotional intelligence assessments.

One of the most popular general assessment tools includes the Myers Briggs Type Indicator (MBTI). Find a local facilitator and have them administer the instrument to your project team. The four different type indicators used in the Myers Briggs assessment provide for sixteen different individual combinations. Map your team against those sixteen combinations and discuss it as a team-building exercise.

You can also administer the StrengthsFinder assessment to help an individual determine their strengths. Once you know the individual's top five strengths, this can provide a basis for your development efforts.

9. Practice Truth Telling Techniques

Take the time to assess your ability to tell the truth with others. Are there situations where you have difficulty telling the truth? Which of the truth-telling techniques pose the biggest challenge for you?

A starting point might be to review the following list and rank your responses in terms of what you do best and what you do least well:

_____ Do you say yes when you really should say no?
_____ Do you have trouble stating what you like and simply go along with what others want?

____ Do you have judgments or beliefs of others that you withhold to avoid conflict?

____ Do you let hurts and resentments build up instead of quickly clearing them up with others?

____ Do you avoid providing truthful feedback for others for fear of their reaction?

____ Are there individuals in your environment who make you feel you need to walk on eggshells when they are around?

Select one area that you want to work on. Set a daily goal for yourself to try and improve in that area. Start slow and build up, just as if you were exercising. For example, if your challenge is saying no, you might make it a goal to say no to at least one unnecessary thing every day for a week. Start with people or situations that are relatively low risk and build up to those who hold higher stakes for you.

If getting clear is your challenge area, determine which individuals pose the biggest struggle for you. If there is a current issue that you have not been clear about, make it a point to meet with the individual to clear it up as soon as possible. If the person you struggle with the most is your spouse or a co-worker, set a goal to get keep short accounts with them. Try to clear up all hurts or resentments on a daily basis. Keep track of how you are doing and celebrate yourself.

10. Evaluate How You Are Co-Creating Your Outcomes

Take a look at your project and relationship outcomes and evaluate how you are contributing to any issues or problems. Do you tend to play the victim? Do you think that things primarily happen to you instead of your making things happen? Evaluate how you are co-creating the relationship outcomes you are getting. Rank your level of satisfaction with your relationship outcomes.

11. What Are Your Relationship Patterns?

Think about your recent experience on projects or in the work environment in general. Can you identify any patterns of relationship breakdowns? In other words, what would be your equivalent of a string of ignorant bosses? Do you have any recurring themes that prevent you from performing at your best?

Determine if you have any relationship patterns or are in some way recreating the same problems with different people over time. This is an area where it might help to get some feedback from a significant other, mentor, friend, or anyone else who has known you for a while.

Once you see the pattern, the next step is to determine your contribution to the situation. Own the part that you played and then think about what you could do differently in the future in order to get different results. Try to identify at least two or three things that you could do.

Now think about your current relationships. Which relationships are at risk for this same pattern of breakdown? What steps can you take right now to break the pattern?

12. Enroll an Accountability Partner

Some of the techniques described above are more challenging than others. If you find yourself struggling with these despite your good intentions, you might need to enroll the help of a friend or accountability partner. An accountability partner can help you to make changes or breakthroughs that you would not otherwise make on your own.

Who would be a good accountability partner for you? See if you can identify someone who will hold the bar high for you. Share your challenges and goals with them and set up checkpoints where you can let them know how you are doing. Keep it fun and encourage them to have high expectations for you.

PART 4

Using EQ to Lead Project Teams

After reading this far, you should have a solid understanding of the first four domains of emotional intelligence and their associated competencies. The following three chapters will discuss the fifth domain of emotional intelligence and provide additional insights into how we can apply what we know to be more successful as a project manager.

In Chapter 7, Project Team Leadership, we will explore what it means to lead projects and how that differs from managing. We'll talk about how to communicate with high emotional intelligence. We will explore the best way to develop a team including selecting and retaining team members. We will also explore conflict management and then we will close with a series of techniques to improve our project team leadership.

Chapter 8 is about creating a positive project team environment. We will look at the difference between projects that have a positive team environment and those that don't and the project manager's role in setting the tone and direction for the project. We will also look at how the team environment is affected by the culture of the organization and what the project manager can do to impact that larger environment.

Chapter 9 deals with excelling with emotional intelligence on large and complex projects. It is my hope that you will use the information in this book to grow as a PM and, if desired, to take on more challenging projects.

7

Project Team Leadership

■ Introduction to Project Team Leadership

Project team leadership is the over-arching aspect of the emotional intelligence framework for project managers. It is about getting the right people on your team, successfully communicating with them and motivating them, and then clearing conflicts and other roadblocks so that they perform and achieve the project objectives. This domain includes the project management competencies of communications, conflict management, and inspirational leadership, as shown in Figure 7-1.

Like the relationship management domain that we explored in Chapter 6, project team leadership builds on the previous emotional intelligence domains.

What the Experts Say About Team Leadership

Though leading teams is critical to project managers, up till now it has not been the focus of emotional intelligence researchers. The emotional intelligence researchers have only indirectly tackled the subject of applying emotional intelligence to team leadership. Daniel Goleman and his *Primal Leadership* co-authors looked at the various emotional intelligence competencies and how they impact leaders. (*Primal Leadership* also discusses six leadership styles that we will explore in Chapter 8). Otherwise, there is little information available to relate emotional intelligence to the leadership of project teams.

Figure 7-1: EQ Model Showing Team Leadership.

As noted in Chapter 7, I chose to designate several of the competencies that Goleman included under relationship management as team leadership competencies. Communications is a core competency for both project management and emotional intelligence. This includes not only empathetic listening as we addressed in Chapter 4, but also consistent and effective communicating with project stakeholders.

Conflict management is the second competency that we will explore. This is another subject that should be very familiar to project managers. Goleman views conflict management as negotiating and resolving disagreements; it includes the following competencies:

- handling difficult people and tense situations with diplomacy and tact
- spotting potential conflicts, bringing disagreements into the open, and helping to de-escalate
- encouraging debate and open discussion
- orchestrating win-win solutions[1]

---

[1]Daniel Goleman. *Working with Emotional Intelligence.* NY: Random House/Bantam, 1998.

Finally, we will look at what Goleman alternatively calls leadership or inspirational leadership. In *Working with Emotional Intelligence,* Goleman defines leadership as inspiring and guiding individuals and groups and includes the following aspects of leadership:

- articulating and arousing enthusiasm for a shared vision and mission
- stepping forward to lead as needed; regardless of position
- guiding the performance of others while holding them accountable
- leading by example[2]

■ Communications

Undoubtedly project managers need to be great communicators. This is one of the most important skills that a project manager should possess. It is hard to imagine anyone who could be successful as a PM without being a good communicator.

> Project managers need to be great communicators.

Not everyone appreciates the need for PMs to be great communicators. It is entertaining to me to hear the criticism of project managers by team members who are new to projects. I have heard quite frequently that "All you project managers do is walk around and talk to people." I wholeheartedly agree with that statement. Walking around and talking to people is one of the important ways that project managers communicate. Unfortunately the individuals who make those types of statements haven't yet seen the value in good communications.

I am also entertained when I hear the following from a new team lead or project manager: "I didn't get anything done today, all I did was sit in meetings." This is typical of those new project managers who were accustomed to being individual contributors. Frequently they will feel frustrated with their apparent lack of contribution and the fact they were in so many meetings. To them I say, "Welcome to project management."

The reality is that for most project managers, a big part of the job is communications. That may take the form of walking around and talking with

---

[2]Ibid.

team members or stakeholders. It may also mean sitting in lots of meetings. That is communications. Communications can also include talking on the telephone, writing e-mails and instant messages, preparing for meetings, creating and delivering briefings, and preparing status reports.

The focus of this section is on how to apply emotional intelligence to improve project communications. Project communications are a rather broad topic and some level of familiarity with the topic is assumed. For project managers who are not familiar with project communications, I recommend that you start with Chapter 10 of the *PMBOK® Guide,* which is dedicated to this topic.

Of course the *PMBOK® Guide* does not address the application of emotional intelligence to communications. For best results, we need to consider our own emotions, the emotional content of our messages, and the emotions of the recipients of our communications. In the next section, we will look at how project managers can leverage emotional intelligence to improve communications with team members and other stakeholders. Then we will look at specific types of communications methods, advantages and disadvantages of each, and ways to improve them with emotional intelligence.

Communicating with Emotional Intelligence

No matter what form they take, communications contain and evoke emotions. Well-planned communications help the project manager to set the emotional tone for the team. Poorly executed communications can trigger negative emotions in the team.

Communicating with emotional intelligence involves applying the domains of self-awareness, self-management, social awareness, and relationship management. Project managers who are competent in each of those domains will do a better job of communicating with emotional intelligence.

If you want to be intentional about your project communications, consider the following steps:

- determine your objective
- understand your own emotions
- choose an appropriate time, place, and mode
- approach others with empathy
- listen and respond to the emotions of others, and not only to the content of what they say
- share your own emotions when appropriate, being as open and honest as possible
- check for understanding and reactions

Determine Your Objective

Determine your objective means to understand the point of the communications. Some examples of communication objectives include:

- recognizing the work of others
- encouraging or motivating team members to work harder
- providing constructive feedback to encourage someone to change their behavior

The key is to be clear about our objectives up front. If we don't set realistic objectives before we communicate, we are not likely to be systematic and we probably won't achieve much.

I have found it helpful to jot down a few bullet points before important meetings. These bullet points might be in addition to an agenda or any other preparation I would do for the meeting. I would typically choose my words carefully since I understand that word choices can affect the emotions evoked.

Understand Your Own Emotions

Understanding our own emotions means we are aware of our emotions, or self-aware as we learned in Chapter 3. This is a necessary first step for good communications. If we are unaware, we won't be able to accurately communicate with others on an emotional level. Our own emotional state will leak out in undesired ways or we will misrepresent how we feel to others. We should start by using the SASHET model introduced earlier to be clear about our own emotions.

Choose an Appropriate Time, Place, and Mode

It is critical that we choose an appropriate time and place for our communications with others. Delivering bad news at the end of the day when your team is heading out the door is poor timing. Even worse timing would be to deliver bad news when you are leaving the office early and won't be around the rest of the day. You need to be careful, though, that you don't stall on delivering news because "the time isn't right." While timing is important, we should not let our own fear cause us to delay the delivery of bad news.

It is also imperative that you choose an appropriate place for the communications. Privacy is critical when discussing personal issues.

I once had a situation with a team member who had failed to meet an important deadline. I made the mistake of addressing the issue with the team member in his cubicle, which was part of the open landscaping in the office. Needless to say it was inappropriate to discuss this person's shortcomings when others could hear the conversation.

Finally, we need to consider the modes of communications that are appropriate in any given situation. It would not be appropriate to use a fax message to fire someone. Nor would it be appropriate to use instant messaging for a tough discussion. Both of these situations would be well served by a face-to-face discussion.

There are also times when we need to use multiple modes of communication. Often, our verbal discussions will need to be supported by a written communication or some other form of documentation to keep in our permanent records.

Approach Others with Empathy

Where possible we must approach others with empathy. We should attempt to think through how they will feel before and after our communications with them. For example, consider if the other party or parties will be scared in anticipation of bad news. Think about how we expect them to feel after we deliver our message. Do we expect them to be happy after we recognize their performance? What will we need to do in order to assure that they take this in the most positive light?

Listen and Respond to the Emotions of Others

As project leaders, we need to distinguish between the content of what people say and the emotions underneath that content. In many situations, it is more appropriate to respond to the emotions than to the actual words that the individual is saying. As an example, we may say something like "you sound disappointed." We may need to lead others to appreciate what they are feeling and help them to articulate that. This includes listening with empathy and using paraphrasing or other playback methods to replay what we hear from others, as we discussed in Chapter 4.

Share Your Own Emotions When Appropriate

We also need to be able to share our own emotions when appropriate. We should strive to be as open and honest as possible. Of course, this doesn't mean that we bare our souls and share everything.

We may also want to practice the truth-telling techniques that we learned in Chapter 6. This may not be appropriate in all situations. Use your emotions to guide you in determining how much to share. Consider your objective for the communication and evaluate whether or not sharing additional information will bring you closer to that objective.

Check for Understanding and Reactions

Just because we delivered a message in a meeting doesn't mean that the recipient understood or retained the message. We need to follow-up with the receiver to make sure that they understand what was communicated. We might also ask for their reaction to the message.

I like to leverage key project team members to check for understanding and reactions. A couple of team members could be trusted to be open and candid about their reactions. I would seek them out after important meetings to see what they heard, what they took away, and any reaction they might have had to the message.

Methods of Project Communications

Table 7-1 provides a summary of some popular modes of communications that a project manager may use, the emotional intelligence advantages and disadvantages of each, and some tips for applying emotional intelligence to each mode.

Use E-Mail and IM Carefully

A word of caution about the use of e-mail and instant messaging (IM) as communication tools. Each of these has its place on project teams. E-mail has been used for several years to support project communications. In recent years IM has rapidly become accepted as a valuable project communications tool. It is the power of these two modes of communication that can make them risky if not used properly.

With e-mail, you can reach a very wide audience in a hurry. This is great if there are important and urgent communications that need to go to that wide audience. It is not so great if you have lost control of your emotions and you want to vent to everyone about how angry you are.

You may not even do this intentionally. I have inadvertently sent email messages to the wrong recipients on multiple occasions. This is especially embarrassing if the message is poorly written, unprofessional, or has a critical tone. More important than proper addressing of e-mails is to think before you even create the message. Go back to the steps we mentioned in this section and think about your objectives and your feelings. Before creating an e-mail, make sure that you need to send one. If you are responding emotionally, e-mail is unlikely to be the best mode of communication.

Instant messaging has similar shortcomings though it doesn't necessarily have the power to communicate the same message to multiple people at the same time. Many people use IM to keep ongoing informal chats going throughout their workday as they work on different tasks. These individuals may have three or four different conversations going on at the same time as they do their work. (I find myself challenged to have one meaningful conversation at

Table 7.1

Method of Communication	Emotional Intelligence Advantages	Emotional Intelligence Disadvantages	Tips for Maximizing Effectiveness
Face to Face Meetings	• Face to face meetings include visual and audio clues that supply the emotional context for the message. • Allows speaker to check for understanding and provide clarification as needed.	• You may only get one chance to say things correctly.	1. Use in conjunction with written communications. For example, hand out agendas and talking points in advance, or follow-up meetings with meeting notes or frequently asked questions.
Phone Calls and Teleconferences	• Opportunity to speak to each other when not in the same place. • Better at conveying emotions than email or other written forms of communications.	• Since we cannot see each other, we miss out on important visual clues. Puts the burden on the communicator to probe for understanding and emotions. • Forces speaker to articulate emotional context better than if the parties were together or could see each other. • Different accents and language proficiencies may create challenges simply to understand the words of another let alone the emotional content or intent of those words.	1. Use in conjunction with written communications. For example, hand out agendas and talking points in advance, or follow-up meetings with meeting notes or frequently asked questions.

Written Reports	• We can choose our words and emotional content carefully. • Written reports provide a permanent record of the communication.	• Written reports lack the ability to clarify or answer questions, or to provide additional detail. • Written communications lack the emotional context provided by visual cues, body language, and tone of voice. This can lead to misinterpretation, de-motivation, or conflict.	1. Be consistent in style and approach with your messages. 2. Get a peer or team member to read over anything written before it goes out. 3. If in doubt about the message, call or stop by the person to provide clarification if needed.
Email	• With emails, we can choose our words and emotional content carefully. • Provides the ability to reach many people in different locations quickly. • Widely used and accepted as the norm for many team communications. • Emails provide a somewhat permanent record of the communication.	• Emails lack the ability to clarify or answer questions, or to provide additional detail. • Email lacks the emotional context provided by visual cues, body language, and tone of voice. This can lead to misinterpretation, de-motivation, or conflict. • Email as a medium tends to be overused and people may miss important information if there is a deluge to sift through.	1. Make an investment in writing clear email messages. 2. Be consistent in style and approach with your messages. 3. When in doubt, let an email sit over night or get a friend to read. 4. Check for understanding by meeting in person, calling or asking for a return email. 5. Try not to overuse email so that the messages you send are read and acted on.
Instant Messaging (IM)	• IM can be a fast and informal way to reach an individual immediately. • Similar to other written forms, it has the advantage of being somewhat permanent.	• Most people do not spend much time crafting instant messages. • Like email, instant messages lack the emotional context provided by visual cues, body language, and tone of voice. This can lead to misinterpretation, de-motivation, or conflict. • Reaches only one person at a time.	1. Treat IM as one more communication tool. Don't use I.M. in unprofessional or inappropriate ways. 2. Do not use for formal project communications. 3. Take care to provide the emotional context for the message.

a time.) Those that have several conversations going run the risk of sending the message to the wrong recipient.

Another risk with instant messaging is the apparent informality. The ability to chat back and forth can cause people to become less professional, or even flirtatious, or to act in otherwise inappropriate ways. As evidence, consider a recent scandal involving a congressman who allegedly sent inappropriate instant messages to a congressional page.

Both e-mail and IM suffer from the lack of context. The same message can be interpreted multiple ways. Without visual clues it might be hard to tell if someone is joking around or if they are angry and dead serious. Two people may read the same message and come away with a different interpretation of the message.

Improving Your Meetings

Most project team members seem to have a dislike for the deluge of meetings that come with the job. Here are some ways to improve your meetings to make them both worth attending and enjoyable.

- Start with meeting objectives and an agenda.
- Monitor the group for emotions and aliveness. If everyone seems angry or bored, it may be appropriate to state that you've noticed this and ask why.
- Always show respect for others, in particular those not present.
- Monitor and address sarcasm and other inappropriate expressions of emotions.
- Address conflict.
- Lead with your own emotions.

Non-Verbal Communications

The focus of the previous section has been on verbal communications. It is important to recognize that we communicate all the time without using words. Non-verbal communications can include body language, touch, the artifacts and items found in your office, your own physical appearance and dress, the actions you take, and even the car you drive. Each of these things sends a message about you even before you open your mouth or write something.

The most important nonverbal communication is actions. It has been said that actions speak louder than words. The actions you take, or the ones you do not take, send messages more clearly than if you had spoken the words. If your words do not match your actions, people will be more likely to pay attention to your actions than your words. As the next section describes, we need to be consistent in all of our communications.

Congruence in Communications

Congruence is a principle that applies to all of the ways in which we communicate. We need to be consistent in the message that we are sending with our words and our actions. We cannot tell someone they are important to us and to the team and then act in ways that send a different message.

In a 2006 episode of the TV program "The Apprentice," a contestant named Allie was continually rolling her eyes during the final boardroom scene when her project manager Tammie was talking. She was (appropriately) called for her behavior by Donald Trump and his leadership team. Her response was to deny that she was rolling her eyes. All the while Allie offered half-hearted praise for Tammie. This was incongruent. It would have been more consistent to simply say that she had no respect for Tammie as the leader. Allie was trying to avoid sounding petty and small by criticizing Tammie, but the eye rolling conveyed that message loud and clear.

Congruence in our communications also means that we are consistent with our actions and words with different groups of people, as well as inside and outside the company.

■ Conflict Management

Conflict Is Inevitable

Conflict seems to be inevitable on projects. From the start, projects are built on a foundation of the conflicting constraints of time, cost, and scope. Further, projects are often created to satisfy the needs of one set of stakeholders, which often conflict with needs of other stakeholders. During the execution of projects, conflict frequently surfaces over contention for resources, rewards and recognition, roles and responsibilities, team member diversity, technical decisions, reporting structures, and even individual personalities.

Lack of emotional intelligence in project team members and stakeholders can also cause conflict. Team members and stakeholders who experience emotional breakdowns or lack emotional self-control are like ticking time bombs. When these bombs detonate, they will frequently take healthy members of the team with them, which could include you as the project manager. Even team members and stakeholders with high emotional intelligence may create conflict with others when they are under stress and pressure.

Project conflict can be disruptive. If not properly channeled, conflict can stifle communication, kill creativity, and squash productivity. Un-managed conflict will create unnecessary distractions and may encourage otherwise good resources to leave the team. Project teams that are not able to manage conflict may ultimately fail to reach their objectives.

Conflict May Be Healthy

In some cases, conflict can be healthy. Properly managed project conflict can galvanize teams, spark creativity, and cause healthy competition. Project conflict is an opportunity for the project manager to demonstrate leadership with emotional intelligence competencies such as empathy, self-control, and relationship management.

Conflict Management Is the PM's Job

Conflict management is an essential part of the project manager's job. The project manager is the one who will make the difference between leveraging conflict or having conflict wreak havoc on the team. Successfully recognizing and addressing conflict is part of the PM's role.

Recognizing That We Have a Conflict

The first step in the process is to recognize that there is conflict. In many cases, it won't be difficult to see. Consider the case where a team member came to me and said, "I won't work for him anymore," then proceeded to tell me about all the shortcomings of this team leader and how hurt she felt.

In another example, two subteams were involved in a decision over two possible technical directions. One team lead calmly described the two approaches and the merits and shortcomings of each. The other team lead simply said, "any idiot can see that this is the only valid approach."

It is not hard to see the conflict in these examples. It would not be hard if we saw or heard two individuals arguing with each other. However, the signals may not always be this clear. We need to be attuned to our environment to pick up on subtle signs that something is wrong. These signs include lack of communications, missed deadlines, poor quality deliverables, or deliverables behind schedule. Team members may reflect the conflict in their communications through sarcasm or the silent treatment. They may also do everything possible to make life difficult for other members, or avoid all meetings.

Traditional Approaches to Conflict Management

Assuming that we do recognize project conflict, how do we go about managing it? We can start with the traditional ways managers have addressed conflicts. There are five traditional modes of conflict resolution available to project managers. These modes are outlined in *Project Management: A Systems Approach to Planning, Scheduling, and Controlling.* The five modes are:

- compromising
- smoothing (or accommodating)
- forcing
- avoiding (or withdrawing)
- confronting (or collaborating)[3]

Let's look at each of these classic modes of conflict resolution from an emotionally intelligent project manager perspective.

Compromising

Compromising is when we search for a solution to the conflict that splits the difference and brings some degree of satisfaction to each party in a dispute. Compromising is characterized by give-and-take from each of the affected parties. Project managers that compromise are not necessarily looking for the best solution; they are simply looking for a middle ground that will be acceptable to both parties.

Compromising takes more emotional intelligence than withdrawing or smoothing because the issue is brought out into the open and discussed. However, compromising doesn't allow for the possibility of a win-win solution. It requires each of the parties in the conflict to give up something. It may encourage tentativeness in team members rather than going all out.

Compromising may be useful when the stakes are not very high and when both parties want to maintain the relationship.

Smoothing or Accommodating

Smoothing is when we minimize or avoid areas of difference. Smoothing managers tend to talk others out of being upset or try to gloss over it by emphasizing areas of agreement. They may establish a subteam to tackle a tough issue to reduce polarization of the team and avoid win-lose thinking.

---

[3]Harold Kerzner. *Project Management: A Systems Approach to Planning, Scheduling, and Controlling.* Hoboken, NJ: John Wiley & Sons, Inc., 2006.

A classic example of smoothing would be the plea "Can we get along here? Can we all get along?" That comment was made by police assault victim Rodney King after the 1992 Los Angeles riots. King was trying to smooth over the areas of upset and disagreement and urge people to just get along.

As a technique for resolving project conflict, smoothing is relatively low in terms of emotional intelligence. Like withdrawal, when we use smoothing we are not dealing with the underlying issue that is causing the conflict. Instead, we are avoiding the issue.

Smoothing can often cause problems to fester and reappear in other ways. Project managers that smooth over conflict force team members to take their issues underground. They will often vent their concerns to others and thereby sow dissention. Team members who are encouraged to smooth over conflict may begin to downplay or withhold bad news. The message they receive from the PM is, do not rock the boat.

We can use smoothing when the stakes are not very high or when we want to maintain good working relationships. Otherwise, it should be avoided.

Forcing

Forcing or suppression is used by managers that see conflict as disruptive to production and try to squelch that conflict. The manager makes it clear that disagreement is not tolerated and will work quickly to deal with any conflict. Any challenge to the manager is viewed as subordination. It is often characterized by a win-lose feeling in the team.

Forcing does not examine and address the underlying cause of the conflict and so is likely to lead to a recurrence of the problem in another form. The project manager's intolerance stifles any real discussion of the conflict and extinguishes the possibility for learning and change.

As you might imagine, forcing takes very little emotional intelligence. The parties involved may see a particular conflict as one in a series of conflicts. Each may feel that if they lose this one conflict, they can even things up later. After a conflict is resolved, the two parties may simply be regrouping and preparing for the next battle.

Forcing is a shortsighted approach to conflict resolution. It should be used only when time is limited, when the long-term relationship is not important, or when no other solution will resolve the situation.

Avoiding or Withdrawing

Project managers who use withdrawal will retreat from an actual or potential disagreement. They avoid disagreeing with others. They may go so far as to physically separate themselves from conflict by leaving the room or even taking a vacation. They may also distance themselves from unpopular management decisions saying, "hey, I am just following orders."

In relation to the other approaches, withdrawal is very low in terms of emotional intelligence. In fact, withdrawal was identified as one of the emotional breakdowns described in Chapter 4. When we use withdrawal to deal with a conflict, we are disengaging from the relationship. We don't tell the truth about our feelings or our wants and needs.

Unfortunately, withdrawal does not solve anything. In fact, with withdrawal we don't even acknowledge that there is a conflict. When we use withdrawal, we aren't really interested in solving the problem. We don't provide the other party the opportunity to work with us to resolve the conflict.

Withdrawal can be successful as a short-term strategy. By separating parties in a dispute, we allow the air to clear and cooler heads to prevail. Withdrawal would be very appropriate in situations where you believe that there is a risk of physical danger to anyone. Withdrawal could also be useful in situations where there is no long-term relationship. If you experience conflict in the last few weeks of a project, you may decide it is not worth working to resolve that particular issue. In all other cases, withdrawal should be avoided.

Confrontation or Collaboration

Confrontation is facing the conflict directly and using problem-solving techniques to work through the disagreement. When we use confrontation, we bring the conflict out into the open so that we can deal with it. Confrontation is what is often described as seeking a win-win solution. Confrontation is the one technique that addresses the underlying cause of the conflict, making it the most economical solutions in terms of personal investment and return.

As you might guess, confrontation is the highest in emotional intelligence of all the conflict resolution approaches. It takes a PM with emotional intelligence (and courage) to confront conflict directly and work to resolve it. PMs may feel scared or inadequate to deal with the conflict.

I was taught an important but embarrassing lesson about using confrontation to resolve conflict. Several years ago I was hired as a test manager for a large systems integration project. I was actually a co-test manager partnering with another manager to complete the testing. I found working with the other manager difficult to say the least. I was organized and had experience with test planning and execution. My fellow manager was experienced with the technology we were using but lacked the skills to organize and execute the testing. I became frustrated. After some half-hearted attempts to talk to my coworker, I told the project director that I had an issue with my co-test manager. His response was to invite me to meet him for lunch that very day.

When I arrived at the restaurant, I was surprised to see the project director sitting in a cozy round booth with my co-test manager. I sat down with the two of them and immediately the project director asked me what it was about my co-test manager that I needed to discuss with him. I was embarrassed, to say the least.

The confrontation with the project director taught me a few things. I learned that I should have spent more time working on the issue with my co-test manager before bringing it to the project director. I learned that the reason the project director paired us up was exactly the issue I wanted to complain about—we had different strengths and skills sets. Most important, I learned that the most direct way to resolve an issue was to confront it directly.

I try to remember these lessons when individuals come to me with issues or conflicts on a project. I try to tell them that the shortest distance between two people is a straight line and that is the most direct way to resolve a conflict.

One final note about confrontation: it is important for project managers to send the message to their team that they are open to confrontation themselves. You want your team to be comfortable bringing issues with you out in the open without fearing reprisal.

Applying Emotional Intelligence to Conflict Resolution

Beyond looking at the levels of emotional intelligence in each of the conflict resolution approaches, we can also use the emotional intelligence competencies to better manage conflicts. We begin with a focus on what each party is feeling.

Conflicts involve both facts and feelings. It is usually easy to get the facts. That is the "he said, she said" part of the transaction. The facts are helpful as a starting point but they are only part of the story. We need to get beyond the facts to understand *why* those facts matter so much to the parties involved. That requires an understanding of the underlying feelings as well as the unstated wants and needs of each of the parties.

It is important to probe to find out what the parties in a conflict are feeling. We need to listen emphatically and pay attention to feeling words and body language. We may even need to ask questions. Recall the example that I described in Chapter 5 where a team member sat with her arms crossed, fiercely insisting "I am not angry." People in conflict usually feel scared, angry, sad, or some combination of all of these things. They may be angry about critical remarks from a co-worker. At the same time, they may be sad because their feelings are hurt and they want to be friends with the co-worker who made the remarks. Finally, they may be scared of a confrontation or scared that they need to leave the project because of that person.

It would be unlikely that a team member involved in a conflict would have the emotional intelligence to openly discuss their feelings. More often, individuals will not be aware of the various mix of feelings they are experiencing. The project manager can lead or coax team members to appreciate the different feelings they are experiencing.

Understanding the feeling is the first step. The second step is to identify the underlying want or need. Some common wants and needs of project stakeholders are shown below:

- want to be recognized
- want to be important
- want to be productive
- want to be promoted
- want to feel part of the community
- need to make more money
- need to express themselves
- need to be liked or loved

When we understand the underlying wants and needs of the affected parties, we better understand their motivation. Then we can work together to address the issue or conflict that is caused by the underlying want and need. We can help each party to the conflict understand the wants and needs of the other party and to achieve their own wants and needs.

You Might Just Be the Cause

Our approach may vary a little if we are a part of the conflict or the cause of the conflict. If we are part of the conflict, we need to first orient to ourselves. The questions that we need to ask remain the same. We need to understand what it is that we are feeling. We will typically be sad, angry, or scared. We go further by asking what it is that we are sad, angry or scared about. What is our underlying want or need in this situation? How does this conflict move us closer to or further from our wants and needs?

Once we understand where we are coming from, then we can evaluate the other person. We start by trying to understand what they are feeling. Then we explore what they want and need in this situation. Then we explore ways to work with them through the conflict. We may want to think it through on our own and then discuss it with the other party. If it is tense or uncomfortable with just the two of you, ask for a peer manager or for a neutral third party to join the discussion.

Calmly leading others through conflict can help strengthen our relationships and build the team. It is also a way for PMs to demonstrate leadership.

■ Inspirational Leadership

The third and final competency of team leadership is inspirational leadership. Inspirational leadership is the ability to inspire others by casting a vision for the individual and the team. PMs with inspirational leaders make work attractive and interesting to the team, create high team morale, and attract and retain good resources.

Vision Casting

Vision casting is the process of stating a future, positive picture of the goals or objectives for the team, assisting the team to understand why they are important, and helping the team to connect with those goals and objectives. Vision casting for projects is the responsibility of the project manager.

One way to cast a vision is through the use of the mission, vision, and values statement for the project or team. The mission is a short statement about the overall objective for the team or what is going to be accomplished. The vision is a statement on how that mission will be accomplished. And the team values are the framework for pursuing the mission.

Consider the following example from a recent project that I managed. I created the picture shown in Figure 7-2 to represent the mission, vision, and values for the team.

The articulation of the team mission had a galvanizing effect on the team and on me as the leader. When I began to leverage this statement, it anchored my decisions and helped me to show others how their work fit into the larger picture. Each part of the mission, vision, and values statement was applicable. For example, I used the mission to help communicate the priorities for everyone on the team. Up to that point, each subteam had focused only on their own part of the project and their own work. The diagrams and words reminded them of the goals of the larger team. The vision was also important as it showed the balance I was striving to achieve between reaching the stated project objectives as well as investing and growing the people.

Team Mission

Team Mission

Collect data
effectively &
with high quality

Prepare data
leveraging team
strengths

Deliver data
in a timely and
useful way to
support our client

Team Vision

Get The Work Done
Do our best to achieve the goals
and objectives of the program

Develop Our People
Increase team capabilities by
developing the team through
challenging assignments and
increasing responsibilities

Team Values

Continuous Improvement

Teamwork

Contribution

Succeed or Fail Together

Timeliness

Fun

Figure 7-2: Example of Mission, Vision, and Values Statement.

Finally, the values were important since they served as ground rules or the code of conduct for the team. We developed the values list by team vote. Once we agreed to certain values, we used them to set a framework for how we would operate.

The biggest impact of the mission, vision, and values statement was that the entire team could understand what we were doing and how their particular part fit into that mission. They also began to appreciate my goals for how we would get the work done and how that would benefit them individually.

■ Additional Considerations for Team Leaders

Building the Project Team

One of the important roles of the project team leader is to build the project team. This includes selecting the best team members, taking steps to retain them, and removing resources from the team when necessary. As stated in Chapter 1, as a PM, you live or die by your resources. The skills, experience, and motivation of the resources will determine what can be accomplished by the team. It is essential that you get the right team and that you are able to retain them until the project is over.

Selecting Project Team Members

Of course we don't always have the luxury of selecting our team members. But we usually have some latitude when it comes to choosing who will be on the team. We need to exercise all the power we do have in order to maximize our chances of success.

Selecting the right team members from the beginning is very important. Many PMs act as if they have little or no say over their resources or that their choices don't matter much. Both of these attitudes will stand in the way of getting the best resources for your teams. Resources are unique, they are not generic or interchangeable. Consider the fact that on IT projects, the best developers outperform the worst developers by a factor of 10 to 1.

Professional sports teams are in the business of trying to win. They take recruiting talent very seriously. Look at how a professional sports team addresses the draft. They understand the importance of identifying strengths and weaknesses of their current team and finding the new players who will fill the gaps and round out the team. A professional football team doesn't just think linebacker, kicker, or center. They look deeper to get just the right skills to complete the entire team. PMs could take a page out of the NFL playbook when it comes to recruiting resources for the teams.

What kinds of factors go into the decision to hire resources? Most people would consider the candidates' technical capabilities, skills, and experience as the key factors. Here are some additional aspects which I think need to be considered:

- the strengths and weaknesses of the candidate versus the strengths and weaknesses of the team
- the candidate's experience with similar projects (size, technology, client)
- the candidate's attitude toward the project and team
- the candidate's personality and fit with the rest of the team
- the candidate's level of emotional intelligence

Of course it will be difficult to assess several of these factors in an interview, including the candidate's level of emotional intelligence. The point is to think beyond the basic questions of skill or experience and begin to look at the dynamics of the team and how each person will fit.

This list even mentions attitude. A good attitude is just as important as having the correct skill sets for the project. I have heard leaders say they hire for attitude and train for particular skills.

Different projects will require different approaches. I once managed a very large project that required hiring a lot of resources. I noticed that we had problems with those resources who up to that point had worked only on relatively small projects. Those resources had a difficult time dealing with certain big project issues like bureaucracy, recognition, and collaboration. Over time I learned to ask an additional question during interviews and that was "What was the largest project team you've worked on?" I began to exclude those people who had worked on teams of only five or six people because they often did not perform well on a team of thirty or fifty members.

The goal of the project manager when selecting resources is to add to the overall team capabilities. We want to select the individuals who will fill gaps, add to the team strengths, and generally bolster the team.

Impact of Organization Structure on Getting Resources

The structure of the organization will affect the project manager's role in selecting team members. Common organization structures include the functional organization, the matrix organization, and the projectized organization. The matrix organization can be characterized as either weak matrix or strong matrix to indicate the power of the PM relative to the functional or resource manager. Let's look at how the PM selects resources in the functional organization, the matrix organization, and the projectized organizations.

Selecting Resources in the Functional Organization

In the functional organization, the PM will likely have little voice in the staffing of the team. The functional manager will make most if not all of the decisions on staffing and the PM will find himself playing the hand they are dealt, so to speak. Resources will typically be constrained and shared across multiple projects. Team-building efforts are going to be more critical than ever in this type of environment.

Selecting Resources in the Matrix Organizations

In the matrix environment, the project manager and the functional manager will share responsibility for selecting project resources. To be successful in this environment, the PM needs to build a strong relationship with the functional manager. Nurturing that relationship will determine the quality and availability of resources we have for our projects.

The relationship building skills that we discussed in Chapter 6 will be especially relevant when it comes to managing the relationships with those functional managers. The key to building the relationship with the functional manager is to understand the goals and objectives of their role.

The primary role of the functional manager is to keep the resources who report to them engaged on projects. The functional manager needs to do this for the high-performers who are easy to keep assigned to projects and are typically over-allocated. The manager also needs to do this for those average or underperforming resources who are harder to place on projects and are often not so busy.

As PMs, we can help the functional manager as well as ourselves. By building strong relationships with the functional manager, we can better communicate our needs as well as negotiate for the resources we need. We can also help the functional manager by providing early forecasts of project resource needs and communications changes in a timely fashion. This is something the functional managers will appreciate and remember.

Selecting Resources in the Projectized Organizations

In a projectized organization, the PM will take on more of the responsibility for staffing the project team. The PM may even have authority over hiring and firing of team members. In such an environment, the PM usually has the luxury (and the responsibility) on hiring decisions.

Tips for Interviewing Team Members

Project managers who don't hire frequently may lack the experience to make good decisions about new hires. We might select the wrong resources or find that people are not as they appear on their resume. We may also find the hiring process to be a slow and costly investment for the PM and key resources. Over the course of a recent long-term program, I interviewed at least fifty resources and hired about twenty of them. I found that the following things helped me to hire the best resources:

- judicious use of others to interview
- in-person interviews
- specific hiring qualities
- template for comparing apples to apples
- pre-screening

Judicious Use of Others to Interview

The judicious use of others to interview means that we involve others in the process when appropriate. Early in my career I used more of a committee approach to selecting resources instead of selecting them on my own. Over time I found that this strategy often produced poor results. It didn't always hold that the individual that everyone on the team liked was the best person for the job. This approach was also very costly due to the number of resources involved in each interview.

Now I tend to rely strongly on my own judgment. I may involve the one or two key people who the individual will work with but I don't ask everyone on the team to interview new people. It is a big investment that has only marginal return.

Face-to-Face Interviews

While we may perform much of our work virtually or remotely, we need to conduct interviews face to face whenever possible. The face-to-face interview provides much more information than one conducted over the phone. In nearly every situation where I conducted interviews solely over the phone, I ultimately regretted that I never had a face-to-face interview.

Specific Hiring Qualities

Over the years I have learned that there is a pay-off when we determine up front, before we interview any candidates, the specific hiring criteria for the job. We need to identify those criteria and use them as a guide during the interview. Otherwise, we can be swayed by individuals who relate well during the interview but may not have the necessary qualifications. After all, people tend to pick those they like and that may include ignoring qualifications.

Template for Comparing Apples to Apples
We can extend the concept of the specific hiring qualities to create a template to be used for interviewing several candidates. The template is especially helpful when you are trying to sift through different resume styles and formats to find specific information. It is much easier to put all the key hiring qualities in one place.

This can be extended even further by having some sort of pre-screening. We can ask the candidate, or our HR department, or the account manager (if working with contract labor), to complete the template for each candidate and pre-screen them for us. This can save us considerable time and effort.

Retaining Team Members

Once we have hired the right people and created a solid team, how do we create an environment that keeps people on the team? It is up to the project manager to create an environment where resources feel valued, can contribute, and can succeed. Those PMs that have invested in their own emotional intelligence will find that they attract and retain others when they:

- lead with inspiration and make work interesting and attractive
- develop others, making the team appreciative and wanting to do more
- make people feel that they are important
- make people feel they are wanted and needed

Removing Members from the Team

In some cases, we will find that we have the wrong people on the team. Removing people from the team is just as important as selecting the right ones to add. When we evaluate whether to retain a resource, we need to consider factors similar to the ones we used when selecting members for the team.

While there are some people who are critical to our teams, PMs should recognize that no one person is irreplaceable. It sometimes happens that individuals (and even PMs) get the idea that they are the most critical part of the team and cannot be replaced. They let their egos get in the way of the work and can lose sight of the project objectives. In some cases this is incurable; the only thing the PM can do is to remove the resources from the team. This takes courage.

Project managers may actually improve their team by subtracting resources. If someone is casting a negative shadow over the team, has a poor attitude, or causes constant conflict, they can reduce overall productivity. The entire team suffers when someone is acting in negative ways. As the project manager, it is important to recognize and address situations where team members should be disciplined or removed.

Once we determine whether to retain someone or cut them from the team, how do we actually make it happen? This can be tough. Do we remove them from the team, ask them to leave, encourage them to leave, or make their environment unattractive and hope they leave on their own? Project managers may even lack the authority to make that decision on their own. In the matrix organization, PMs may need to work with the functional manager to remove someone from the project team.

When we do remove someone from the team, we need to consider how to best communicate that to the rest of the team. If we don't explain it, others may feel that they will be targeted next.

Better Decisions Through Emotional Intelligence

One of the ways in which project leaders can leverage emotional intelligence is making decisions. We talked in Chapter 1 about emotions being information and how that information is like personal radar. This section will discuss how to go about leveraging that emotional information to make better decisions.

Negative emotions should be monitored closely during decision making. In Chapter 3 we talked about how our emotions can lead us to make poor decisions or to react without thinking, resulting in emotional breakdowns. We can make terrible decisions if we let ourselves be swayed by fear, sadness, or anger without looking at the cause of those negative emotions. When we recognize that we are feeling scared, sad, or angry, we can look beyond the feeling to the underlying cause. This will allow us to take in the emotion and any other issues, and reframe the decision to include a full view of the situation.

In fact, David Caruso and Peter Salovey argue that each of the emotions serve us differently for different types of decisions. Their research shows that people in a sad mood can often develop more persuasive messages and better-quality arguments than people in a happy mood. Conversely, people in a happy mood may have more creative arguments than those who are sad.[4]

---

[4]David R Caruso and Peter Salovey. *The Emotionally Intelligent Manager: How to Develop and Use the Four Key Emotional Skills of Leadership.* Hoboken, NJ: John Wiley & Sons, Inc., 2004.

Which makes sense, because when we are sad or scared, we tend to be overly pessimistic. We have a hard time seeing that something is working and we pick apart a plan and find all its faults. We are more likely to say no; even when it might serve us better to say yes.

Ironically, individuals who are in positive moods can make some very poor decisions. They will tend to underestimate the risk of negative events. When we feel happy, we may overlook key information, neglect to plan for contingencies, or gloss over negative data. We may be overly optimistic about project outcomes and fail to consider relevant risks. We may say yes to additional work or deliverables when we should say no.

Anger is a powerful emotion that helps motivate us to act. Anger can give us the power we need to make important changes or to simply get us moving when we are scared.

The starting point, then, for using emotions as input to decisions is to understand what we are feeling and, as noted in Chapter 3, to understand as much as possible why we are feeling that way. That understanding should lead to using our underlying emotions to balance our decisions. We need to understand what our gut feeling is telling us. If we feel uneasy about the interview with the candidate for the open developer position, what is behind that feeling? Armed with that information, we can approach a decision differently.

The second part of decision making with emotional intelligence is to understand and incorporate the feelings of those around us. What do others feel about this decision or the underlying issues? What is their position and why? This is where we use our social awareness skills to understand others. We can use our empathy to put ourselves in their shoes and identify what they are likely to feel. For individuals we know well, we can use our understanding of their typical emotional state. If others tend to be overly happy or sad, that might influence the way they evaluate a particular situation.

Once we understand the emotional landscape, we can look past the emotions to the principles involved. We orient to principles when we make a decision that is grounded in the values of the team and the organization. We may be scared about a decision to bring on a new resource or try a new technology on the project but we need to see past the fear and look at the benefits we are trying to obtain. We need to make the best decision at the time in spite of how we might feel.

Getting Support

My mentor Rich has often said that big goals require big support. If we are going to live big as project managers and leaders, we need a lot of support. A

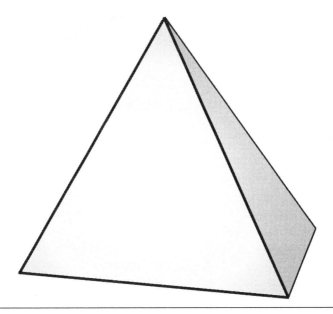

Figure 7-3: Support Base for a Pyramid.

good metaphor for support is the great pyramids. Think of the pyramids and the size of the base relative to the height of the peak. The higher the pyramid, the larger the base needs to be, as shown in Figure 7-3.

"Big goals require big support"
—Rich Blue

So what is support? In this context, we are using support to mean the emotional support and help of others. It could be help in the form of encouragement, accountability, listening, feedback, or coaching and mentoring.

Getting support is a relatively new concept for me as it may be for many project managers. I used to be the type who got it all done on my own. I was independent, and I rarely asked others for help and saw it as a weakness if I did.

I've come a long way in this area. I now participate in a men's small group that meets weekly to provide emotional support as we work at being husbands, fathers, and leaders in our careers. I participate in two running groups that recently helped me qualify for the Boston Marathon. One running group meets weekly and focuses on speed work and racing. The other meets monthly and focuses on creating community and emotional support for running. I am an active member of my local church. I have participated in two personal growth retreats every year for the last four years. This book actually sprang from my work with three different mentors and I am honored to have different people involved in reviewing my writing and providing feedback. I have a team who holds me accountable to my weekly writing goals. Finally, my wife Norma has been an inspiration and source of support through all my work.

I feel like an evangelist when it comes to getting support and including others. In many different areas in my life, I feel like a race car driver with a pit crew who is supporting me. They watch my back for me. When I need something, I ask them for help. I don't see how it is possible to be successful without enrolling others in supporting us. We need to enroll others to allow them to participate in our goals and objectives, and ultimately in our success.

One of the reasons many people do not ask others for help is that they don't want to burden others. This is a fallacy that is easily debunked. Consider for a moment when others have asked you for support. This could be to participate in an informational interview, or to come into your office and vent, or to get advice, or to provide coaching and feedback. Most people feel flattered when asked and are happy to help. I know I do. Unfortunately, I sometimes forget to apply that to others. So I hesitate to ask when it could really help.

There is another irony of asking for help. When you ask someone to help you with something, they become invested in you and want to see you succeed. Once someone invests in you, they are no longer separate from your success. When you succeed or fail, you reflect their input and help and by extension they succeed or fail. So those who invest in you want to see you succeed. Instead of being bothered by your request, they become part of your team and take an interest in your success. And the opposite is also true. If you exclude people from helping you, you deny them the opportunity to be part of your success.

A good friend of mine was recently responsible for organizing a fund-raising event for a high school coach who had non-Hodgkin lymphoma. He almost hesitated to invite me to the event because it cost $100 per person and I did not even know the coach. Fortunately, my friend did ask, and I went to the event. I was so affected by the kind words spoken by the friends and family of this coach that I walked away inspired and thinking about my own life. Later, I thanked my friend for including me. I personally benefited because I was impacted by the event. And I was happy to be able to help him. Far from feeling obligated to participate, I felt honored to be a part of this celebration of the coach.

Take a moment and think about your own support team. How would you rate yourself on getting other people involved in your success? Are there areas of your life where you are good at getting support? What are the areas where you tend to fly solo and go it alone? What stops you from involving others in your support?

■ Techniques for Improving Project Team Leadership

1. Techniques to Improve Team Communications

Plan your communications in advance whenever possible. Think through the emotional content, your own feelings, and the emotions of the recipients.

Practice your communications. You can do this alone, with your spouse or kids, with a peer or trusted co-worker, or with your boss. This is especially important for PMs who get nervous in front of groups.

Speak from the heart by sharing your emotions. Be honest, though, and don't try to be manipulative or to cover up your emotions; it doesn't work.

2. Techniques for Conflict Management

Expect conflict and lead by example when it comes to resolving it. Let people know that your style is to be open and take on conflict directly. Refrain from shooting the messenger so that people are willing to bring conflict to you.

One technique that I used successfully on a recent project involved the opportunity for team members to vent. When I sensed there was pressure on people or that conflict was brewing, I would add a block of time to my weekly team meeting and call it "Open Rant." Each person would get sixty seconds or so in the meeting to rant about anything they wanted. They did not have to fear reprisal; the team simply held the space for each person to get something off their chest if needed. Not everyone used the time, but the ones that did were able to blow off some steam.

3. Create a Mission, Vision, and Values Statement for Your Project Team

Many people think of a mission, vision, and values statement as something done only at the company's strategic level. It is also possible to create a mission, vision, and values statement for your project team. Keep it as short and focused as possible. Include your team in the process and the outcome.

4. Cast a Vision for the Team

Whether you use a mission, vision, and values statement or simply talk about your vision for the team, be an evangelist about it. Continue over the life of the project to talk to the team about your vision, why you are excited about it, and how their work fits into that vision. Describe for them the outcomes you see for each team member and the overall team, and encourage them to embrace the goals and objectives for the team.

5. Become a Talent Scout

Getting the best resources is important to the success of the project. The project manager should view themselves as a talent maven. They should be constantly on the lookout for new talent to add to their team or to keep in the back of their mind for some future project. When you are impressed by another professional in your field, you should be thinking about how to get them on your team. Add people to your team who are so good they scare you.

6. Become Systematic About Screening and Hiring Resources

PMs that want to lead better will work to develop systematic ways of interviewing and selecting new resources. This is not something that can be left to chance. Develop systems and processes that allow for repeatability and that serve the needs of the project. This might include a checklist for hiring, a skill set template, a two-on-one interview process, or anything else that leads to better selection and hiring.

7. Tools to Address Team Strengths and Weaknesses

Try using the StrengthsFinder assessments for your entire team. The results can be plotted and used as a basis for discussion. This makes for a great off-site team-building exercise early in the life of a project.

In a creative use of the StrengthsFinder, I know of one company who conducted assessments of their top seventy-five managers. During an offsite retreat, they posted the StrengthsFinder results anonymously and let the management participants use the results to select the leaders for the retreat. The results were interesting and not what they would have been if they had simply used the organization chart to organize the retreat.

8. Expand Your Support Base

Try expanding your support base by getting more people involved in your success. The following list includes many ways to engage people in what you are doing. You will notice that many of these start with "ask." We need to view an "ask" as an invitation for someone to participate and share in our journey.

1. Enroll your spouse or significant other in your success. Ask them to participate by giving you feedback and emotional support. Or, invite them into the planning of a large goal and then request that they hold you accountable to work toward that goal.
2. Brainstorm about who would be the best person or people to coach or mentor you to reach your particular goals without regard for whether or not you know them personally or think they would help. Then reach out to them and ask for their help.
3. Ask someone to be a coach or mentor. If you don't currently have any mentors, identify someone you respect and ask them if they would be willing to mentor you. If you can afford it, hire a professional coach with expertise in your domain. As an example, I recently hired a personal trainer to help me achieve my goal of qualifying for the Boston Marathon.
4. Ask someone on your current team for feedback on the job you are doing. Be open and receptive.
5. Develop an open relationship with a peer that will provide you with a sounding board for your ideas, challenges, and conflicts.
6. Join some type of support team. This could be a weekend running group, a church group, a 12-step program, a professional organization, or whatever else meets your needs.

8

Creating a Positive Team Environment

In the previous chapters, we explored the various aspects of emotional intelligence and project management. We started by looking at emotional intelligence for the project manager, then we broadened our view to include interactions with members of the team and other stakeholders.

This chapter looks at how project managers can leverage emotional intelligence to create an environment that is positive and productive for the project team. There is a direct correlation between the team environment and the productivity and satisfaction levels of the team members. Whether intentional or not, the PM sets the overall tone and mood of the project. Through their actions and communications, PMs can create either resonance or dissonance in the project environment. We will look at ways that PMs can carry out their responsibilities and contribute to a positive team environment. Finally, we will finish the chapter with a list of techniques that PMs can put to work immediately to improve the environment of their projects.

■ What Makes a Great Project Team

A World of Difference

If you have been involved in enough projects, you will have experienced some project teams that were good, or even great, as well as some teams that were perhaps not so great. Take a moment and think about a project team that was really terrific. If you are like most people, you can recall a project that was fun to work on; you even willingly worked extra hours. You likely felt happy and excited to be part of the team and sad when the project ended or when you left.

With the memory of that project in mind, think about the things that made that project so enjoyable. What was it about that project team that made you willing to work extra hours or go the extra mile to help others? What was it that made you sad when your time on the project ended? To the point, what were the characteristics of that project that made it so great?

I often ask my students about the projects they felt were great and what characteristics made those projects great. Most students respond that the best projects had the following characteristics:

- interdependence among team members
- diversity of team members
- mutual respect
- the work was challenging
- they shared common goals
- commitment of everyone
- high performance of all members
- synergy among members

While not a scientific study, I have found the results consistent across classes. These characteristics are the context of the project. If they are not part of the values of the project, or if the values conflict with these, the project environment is going to suffer.

Think for a moment about projects that you have been on that were not so great. Can you recall a project that you did not enjoy and could not wait to leave? Most people have at least one of these types of projects on their resume. Let's hope you were not the PM. What was it like to be in the middle of that not-so-great project? What made you want to leave? How did the project fall short of your hopes and expectations? How would you characterize the environment of that project?

It is amazing how two projects can vary so widely in terms of team morale, productivity, satisfaction levels, and motivation. There is a world of difference between project teams with a positive environment and those without it. Given the two choices, it seems clear that most people would prefer to be part of a project team that has a productive and positive environment.

There is a world of difference between project teams with a
positive environment and those without it.

As project managers, we want to create the best possible team environment to attract and retain great team members and to help them to be
productive. If we want to get the best from our teams, we need to create an
environment that will support our team members and encourage them to
perform at their best. The project manager is responsible for creating that
team environment. They set the stage so that the team can do their best work.

Resonance and Dissonance in Project Leaders

Another factor in establishing a positive environment is the level of emotional
resonance or dissonance created by the project leader. In *Primal Leadership,*
Daniel Goleman and his co-authors discuss the concepts of resonance and
dissonance as they apply to leadership. Resonant leaders are those who can
manage and direct feelings to help a group meet its goals.

Resonant leaders form strong bonds with people and create a sense of
oneness across a team. Those leaders are in harmony with the team.

While resonant leaders create harmony with the team, dissonant leaders
do the opposite. Dissonant leaders create discord and emotional disconnects.
Their messages sound off-key because they lack empathy or are unable to understand others. They transmit negative emotional messages that fall flat or
worse, disturb others and create conflict. The caveman manager that I discussed
in Chapter 4 would be a dissonant leader as would the difficult and at-risk
individuals we discussed in Chapter 6.

While there is no 12-step program to cure dissonant leaders, there are
steps that project managers can take to become more resonant. PMs can start
by becoming more proficient at the emotional intelligent competencies that
we introduced in the previous chapters. They can develop their self-awareness
and social awareness in order to better understand themselves and others.
They can show empathy toward others and place themselves in the shoes of
the members of their teams. They can work to create messages that connect
to the emotions and wants and needs of others. They show how each team
member's personal goals and objectives relate to the team's goals and objectives. They emphasize the common purpose of the team and focus on getting
people pulling in the same direction.

PMs can evaluate their own leadership style and even learn new styles of leadership. Goleman and his *Primal Leadership* co-authors discuss four resonant leadership styles and two dissonant leadership styles. We are going to explore these leadership styles in detail in Chapter 9 and will provide some tips and techniques for leveraging these styles.

■ How PMs Set the Tone and Direction for the Project

The PM is responsible for the tone and direction for the project. Like the captain of a ship, the PM's leadership is an invisible force that guides the team.

PMs who are intentional about setting the tone and direction for the project create safety in the project environment. By this I do not mean physical safety, though that is important to the project team. A safe environment is one where expectations and standards for behavior and performance are clear. Project managers create a safe environment by setting standards, enforcing the rules, addressing conflict, holding others accountable, and recognizing others. This safe environment encourages team members to take risks, flourish, and perform at their highest.

Have you ever been in an unsafe environment? Unsafe environments are characterized by a lack of team norms, values, and rules. There may appear to be no one in charge in unsafe projects, there is an undercurrent of dissatisfaction, and everyone complains about everyone else. Priorities are often not stated and conflict goes unmanaged.

In the next sections, we will look at how PMs set the project tone and direction by their handling of the following key PM leadership responsibilities:

- establish team values
- enforce the rules
- stand up to management
- hold others acccountable
- recognize individuals

Establish Team Values

We talked about team values as part of the mission, vision, and values statement in Chapter 7. As PMs, we need to create team values and ensure that they become more than just words on a page. The team values are the norms of the project team; they are an agreement on how the team will act and treat each other. As PMs, we need to model the team values, communicate them to the project team, and hold the team to those values.

PMs should work early in the life of the project to establish team values. These values can be established as part of the mission, vision, and values statement or they might be identified separately. It is usually best to create the team values with the help of the project team though there may be times when it is better for the PM to set the team values independently.

Once we establish the values, we need to make sure that the team lives up to them. We do this by acknowledging team members who demonstrate the values. Several years ago I was one of eight project managers on a large program team. Our core team of project managers, together with the program manager and sponsor, created the team's value statement during an offsite meeting. Rather than simply writing the values down and forgetting them, the project sponsor had the values printed on memo pads that were freely distributed to all 100 members of the program team. The project sponsor also set up a simple recognition system based on those team values. The recognition system made it easy for any member of the program team to acknowledge and reward any other team member for demonstrating one of the team values. In this way, the program sponsor provided a mechanism for reinforcing the values of the team.

We can also reinforce the values by calling out behavior that is not in line with the values. If a team member is not playing by the rules or is demonstrating bad behavior, we can take them aside and discuss their behavior. We should not tolerate behavior that is contrary to the team values.

Enforce the Rules

In a similar way, the PM needs to be willing to enforce the team rules. Rules, the way that the PM expects others to behave, can include everything from being on time for meetings to requesting vacation time. An example of an expectations list is shown in Table 8-1. This list identified the expectations I placed on the team leads reporting to me on a particular project. The format provided a means for the team leads to do a self-check that also served as a basis for discussion between me and the team lead.

Once the rules or expectations are made clear, it is up to the PM to enforce those rules. When someone on the team is out of line, the other team members will look to the leader to see if they are going to address the issue. Inaction sends a clear message that the rules are not important or that they do not apply to everyone.

Table 8-1: Expectations List

Expectations for Team Leads	Never	Rarely	Often Times	Very Often	Always
Show up on time for meetings	1	2	3	4	5
Review deliverables from an end users perspective	1	2	3	4	5
Lead by example	1	2	3	4	5
Conduct ongoing reviews of performance	1	2	3	4	5
Attend the weekly status meeting prepared to discuss status and issues	1	2	3	4	5
Log and work the team issues; escalate as appropriate	1	2	3	4	5
Conduct regular one-on-one meetings with each team member	1	2	3	4	5
Conduct regular status meetings with your team	1	2	3	4	5
Provide input to or prepare weekly status reports	1	2	3	4	5
Follow the program reporting structure	1	2	3	4	5
Invest in people	1	2	3	4	5
Get coverage when you will not be at work & notify stakeholders	1	2	3	4	5
Follow through on commitments	1	2	3	4	5
Tell the Truth	1	2	3	4	5
Create a fun and professional environment	1	2	3	4	5

For a PM, enforcing the rules may feel like being the heavy, or being a bad guy. A project manager may be afraid that they will not be liked or that others will get angry with them. They may want to avoid conflict because that is easier in the short run. This can be a defining moment for a leader.

Enforcing the rules has a major impact on the environment of the project. Even a seemingly little thing like making sure that people are on time for team meetings can make a difference to the project team. In *The Tipping Point,* Malcolm Gladwell discusses the Broken Windows theory, which links the existence of broken windows in an area to a rise in crime. Essentially it says that crime results from an environment where crime is permitted. The existence of broken windows or graffiti acts as a sort of environmental indicator that crime is tolerated. Individuals who normally would not commit crimes might be tempted to do so if they saw those environmental indicators or if they saw crimes going unpunished. However, if the police crack down on the broken windows and the graffiti and other petty crimes, the overall crime rates would drop significantly.

In the project environment, the project manager is the rough equivalent of the chief of police. The PM needs to enforce the rules. When we enforce the rules, we risk upsetting people, being disliked, or creating conflict. This can be very uncomfortable and scary. We need to push through our fear and address the issue as quickly and directly as possible.

Some project team members will actually get a kick out of breaking the rules. They will test the PM to see if they are serious about enforcing the rules. I have seen this manifested in people who fail to ask approval before spending project funds, those who are chronically late to meetings, and those who disappear on vacation without letting anyone know. As noted previously in this text, this could be a sign of passive aggressiveness. It could also be a team member testing the limits, like a small child will test their parent's limits. Like good parents, a project manager needs to address the issue as directly as possible, including establishing consequences.

There must be consequences for those individuals who break the rules. It is preferable to use positive consequences instead of negative ones. PMs may also want to have ready some lighthearted consequences for first-time offenders or for minor offenses. I have heard of teams who build up a small slush fund by requiring anyone who is late to a meeting to contribute one dollar. Some teams have progressive consequences that start out fun and quickly get less fun if the offense is repeated. This could escalate into the offender being removed from the project team at some point. In most cases however, the best consequence is simply to talk to the offender and ask them to change their behavior.

Here is one final note about enforcing the rules. The best approach is to create an environment where everybody is part of enforcing the rules. In this way, the PM doesn't always have to be the only enforcer. The team can often exert peer pressure to get compliance. To encourage everyone to play a part, the PM needs to send a clear message about the expected behavior and let it be known that they expect everyone on the team to enforce the rules.

Standing Up to Management

There are times when the PM will need to stand up to management on some issue. Examples include when PMs disagree with a decision or when they need to push back on a proposed change in scope, budget, resources, or timeline. In this context, management means the PM's boss, major stakeholders, or the client.

The project team wants to see the PM stand up to management, major stakeholders, or even the client once in a while. They want to know that their leader has the backbone to go to bat for them when needed. They want to feel like the PM has their best interest in mind.

PMs that are unwilling to stand up to management may be viewed as weak or as a pushover. Team members will feel sold out and resent the downstream impacts of PMs who are unwilling to push back. "It all rolls downhill" is a common refrain from frustrated team members. But it is not just team members you need to be concerned with. Managers, major stakeholders, and clients will become wary of PMs who never push back; they will see the PM as weak and ineffective.

That doesn't mean the PM should fight every decision that goes against the team. PMs need to choose their battles. Bob was one of my project managers who fought every decision and change. He opposed every idea that was not his own. He resisted organizational changes, he fought a physical move of his team to bring them into proximity with the rest of the program, he challenged budget cuts, and he resisted attempts to meet the aggressive delivery schedules our client requested.

Bob was a pain for me to manage. He cooperated only when he was getting his way. Otherwise, he was stubborn, argumentative, and often ineffective.

The problem with Bob was not his unwillingness to fight for his team. It was his inability to know when to fight. He didn't know how to choose his battles and his approach of always being willing to stand up to management did more damage than good. His approach did not serve him or the overall team well. As his manager, I often thought about replacing him with someone who was more cooperative.

We also need to consider the long-term consequences of pushing back. We don't want to create ill will or enemies. In particular, we should be careful to follow the chain of command when we disagree with a decision or an issue. In most environments it is acceptable to disagree with your boss. It is usually not a good idea to argue in public with your boss, nor is it good form to go over your boss's head or around them without trying to resolve the issue with them first. In fact, we should always strive to resolve issues at the lowest possible management level before escalating. We should exercise extreme caution any time we are about to go over someone's head, in particular our own boss. Going over your manager's head or skipping levels makes sense only as a last resort. The potential for creating long-lasting conflict is high, and every attempt should be made to work things out first with the manager.

Hold Others Accountable

The effective use of accountability is a powerful lever for the PM. PMs don't perform the work of the project; they direct and make sure that others do that work. Holding others accountable is crucial when we don't have direct authority over team resources.

One way that PMs hold others accountable is by gaining agreement on goals and deliverables, stating our expectations for each person, and publicizing team roles and responsibilities. We make the commitments public and then we support others to complete the work as appropriate.

There are three key parts to accountability. The first is to get agreement on the work to be performed. Accountability is not possible without buy-in from the person performing the work. The second part of accountability is to make that agreement public. Project managers publicize commitments through action item lists, status reports, responsibility assignment matrixes, and project schedules. The third part is to followup. As PMs, we need to be proactive to make sure the team members are performing the activities and following through on their commitments.

Some individuals need to be held accountable to perform at their best. When we remind others of their commitments, they will usually work to meet those commitments.

PMs should be prepared for individuals who are unwilling to be held accountable. I once worked with an individual whom we nicknamed "Teflon Don" based on his ability to avoid being accountable. Don was good at avoiding responsibility for tasks. I realized that it was difficult for me to assign work to Don and it made me uncomfortable to hold him accountable. I wanted to downplay what I needed from him and when. However, that did not serve me very well since Don rarely delivered anything on that project.

Like Don, some people wriggle out of responsibilities or ignore them completely. Project managers who avoid conflict may be scared and find it difficult to bring up the item. It takes courage to pursue individuals and hold them accountable, especially if they are senior to the PM. For example, I used to find it very difficult to hold certain people accountable including my boss, major stakeholders, clients, and anyone I considered senior to me. Once I recognized this tendency to be scared and play small, I pushed myself to change. I made sure that I recorded the required actions, got agreement on those actions, publicized them, and followed up with the responsible party to remind them of their commitment.

PMs don't just sit by and watch if others fail on their commitments. Project managers support others by reminding them of their commitments, clarifying expectations, and requesting periodic updates. If needed, the PM should also offer support or suggest creative ways to accomplish goals. However, the PM should not take the responsibility back from the owner or let them off the hook.

I once taught a class where the importance of accountability became crystal clear. It was a two-day course, and early in the first day a number of the students requested that we take a thirty-minute lunch instead of the planned sixty-minute lunch. This would allow them to end the day sooner and avoid some of the rush hour traffic. We discussed the proposal as a group and everyone agreed to the change. What happened next was not surprising. Only about half of the students were back in their seats and ready to start after thirty minutes; the others were missing. Students continued to arrive back from lunch over the next thirty minutes right up until the original commitment time.

It would have been easy to let this go. After all, the students paid for the class and it was up to them to get the most out of it. However, this course was about emotional intelligence for project managers. PMs need to appreciate deadlines and the importance of sticking to their commitments. So after everyone returned, we spent some time talking about the incident. We recognized that everyone had agreed to the change yet some individuals did not live up to their end of the bargain. That behavior penalized the entire class. We also talked about the message that tolerating this type of behavior would send to the team and how other behavior would deteriorate. The message I sent was that people would be held accountable. It was not surprising then that everyone returned from lunch and breaks on time from that point forward.

This unplanned incident turned out to be one of the most talked-about parts of the course and perhaps one of the most important lessons in leadership that those students received from the course. It was a great reminder to me of the importance of holding others accountable.

Recognize Individuals

We briefly discussed recognition in Chapter 6 on relationship management. I said that recognition is one of the most powerful and underused tools in the PM's arsenal. In addition to building relationships with others, it is one of the ways that the PM sets the tone of the project environment.

In their book, *The One Minute Manager,* Kenneth Blanchard and Spencer Johnson introduced the phrase "Help people reach their full potential. Catch them doing something right."

> "Help people reach their full potential.
> Catch them doing something right."
> —Ken Blanchard and Spencer Johnson[1]

There is genius in that phrase. One of the things I appreciate most about my mentor is when he says "Anthony, my vision for you is. . . ." It is as if he is holding the bar high for me; he can see me performing at even a higher level than I believe is possible.

That is the model I try to follow for my team members and I encourage you to do the same. Look for the best in each person. Try to see beyond their current performance to their true potential. Hold them to that higher bar and encourage them to reach for that level of performance.

The second part of Blanchard's phrase is pure brilliance. "Catch them doing something right" encourages us to be on the lookout for ways to recognize people's goodness. We seek out the best in others and we acknowledge it.

The more natural tendency for me and many others is to focus on what people are doing wrong so that I can criticize or discipline them. It is a habit that I acquired from my critical father. Like any other habit, it can be broken and replaced with better habits. The first step is to recognize that you have a problem. I know that I am most critical when I feel scared or angry. I try to use this awareness to make the shift to being on the lookout for the best in others.

Do you look for the best in others? Or are you looking for the things that are wrong or need improvement? Whichever approach you are taking, it is part of the tone of the project. It becomes one of the unstated values and it affects the behaviors of everyone on the team. We send a clear message to the team when we give recognition or when we withhold it. Team members

---

[1]Kenneth Blanchard and Spencer Johnson. *The One Minute Manager.* NY: HarperCollins, 1981.

will pay more attention to what is rewarded than to what is said. The recognition informs the team on what is important to the project team leader.

There are many opportunities to catch people doing something right. We can recognize and reward individuals for their contribution to the team, for specific results and outcomes, to reinforce the values and expected behaviors of the team, to build morale, and to motivate people.

Once we catch someone doing something right, we need to recognize that behavior. How do we do it? There are nearly infinite ways to recognize people. I have used public awards, certificates, thank you notes, lunches, and many other approaches. One of the best and easiest ways to recognize people is to simply stop by and thank them for their work. You can also thank them in public, in a department meeting, for example. Either way, thanking people doesn't take a long time or cost anything. Tie your thank you as closely as possible to something that the individual did well. It is better not to wait to recognize others.

As PMs, we want to create a healthy and productive environment. We can use the rewards to create an environment of gratitude and recognition.

■ The Team Within the Team

Up to this point, the discussion about the project team environment has largely ignored the broader organizational environment, the department, division, or company environment that surrounds the project. This could include a client organization, if that is where the project team is performing.

The reality is that project teams don't operate in isolation. They are affected by the organizations around them. Project managers cannot afford to ignore the broader organizational environment.

That organizational environment or context will impact the project manager's efforts to create a positive project environment. If the organization environment is positive, the project manager will have an easier time creating a positive project environment.

Negative Environments

PMs need to be concerned about the organizations that are not so positive. For example, I once worked for a small company whose CEO was trying to change the culture from a friendly and collegiate environment to one that was professional and client focused. I was inadvertently caught in the crossfire of this organizational culture change as I led a large project team with a priority on meeting client needs and expectations. In several cases, my style of delivering what the client needed collided with the longstanding culture of scholarly debate. In one memorable incident, the CEO told me to keep doing what I was doing. He said that he would "deal with any ruffled feathers." I felt happy and supported in my work and that helped to reinforce the client-focused team environment.

What if the larger environment you are working in is not positive? Can you create a positive project environment? Absolutely! I believe this is something the best project managers do naturally. They don't let a negative organizational environment corrupt a positive project environment. They send the message to their team that the project is different. They communicate the values and rules of the project team, reward those team members who are in alignment, and enforce the rules.

In the classes I teach I often hear people say "that won't work at my company," or "they won't let me do that." I don't know if the statements are true or not. I do believe that the students who make these statements believe them to be true. Either way it is clear that the students don't feel empowered. In most cases, what is lacking is not permission for PMs to create their own environment, but the PM's courage to take risks and be different. PMs have the responsibility to do what is best for the project and the company. This takes courage. PMs often have more power than they think when it comes to choosing their own destiny. There are probably very few rules imposed on PMs, in particular when it comes to setting the mood, tone, and direction for the project.

If you find yourself in a negative environment that stymies any opportunity to create a positive project environment, consider leaving. Why waste your talent on an organization that is not positioned to leverage it? Don't go home at night thinking that you could be something if only management would let you. Don't be a victim to a negative workplace.

At a minimum, if you cannot leave the negative organization, at least don't let yourself be contaminated by the environment. Don't compromise your own standards for behavior. Be as positive as possible and maybe through a merger, management change, or re-organization, the organization will catch up to you.

■ Techniques for Creating a Positive Team Environment

1. Assess How Team Members View the Team Environment

I have found it helpful in the past to poll my team to see how they feel about the team environment. Most team members will be flattered if you ask how they think you are doing in this area. Consider a mini-assessment which will evaluate how you are doing in terms of creating safety, establishing and communicating values, and resolving conflict.

One of my favorite mini-assessments was one I created and used frequently on different project teams to gauge overall team morale. This team healthcheck mini-assessment, shown in Table 8-2, was used to track the health of a large project team on a quarterly basis over the course of a 3-year program. I plotted the quarterly scores and used them to see trends and spot potential issues. You can use this tool as it is or tailor it to meet your specific needs.

2. Put It in Writing

PMs may choose to document their expectations for their team members to make sure those expectations are clear. Consider working with the team members to create a set of values, rules, or expectations for team behaviors. Use the example expectations list provided in Table 8-1 as a starting point for your own list of expectations. Here are some additional standards to consider:

1. deadlines for intermediate and final deliverables
2. quality standards for deliverables
3. status reporting deadlines

Table 8-2: Team Healthcheck Mini-Assessment

Team Healthcheck				
Strongly Disagree	Disagree	Neutral	Agree	Strongly Agree
1. I know what I need to do my job effectively — 1	2	3	4	5
2. I know what is expected from me on this project — 1	2	3	4	5
3. The work I am doing is satisfying and rewarding — 1	2	3	4	5
4. Communications on this project are effective — 1	2	3	4	5
5. This project is fun — 1	2	3	4	5

Comments: _____

4. time reporting standards
5. weekend work
6. requests for time off
7. conflict resolution

3. Establish Clear Accountability and Hold People to It

There are a number of tools for making sure that project accountability is clear. My favorite tool is the responsibility matrix. An example template for a responsibility matrix is shown in Appendix D. You can also find sample templates on the Internet or make up your own.

When developing a responsibility matrix, list the major deliverables or work assignments in the left-most column. List the responsible people across the top. Use the RACI convention to indicate the role of each of the persons for each deliverable or work assignment, where R = responsible, A = accountable, C = consulted, and I = informed. There should be just one person listed for the responsible and accountable columns.

Once you have established responsibility and accountability for deliverables, you need to hold others to it. Rate yourself on how you are doing in this area. If you are not doing as well as you would like, think about what you need to do to make it better. Are you better with some individual team members and stakeholders than with others? Try to understand what is behind the resistance you feel; it may be your desire to be liked. Determine what steps you need to take to improve in this area.

4. Hold Others to Your Highest Vision for Them

Just as my mentor has done for me, position yourself to hold others to a high vision. Dedicate a chunk of quality quiet time to think about each person on the team and their true potential. Try to see them at their very best. Envision what their future could look like and how you see them succeeding.

Then set up a time to talk about that vision with the individual. Tell them how you see them and encourage them to live up to your vision for them. On an ongoing basis, remind them of how you see them at their best. Continue to adjust your vision to the reality of their growth.

5. Catch People Doing Something Right

Develop the habit of catching people doing something right and make it part of your leadership style. Make it a point to track your efforts for each individual. Give more to those people who are junior or new to the team to help them integrate.

Establish systems so that you are able to follow through on your good intention of seeing the best in others. One simple way is to use your team roster to create a tally sheet. Track the times you were successful in catching each team member in the act of doing something right.

You might want to create more sophisticated measures for yourself if you are having trouble breaking the habit of catching people doing something wrong. Set a target and track your rate of positive versus negative comments. Reward yourself for achieving your goals when you do. When you don't, make it a point to up the ante in the next week.

You can also enroll others to support you in this area. Ask your boss, a coach or mentor, or a peer for support and accountability. Or, if you fall short on follow through, ask someone to help you to set a standard or goal for yourself and to hold you accountable to that goal.

You can also spread the wealth by getting everyone involved in identifying positive behavior. Let team members know that you are on the lookout for people doing something right. Encourage them to identify and bring forward examples of people performing well. This will go a long way toward creating an environment of acknowledgement. While you are at it, try to catch stakeholders doing things right also.

6. 1001 Ways to Recognize People

Some time ago I stumbled across a book titled *The 1001 Rewards & Recognition Fieldbook.* The title helped me to appreciate that the ways to recognize and reward the individuals on our teams are nearly unlimited.

Do a self-check to see how you are doing in this area. Make a list of the people on your team and track how many times you recognize their work over the course of a week. See how creative you can be in recognizing the work of others. No one ever complained about too much recognition. Let people know that you are serious about recognizing and appreciating the efforts and results of the team.

7. Fix Your Broken Windows

You can apply the broken windows theory to your project environment. Take a moment to conduct an honest assessment to see if there are any rules or standards that people don't adhere to in your environment. Develop an inventory of the rules and standards, and if there are lapses, develop action plans to address any regulations that are not being followed.

You can get the team or key members of your team involved. Use their input in those areas where you may have blind spots.

Leveraging Emotional Intelligence on Large and Complex Projects

■ Are You Ready to Lead Large and Complex Projects?

Many project managers see career progression as taking on larger and more complex projects. PMs who want to succeed with these projects must have high emotional intelligence. It is possible to get by on small or even medium-sized projects with low emotional intelligence, but there is very little room for error on a large and complex project. There are too many stakeholders and too many opportunities for breakdowns.

I personally prefer large projects to smaller ones. Larger projects have a higher risk than small projects, but they also have a much greater reward. Often the increase in risk is less than the increase in reward. This is because large projects usually get a high priority within the organization, which makes it easier to attract good resources. Small projects are often given a low priority and are frequently understaffed, which can make them even more risky than bigger projects. For a small increase in risk, larger projects provide more visibility, recognition, and personal satisfaction. I generally recommend that people step up, take on the risk, and go for the large and complex projects.

If the thought of managing a large project intimidates you, this chapter should be of interest. We will look at the characteristics of large and complex projects and how emotional intelligence plays a role in our success with those projects. We will discuss what Daniel Goleman calls the six different leadership styles of inspirational leadership and how good leaders need to select the style appropriate to the situation. We will look at the characteristics of each of the inspirational leadership styles and discuss when to use each style. We will also explore the various emotional intelligence competencies that underpin those leadership styles. We will explore the world of virtual teams and look at ways to bring emotional intelligence into those virtual teams. We will close with a set of techniques intended to help you be successful when you manage large and complex projects.

■ Characteristics of Large and Complex Projects

While all projects are different, large and complex projects tend to have similar characteristics that differentiate them from small projects.

Stakeholder Conflict

All projects come with conflict. On large projects, various stakeholders will often conflict about the goals and objectives of the project. Some groups will receive benefits, and others will experience greater costs or penalties. This leads to built-in conflict that may be in the open or that may be underground.

Layers of Staff

Large projects tend to have large project teams. The larger the team, the less direct contact the project manager has with each team member. The largest projects will have subteams headed up by team leaders or project managers. This affects the project manager's communication plan and approach as well as their choice of leadership style.

Vendors and Subcontractors

Large projects are more likely to include vendors or subcontractors than small projects. When dealing with vendors and subcontractors, the project manager needs the ability to negotiate with, direct, and lead those third parties in order to achieve the goals of the project.

Importance to the Organization

Large projects are usually more important to the organization than smaller ones. There is a larger investment in resources, greater expectation for returns, and a higher priority placed on their success. While it is usually desirable to lead those critical projects, the priority, importance, and visibility can place pressure on the project manager and key stakeholders to succeed. A lack of strong self-management skills can lead to emotional breakdowns that disrupt the team and undermine the project manager's effectiveness.

Role of the Project Manager

With a large team, the project manager's role is less likely to be related to the deliverables and more likely related to leadership, stakeholder management, facilitating, coaching and mentoring, and delegation.

Virtual Teams

With the increase in team size comes an increased likelihood that there will be a virtual component of the team, that is, some of the team will be working remotely. PMs have to deal with time zone and cultural differences and this work is frequently done over the phone. We will look specifically at tools and techniques for applying emotional intelligence to virtual teams in this chapter.

■ Concerns for Large-Scale Project Managers

As project managers take on large and complex projects, the types of issues that they deal with will change. PMs that manage very large and complex projects have some unique concerns.

It's Lonely at the Top

The bigger the team that the PM is managing, the more likely it is for the PM to feel isolated and alone. With a small team of three or four members, it is likely for the project manager to feel like part of the group. However, when a project manager is managing seventy or more members, it is easy to feel isolated. As projects grow in size, the likelihood that the PM will be isolated increases; in particular if the PM has many direct reports. Team members are less likely to engage you in conversation, invite you to lunch, or include you in activities outside work. Project managers can begin to feel sad, lonely, and isolated.

PMs can overcome the loneliness by investing in the relationships with team members and by reaching out to others for support. Team members who are uncomfortable initiating conversation with the "boss" may welcome invitations from the project manager for conversation or for lunch. In addition, the PM should be using regular one-on-one meetings to develop and invest in the relationship with each individual.

The project manager should also develop a support network of relationships to lean on when needed. The network could include the relationships with their own manager, peers, and mentors. It may also include relationships outside the work environment, such as family, spouses or significant others, support groups, fellow members of professional organizations (like PMI), and coaches.

Role of the Project Manager—Delegation

Managing large and complex projects requires us to step away from the day-to-day details, activities, and deliverables. Project managers need to be focused on leadership, stakeholder management, facilitating, coaching, and mentoring. Stepping away from the day-to-day aspects of the project does not mean abandoning them. It does mean delegating the responsibility for those deliverables and activities and holding others accountable for the results.

Delegation can be challenging for project managers. It is especially challenging for those with subject matter expertise or those accustomed to being involved in the details. The reason that delegation is challenging is usually rooted in fear and a lack of trust:

- PMs do not trust their subordinates to do it right (or to do it their way)
- PMs do not trust their subordinates to get it done on time
- PMs are scared that if the subordinate does the work, the PM may not be viewed as valuable
- PMs are scared to not to be in control over the activity and how it will reflect on them

Delegation is a critical skill for project managers who want to grow and take on larger projects. If you are not good at delegating, try the following to improve your delegation skills:

- Use the self-awareness techniques to understand the emotions that come up for you around delegating. Are you scared, and if so, what are you afraid of?
- Be aware and mindful of your desire to control. Practice letting go of how the work gets done and focus only on the results.

- Practice delegating as a learning experience for you and for the delegatee. Start small and work your way up, developing yourself and your resources as you go. Talk about the experience with them before, during, and after.
- Develop a responsibility matrix (see Appendix D) and use it to identify responsibilities and hold others accountable.

Importance of Business Skills Versus People Skills

The application of emotional intelligence has focused on improving our interpersonal skills. This does not mean that technical and business skills are not important. In fact, to be effective and manage large and complex projects, PMs must have people skills, business skills, and some level of technical skills. The exact mix of required skills is going to vary based on the industry, project type, and organization.

Those PMs with a strong set of interpersonal skills who also understand and can speak the language of the business will succeed over those without the business skills.

The reality is that running a large project is a lot like running a small business. In large-scale projects, we need to pay attention to both business matters and people matters. We need to balance the other core project management skills like contract or integration management with EI skills like empathy and self-awareness. We need to apply the correct leadership style to the project.

■ Applying Different Leadership Styles

In the large project environment more than any other place, the project manager has to be flexible in approach and have the ability to vary their leadership style. In *Primal Leadership*, Goleman and his co-authors described six inspirational leadership styles. Four of those styles are considered to be resonant, that is, these styles cause a positive effect on the team environment.

- visionary
- coaching
- affiliative
- democratic

The remaining two leadership styles are considered to be dissonant. The dissonant leadership styles are those that cause disturbance or disruption in the team environment.

- pacesetting
- commanding[1]

Let's look at each of these styles in detail to see how project managers can apply them and to understand the underlying emotional intelligence competencies. We will also look at some of the considerations that go into deciding which leadership style is appropriate for a given project. As you read about each of the leadership styles, think about your own project history. See if you can determine your own dominant leadership style.

Visionary Leadership

Visionary leaders tell people where they are going; they provide the vision and the big picture. On a project, visionaries describe the end goals but leave individuals plenty of latitude on how to achieve those end goals.

The attraction of the visionary leader is their ability to connect the individual's work with the vision for the project so that team members understand how their work fits into the big picture. Team members benefit from a leader who shows them not only how what they do connects with the vision, but also why what they do is important. Visionary leaders help the team members to resonate with the project goals and objectives.

The visionary leader relies heavily on the emotional intelligence competencies of self-awareness, self-confidence, and empathy. In particular, empathy is critical as the visionary needs to understand where people are in order to help them connect to the bigger picture. Vision casting is also an important emotional intelligence competency for visionary leadership.

Goleman's research indicates that visionary leadership is the most effective style of leadership. However, there is a caveat to the use of the visionary style. That is when there are many experts or more senior people reporting to the project manager. In those cases, the vision casting by the PM may fall flat and fail to resonate with those experts or senior people. The visionary may fail to get the appropriate buy-in. Otherwise, the visionary leadership style would be appropriate to any type of project. It would be especially beneficial to projects that are in recovery mode or those that are stalled and need a fresh vision to energize the project team.

---

[1]Daniel Goleman, Richard Boyatzis, and Annie McKee. *Primal Leadership.* Boston: Harvard Business School Press, 2002, p. 55.

Coaching Style

The coaching style focuses on personal development rather than on the accomplishment of tasks. A PM with a coaching style sees the project as the vehicle for the development of the members of the team. The goal of accomplishing the project is almost secondary to the goal of helping people to learn and grow. The project becomes the vehicle that we can use to help people stretch, grow, and develop. The key outcome for the coaching style leaders is the growth of the team members.

I had an excellent manager named Rick for several years; he was a terrific example of the coaching style leader. We worked together on three large projects over the course of about four years. Rick showed great interest in my development and he encouraged me to share with him my long-term goals. In return, he showed me how my current assignment would benefit me and how it connected to my long-term goals and objectives.

One hallmark of Rick's style was his use of one-page weekly objectives. He worked with me to break down my responsibilities into weekly goals that fit on one page. We sat down together each week to develop the objectives. We started by reviewing the goals from the previous week, discussing in detail the progress that was made and any hurdles or issues. Then we would jointly set the objectives for the next week. Though the document would have appeared cryptic to an outsider because of our shorthand notes, we both understood precisely what it meant. Our initials at the top of the page indicated that both of us were committed to the goals.

The one-page objectives worked for that relationship, but they are not necessary to use the coaching style. It is critical, though, that the project manager be involved with the team members at a detail level. The project manager coaches the team member with specific steps and provides encouragement and feedback as they perform.

Another key to the coaching style is the manager's belief in the ability of the team member. I always felt that Rick firmly believed that I could do anything. He didn't seem to think that I had any limitations and his one-page weekly objectives often included stretch goals that I would not even have attempted had he not encouraged me to believe they were possible.

Rick's belief in me encouraged me to try to accomplish the goals even when I didn't see a way to make them happen. Once I ran into some trouble meeting key project milestones. I wanted to take the easy route of pushing out the schedule. This would delay the entire project, cost my company money, and disappoint the client. Rick told me flat out to go back to the drawing board and come up with a solution that did not involve delaying the project. His confidence that I could do it encouraged me to look for that creative solution. I chose to believe that there must be a creative solution if Rick thought that there was one. As it turned out, I was able to come up with a creative solution and we held the line on the dates.

It is easy for me to understand why the coaching style leads to high motivation levels for the team members. I felt motivated to meet the high expectations Rick had for me. I wanted to do what he asked me to do. In fact, I continually raised my own internal standards and expectations based on his expectations for me. If he thought I could do it, then I chose to believe that I could.

The coaching style works best when employees seek direction and feedback and are willing to partner very closely to get agreement on the work to be performed. It requires a high level of trust between the coach and the team member.

The coaching style doesn't work when trust is lacking, when team members are not interested in getting input on their performance, or when the team member feels micromanaged. On a recent project, I consciously applied the coaching style to four different junior members of the same team. With two of the members, I was very successful. Those two team members saw my involvement with them as an investment and kept requesting feedback on a regular basis.

The coaching style failed with the other two team members who saw the same style as de-motivating, critical, and micromanaging. These team members did not like my close involvement and found the coaching demeaning. They wanted to have the latitude to work without checking in with the boss. The main differences in these relationships were the emotional intelligence level of the team members and the level of trust. In those cases where the team members were secure about their role and believed that I had their best interest in mind, it worked great. When the team members had low emotional intelligence or did not trust that I had their best interest in mind, the coaching styles failed.

Affiliative Style

Affiliative leaders are great relationship builders. They tend to focus less on tasks and goals and more on building relationships with their team members. Affiliative leaders create an environment of harmony and friendly interactions. They work to nurture personal relationships using empathy and conflict management.

With affiliative leaders, feelings and relationships are a clear priority. Taken to an extreme, feelings are given priority over results. Affiliative leaders may find themselves wanting to be liked and they may make decisions that place a priority on being liked. Team members may view affiliative managers as soft or indecisive. Team members may also feel they are in the dark about the project direction and their work. They may feel left on their own to make decisions.

I once worked for an organization that emphasized the affiliative style. The company had grown quickly from a partnership between the two founders to being part of a large corporation at the time that I joined. Yet the cooperative nature of the original partnership was part of the DNA of the company and a priority was placed on everyone getting along.

My manager at this company was named Tom. He ran the project management office, which included all the project managers as well as the standards for project management. I was helping Tom with the development of the standards for project delivery including methodology and best practices. I was continually frustrated by Tom's insistence on getting input from all areas of the company and including others in the discussion. In our efforts to get cooperation from across the company, it was not possible to get consensus without watering down the methodology to the point where it was unusable.

Tom was ineffective because of the priority he placed on everyone getting along and on being liked. He was very good at relationships; unfortunately, he was not able to get the results he needed from the project management office.

The affiliative style of leadership works best when you are trying to improve morale and communications or repair broken trust. The affiliative style will not work as well when leaders fail to do the right thing in order to be liked.

Democratic Style

The democratic style is similar in some ways to the affiliative style. Democratic leaders tend to take input from many sources. This input leverages the experience of the team, provides for better decisions, and gets buy-in from the entire team.

Early in my career I worked for a democratic manager named Charley, who was responsible for a corporate-wide competency center. In his role, he supported engineers and engineering managers across the company. In turn, funding for the competency center was provided by each of those engineering managers.

What worked well for Charley was his willingness to get input from everyone. He was a good listener and would spend the time it took with the engineers he supported to find out what they needed. As a former engineer himself, Charley was empathetic to their situation and could place himself in their shoes.

The downside to the time Charley spent working one-on-one with the engineers was the lack of overall direction for our group. Those of us who worked for Charley felt like we didn't know where the group was heading. We seemed to spend more time talking about our work than actually completing work. For example, we were always preparing presentations on the projects we were working on at the competency center and their value to the engineers. We were busy trying to sell the value of the competency center rather than being busy completing the work required.

A big disadvantage of the democratic style, as demonstrated by Charley, is a perceived lack of decision making. Democratic leaders may seem like all talk and no action. They are often struck by delays and conflict. Further, there are times when consensus doesn't make sense and it is more important for the leaders be decisive.

Pacesetting Style

The first of the two dissonant leadership styles is the pacesetting style. Pacesetters are usually individuals with a high personal drive to achieve. The pacesetting leader expects excellence and models that to the team. They have high expectations for performance and for continuous improvement. Pacesetting leaders tend to put pressure on everyone on the team to perform at their very best.

The pacesetting leader places a high priority on the results and this can hurt their relationships with team members. Pacesetters often lack empathy; they tend to believe that everyone thinks like they do. Like perfectionists, pacesetters often feel dissatisfied with the current performance and want to continue to improve it. The pacesetter's message that they are dissatisfied with the current performance can lead to alienation of team members who feel blamed and criticized. Team members may feel that they cannot do enough to measure up.

I have seen the pacesetting style used by Mike, a friend of mine who runs a privately held chain of restaurants. Mike is obsessed with competition and improvement. Whether he is at work or at play on the golf course, he is competing and pushing everyone around him to do better.

Mike and I share an interest in running. His pacesetting style comes through in his training, when he pushes himself hard to run as fast as he can. Not only that, he encourages everyone around him to push themselves. Once when we had planned to run ten sprints of 800 meters each, I mentioned that I wasn't going to run all ten. Without flinching he said that anyone who didn't run all ten sprints was a wimp. That comment made my competitive juices flow. However, I was not surprised when he pushed himself so hard during training that he injured himself.

A well-known pacesetter is Michael Jordan. Jordan's style of play and leadership on the basketball court sent the message "keep up with me if you can." Jordan was always pushing himself and his teammates. He played hard and expected those around him to play hard as well.

A couple of Michael Jordan quotes reflect his pacesetting style and his obsession with winning. Jordan once said that "There is no I in team, but there is in win." He also said "I play to win, whether during practice or a real game. And I will not let anything get in the way of me and my competitive enthusiasm to win."

The danger of the pacesetting style is that the team can begin to feel like nothing is good enough. Pacesetting managers never seem to be satisfied with the current performance. They overlook the positive and tend to focus in on what is not yet working or what can still be improved.

I have unwittingly applied the pacesetting style in previous projects. While it is not my dominant style, I have found it easy to focus on continuous improvement and lose sight of the needs and feelings of my team members. I didn't take the time to acknowledge what was working and recognize people for that.

There are times when the pacesetting style is appropriate. It works best when you are leading a team of experienced and competent professionals. It also works well when paired with the visionary or affiliative styles. It doesn't work well when used exclusively or when you are dealing with inexperienced team members who need more positive encouragement and feedback. It doesn't work with team members who don't perform well under the pressure exhibited by the pacesetting leader. In any case, the pacesetting style should be used sparingly.

Commanding Style

The commanding style is one in which the leader requires everyone to do it their way. Project managers who use the commanding style don't want questions, they want compliance. They are reluctant to share power and authority and they rarely take the time to explain themselves fully. Like the parents of a small child, commanding leaders may come across as saying "just do it because I said so."

I had a manager named Bob who used the commanding style. Bob was recruited to take over and turn around a large program that had failed. The program included three major projects and several hundred team members. I was part of Bob's recovery team.

Bob quickly made it clear to everyone that he was in charge and that things were to be done his way. He also made it clear that the failed policies and practices of his predecessor would not be tolerated. He was ruthless about enforcing his way and showed no compunction about removing individuals from the team even for minor issues. He would joke about firing individuals from the team and kept a running tally of the number of "drive-by firings" he had performed.

Bob was highly successful in the program recovery and earned himself an award from the chairman of the company. In this situation, the commanding style worked because it was appropriate. Bob's military background contributed to his command and control approach, which is characteristic of the commanding style. Bob needed to be clear about his expectations for people and he demanded that people change from the ways of the previous program manager. Unfortunately for Bob it was the only style he knew and he used it in every situation.

Bob was a lot like my dad so initially I found it easy to work for him. His style was both familiar and predictable to me. Bob was extremely critical and often seemed to be personally attacking me or other team members. Eventually, however, his style of leadership took a toll on me.

Like other leaders relying on the commanding style, Bob lacked the people and relationship elements of the affiliative or democratic styles or the attraction of understanding the big picture that is characteristic of the visionary style.

The commanding style should be used sparingly. It works best during emergencies or crisis situations, such as during a project turnaround, when there is no time to explain the rationale behind every decision. Otherwise, the commanding style takes a toll on the team and should be avoided.

Application of the Leadership Styles

Table 9-1 shows each of the styles, the underlying emotional intelligence competencies required for the style, project situations to apply that style, and any traps or situations not to apply the style.

Table 9-1: Leadership Styles

Leadership Style	EI Competencies	When to Apply	Traps/When not to Apply
Visionary	• Inspirational Leadership • Self-Confidence • Self-Awareness • Empathy	• Apply as often as possible, in particular when PM wants to inspire team to grow and be creative.	• When team members are more senior or have unique expertise and PMs vision-casting will sound hollow.
Coaching	• Developing Others • Self Awareness • Empathy	• When team members trust and want the leader to invest in them. • When developing people is important.	• Team may lose sight of project goals in efforts to develop people.
Affiliative	• Relationship Management • Empathy • Conflict Management	• When it is important to bring team together or when healing team divisions is necessary.	• Some affiliative leaders fall prey to being liked by others or lose sight of the project goals and objectives.
Democratic	• Teamwork and Collaboration • Conflict Management • Influence	• When the leader needs to get the input from the team to make decisions; to reach consensus.	• Leader must be open to input from the team. • Team must have valuable input to offer. • Team members may find leader indecisive or bogged down in endless meetings.
Pacesetting	• Achievement • Initiative	• Works well when used with either the visionary or affiliative styles, or when leader applies empathy and self-management to counter the pressure placed on the team. • Works to get the best performance from an experienced and competent team.	• Pacesetters often lack empathy, self-awareness, communications skills, and emotional self management; may communicate that goals are more important than people. • Team members may feel anxious, criticized, and unappreciated.
Commanding	• Influence • Achievement • Initiative	• Emergencies, crisis, or turnaround projects. • When leader is significantly more experienced than the team.	• Use only in those situations where appropriate and balance with other styles.

Most leaders have one dominant style of leadership. Based on the descriptions above, were you able to identify your dominant style?

Good leaders are able to use different leadership styles in different situations. To excel on large and complex projects, we need to be able to switch and adjust our leadership style to the needs of the situation. Daniel Goleman likens the various leadership styles to the golf clubs a player has in their bag. Each club has a different application. The more clubs that a player has, the more flexibility they can bring and the greater their chance of success.[2]

Consider what steps you need to do to expand the styles available to you. In particular, if you rely predominantly on the dissonant leadership styles, a quick win for you will be to incorporate one or more of the resonant styles.

■ Applying Emotional Intelligence to Virtual Project Teams

The Challenges of Virtual Teams

Increasingly, we are working in teams that have at least some virtual component. On large-scale projects, virtual teams are almost a given. By virtual teams, I mean that people are working in different physical locations and not working side by side or face to face. It is not uncommon to have executives in one location, end users in another, and development teams in a third. Often, the team members are in different time zones, which adds further complexity. There are often cultural differences to be considered.

Emotional intelligence is more important than ever for virtual teams due to the reliance on the telephone and e-mail for communications. Neither medium allows for seeing the face or body language of the team members and that makes communications and relationships more difficult.

I have been part of the leadership team for two very large programs with considerable virtual components. In the first case, we were implementing an enterprise-wide solution across a multinational corporation using a team of over 120 from around the world. In another program, we were developing and implementing solutions for a country in the Middle East. We used over 100 resources spread in locations from the Middle East to the West Coast of the United States. Keeping everyone on the same page with a virtual team can be a struggle for project managers. Many of the following tips and techniques were learned from these program experiences.

---

[2]Ibid., p. 54.

Emotional Intelligence Helps Virtual Teams

Applying EI techniques in the virtual environment may be more important than anywhere else. Here are some ideas for making virtual teams work for you.

Face-to-Face Meetings

To get the most out of virtual meetings, make it a point to have at least one face-to-face meeting with each team member early in the project. This will help the communications later when you cannot see the team members' faces or read their body language. I also recommend that you make it a point to meet in person over the course of the project if that is possible.

When I had a virtual team working for me on the other side of the globe, I initially did not think it was necessary to travel there just to meet with them. However, I did travel there on several occasions. I learned that even if I was visiting there for other reasons, I could still make time to meet with people one-on-one and in groups in order to connect. In fact, I made it a point to go out to lunch to get to know them personally and understand their goals and objectives. The meetings I had served me over the life of the program.

Another application of the face-to-face meeting is when part of the team is local and part is working virtual. When some team members are dialing in, the local team members may gravitate toward calling in from their desks or homes instead of coming to a central meeting location. I have been on calls where individuals in side-to-side cubicles both dialed in to the same teleconference. Their logic is that since everyone cannot be together, there is no reason for the local team to get together. This approach tends to be isolating and it works against the PM. Team members are more likely to be multitasking than engaging with one another at these types of teleconferences. A better approach is to stress the importance of face-to-face meetings and request that individuals make it a priority to meet as a group. This may not always be possible, but it will be more likely if the PM requests it.

Leverage Technology

Use technology to improve your communications with remote team members. The ways to do this are limited only by your creativity. Technology enablers include the use of instant messaging (IM), satellite or cell phones, text messaging, bulletin and discussion boards, blogs, a project web site, voicemail distribution lists, video conferencing, teleconferencing, e-mail, and collaboration tools.

The key is to make the technology work for you and the team, not against you. For example, some project managers are not familiar with IM and may view it as a tool for goofing off. Rather than fight it, or outlaw it at your company as a leader I know recently did, embrace it. Get on board with it yourself and use it to connect to the more technically savvy members of your team.

Once on a project we used a map as a low-tech way of staying connected. A key team member left his home in the States and traveled between London and Shanghai. He was still a project leader and still dialed in to the project teleconferences. We used a world map and a small icon of him and his family to track where he was over his travels. In this way, we were able to better connect with him. He was more than simply a disconnected voice on the phone.

In the same way, consider including pictures of all team members available in a central location or on the project web site. It will help others on the team to feel connected to those in remote locations.

Make Communications Work for Everyone

Good communications planning and stakeholder relationship management should help to identify and resolve communication needs. However, recognize that on virtual teams, it is easier than ever to get disconnected. PMs should constantly evaluate the regular communications and make sure that they are sufficient and that all stakeholders' needs are being met. On every project there is invariably an occasion where some stakeholder steps forward and says, "I didn't know that," or "I never heard about that."

Don't be afraid to experiment with your communications. During intense periods of activity, it may be necessary to coordinate across all the work sites with a brief "stand up" type meeting once per day. Or, it may be appropriate for each team to hand off their work at the end of their day when you have teams spread across time zones.

As the PM, it pays to be aware of the amount of time you spend with each stakeholder and those reporting to you. With a virtual team, it is very easy to spend more time and better quality time with those who are located near you than those who are remote. You can counter this by investing more in those who are remote. If you spend thirty minutes per week with each direct report in a face-to-face meeting, consider spending forty-five or sixty minutes on the phone with those who are remote.

Try to be consistent across locations. If you have an all-hands meeting in one location, either have others dial in or repeat the meeting with those who are remote. Develop and share frequently asked questions with the entire team. Archive and distribute minutes from those meetings for any individuals who are not able to attend.

Use Humor

When it works, humor helps us to connect with each other and to see each other in a more positive light. It can bring levity to situations and lighten tensions so people feel more comfortable.

Humor can also work against us, in particular in the virtual environment when facial expressions and body language are not available to indicate that someone is "just kidding." In virtual environments, it may not be possible to hear others laughing or to get the responses of others to our own humor. Humor, when it doesn't work, can highlight the differences between people and serve to alienate us.

As a general rule, humor works best when team members know each other. When individuals do not know each other, humor can be easily misinterpreted or misconstrued.

Self-deprecating humor works better than poking fun at others. In general, PMs should avoid joking about others, especially if they are not present. Joking about others can cause distrust and alienation among the team.

As a project manager, I create an environment where people know that I try not to take myself too seriously. I joke about myself and point out the things that I do which people find funny. At one point another PM pointed out that my jokes were not very funny and offered to raise his hand in meetings so that others would know I was joking.

Injecting humor into our written status reports can breathe some energy into what are often very lifeless documents. Use of humor can make the document more interesting and easier to read and may lead to more status reports actually being read.

I once had a project manager who wielded humor very effectively as part of a large virtual team. His daily status report from the client location in the Middle East included a mini trivia quiz at the top. Every day he added a movie quote to his status report. Between his use of humor and the movie quotes, he created a report that was well read by the rest of the team.

Build Relationships Off the Call

Virtual teams are often characterized by a seemingly endless series of teleconferences, which tend to be formal and typically lack opportunities for developing interpersonal relationships. Individuals can be lost in the formality and structure of all of these teleconferences. Relationships with team members may be superficial and the team members may view the PM as lacking in warmth and personality.

To improve relationships and make teleconferences more personal, use the time off the call to invest in and build relationships with virtual team members. Don't limit your investment in them to the structure of a regular meeting. Use the time off the call to let your true nature show. Be as informal as possible and encourage them to talk and to share their concerns, interests, hobbies, and objectives.

■ Emotional Intelligence Techniques for Large and Complex Projects

1. Learn to Identify Leadership Styles

You can use your prior experience to help you identify different leadership styles. Make a list of the PMs and other managers you have worked with over the last five or even ten years. For each one, identify the emotional intelligence competencies you experienced with them. See if you can identify their dominant leadership styles. Evaluate, if possible, whether they used different styles with different team members.

2. Identify Your Dominant Leadership Style

In this exercise, you will determine your own dominant leadership style. Start with the list of EI competencies. Based on what you know about those from the earlier chapters, list the ones that you feel are your strengths. Then re-read the descriptions of the six leadership styles. Is one of them clearly your dominant style? Or do you believe that you use multiple styles?

Take this exercise one step further by getting input from others. Ask those on your current team to review the list of characteristics of each of the leadership styles and see if they can determine your dominant style. You can expand the discussion to your boss, spouse or significant other, and perhaps even your own children as appropriate. Get as much input as possible to see yourself as others see you.

3. Build New Leadership Muscles

Once you determine your own dominant leadership style, select another style that would best complement it. If you don't currently use visionary leadership, that would be a great choice since research has shown it to be the most effective.

Having selected the leadership style, start with the underlying emotional intelligence competencies for that style. Once you determine which competency you need to strengthen, go back to that competency in the previous chapters. Review the various techniques provided for improving that competency.

If you need help, consider enrolling someone in this process. A mentor or even a member of your team would be in a good position to help track your progress and provide feedback as you build those new leadership skills.

4. Improve Your Delegation Skills

If you find delegation difficult due to fear or control issues, or if you just want to improve, there is no time like the present. Decide today to begin to practice delegating. Start small and perhaps with someone whom you trust the most. Gradually increase your level of delegation while you monitor your feelings and emotions around the process. Track your progress and celebrate your successes in this area.

Alternatively, identify someone in your work environment who is good at delegating and ask them to help you to improve. Find out what works and doesn't work for them and try those techniques for yourself. Set goals and ask them to hold you accountable for the results.

5. Check the Roster for Your Virtual Team

If you are managing a virtual team, take the time to walk down through the roster of team members. Are you connecting with everyone on the team and especially those whom you don't see? Make a note of how much time you spent in the last few weeks with each of the team members. Is that amount appropriate for the size of the team and the role of the individual? Are there any team members who are not getting enough of your time and attention?

Consider polling your virtual team members to find out how well connected they feel to you. Put together a short survey or simply call each of them. Either approach will provide valuable feedback. Calling them may reveal information that a written survey will not. However, team members may be more forthcoming with a survey than they would with a phone call.

6. Work on Relationships "Off the Call"

If you are leading a virtual team, what steps are you taking to build relationships? If the communications are typically conducted through a series of conference calls, select a member of the team you don't know well and choose to work on that relationship. Make it a point to call them or visit them off the call and get to know them on a personal basis.

■ Epilogue

You have learned about why emotional intelligence is important to project managers, and how to apply it to become a better project manager. You have also learned in Chapters 1 through 9 about a set of tools and techniques that you can use to improve your level of emotional intelligence and your project success. Each chapter included techniques and mini-exercises for improving your level of emotional intelligence. If you skipped over any techniques or exercises, I recommend that you go back to those that hold the most potential for your improvement. Try the techniques and exercises, even those that seem silly, and see if you can improve your competency in each area.

We can always improve in the area of our people skills. And the great news is, no matter what our starting point is, we all have the ability to improve our level of emotional intelligence. I still find myself learning and growing in the area of emotional intelligence. I occasionally take a step backward and fall into old habits or make mistakes. However, when I do that, I recover faster. I try to remind myself of how far I have come and how much better I am at managing my emotions than I was in the past. And I try not to take myself (or others) too seriously.

The following Appendixes contain additional tools and more information that project managers may find helpful for improving their level of emotional intelligence. Useful tools include the Emotional Tally sheet in Appendix A and the Emotional Intelligence Assessment Checklist in Appendix B. Though certainly not unique to emotional intelligence, the Stakeholder Management Tool in Appendix C and the Responsibility Assignment Matrix in

225

Appendix D are valuable tools to project managers trying to improve their emotional intelligence.

Appendix E provides a list of Hollywood movies that are helpful to individuals trying to learn more about emotions. Appendix F contains a list of magazines and journals dedicated to the topic of emotional intelligence. For individuals seeking books on emotional intelligence, Appendix G provides a starting list. Appendix H lists classes and training providers on emotional intelligence and related topics. Appendix I lists web sites on the topic of emotional intelligence.

Appendix J provides information about some of the most popular assessment instruments available for measuring emotional intelligence. Last, Appendix K contains information about a survey that I conducted in 2005 of over 100 project managers to determine interests and attitudes about emotional intelligence.

Appendixes

Appendix A
Emotional Tally Sheet

The tally sheet shown in Figure A-1 is helpful for tracking and identifying patterns in your emotions over the course of a week.

The tally sheet shown in Figure A-2 is helpful for tracking multiple individuals at the same time, for example, in a meeting.

	 Sad	 Angry	 Scared	 Happy	 Excited	 Tender
Monday						
Tuesday						
Wednesday						
Thursday						
Friday						
Saturday						
Sunday						
Total for Week						

Figure A-1: Emotional Tally Sheet (1)

	Sad	Angry	Scared	Happy	Excited	Tender
Tim						
Dennis						
Jim						
Z						
Cortney						
Bill						
Barry						
Stephen						
Rick						
Neale						

Figure A-2: Emotional Tally Sheet (2)

Appendix B
Emotional Intelligence
Assessment Checklist

1. **Automatic or Default Emotion** *Does the individual have an overriding or default emotion? Are they predominantly happy or sad? Put a check mark beside the top 2 emotions they experience on a regular basis.*	☐ Sad	☐ Happy
	☐ Angry	☐ Excited
	☐ Scared	☐ Tender

2. **Self-Awareness** *How self-aware is this individual? Do they know what they are experiencing at any one time?*	**Self-Awareness Rating**
	Not Very Self-Aware Aware Very Self-Aware 1 2 3 4 5 6 7 8 9 10

3. **Expressiveness** *How emotionally expressive is this individual? Do they express emotions in what they say, how they say it, or through their actions?*	**Expressiveness Rating**
	Not Very Expressive Expressive Very Expressive 1 2 3 4 5 6 7 8 9 10

4. **Self-Management** *How effective is this individual in self-management? Does this individual apply self-control for both positive and negative emotions?*	**Self-Control Rating**
	Poor Some Good Self-Control Self-Control Self-Control 1 2 3 4 5 6 7 8 9 10

5. **Emotional Breakdowns** *Does this person experience emotional breakdowns?*	☐ Angry Tirades ☐ Door Slamming ☐ Email Letter Bomb ☐ Withdrawal & Isolation ☐ Holding Grudges & Getting Even	☐ Criticizing ☐ Sarcasm and Inappropriate Humor ☐ Playing the Victim

6. **Stinking Thinking** *Does this individual experience stinking thinking?*	☐ All or Nothing Thinking ☐ Using Always and Never ☐ Being Negative	☐ Filling in the Blanks ☐ Should Statements ☐ Personalization and Blame

7. **Changes and Surprises** *Look at how they react to changes or to surprises. Are they open and receptive? Or shut down, reactive, and negative about new things?*	**Handling Changes and Surprises**
	Not Very Receptive Receptive Very Receptive 1 2 3 4 5 6 7 8 9 10

8. **Stress** *They say that stress will reveal a person's true character. How resilient is this individual under pressure? Are they graceful or are they mean and vindictive?*	**Handling Stress**
	Not Very Resilient Resilient Very Resilient 1 2 3 4 5 6 7 8 9 10

9. **Social Awareness** *How aware is this individual of their environment and the people around them? Consider their level of empathy toward others, their organizational awareness, and their ability to set emotional boundaries.*	**Empathy**
	Not Very Empathetic Empathetic Very Empathetic 1 2 3 4 5 6 7 8 9 10
	Organizational Awareness Not Very Aware Aware Very Aware 1 2 3 4 5 6 7 8 9 10
	Emotional Boundaries Poor Boundaries Some Boundaries Good Boundaries 1 2 3 4 5 6 7 8 9 10

Figure A-3: Emotional Intelligence Assessment Checklist

Appendix C
Stakeholder
Management Tool

The stakeholder management tool is used to identify stakeholders and organize information about them. See Figure A-4 for an example of a blank template. Figure A-5 is an example of a stakeholder management tool that has been partially completed.

Stakeholder	Priority	Position	Role on Project	Stakeholder Objectives	Facts, Passions, and areas of interest	Communication Style	Emotional Connections and Relationship Strategies	Action Steps to Maintain and Nurture this Relationship

Figure A-4: Stakeholder Management Tool, Blank

Stakeholder	Priority	Position	Role on Project	Stakeholder Objectives	Facts, Passions, and areas of interest	Communication Style	Emotional Connections and Relationship Strategies	Action Steps to Maintain and Nurture this Relationship
Debbie Brown	H	+	Executive Management	• Increase role and visibility of her organization	• Strives for excellence • Enjoys fine dining & likes to try new restaurants • Likes to work over lunch • Has 3 children	• Prefers informal communications and welcomes voicemail updates • Likes to go out and talk shop over lunch	• Stay in touch; keep Debbie informed and current	• Schedule regular lunches (1 per month) • Find ways to provide interesting updates from the "project front lines"
Bob Hague	H	N	Client	• Use project as stepping stone for better job • Look as good as possible • Maintain control over other client stakeholders	• Interested in database technology • Concerned with project's impact on career • Can be hard on his own staff • Starts early each day and leaves early	• Prefers written status reports and updates • Dislikes all meetings	• Maintain formal and informal communications • Keep very short accounts	• Submit well written and accurate status reports • Bring issues to him immediately • Make it a point to stop by for informal chats • Provide advance notice of staffing changes
Jim Smith	M	+	Subcontract Labor Manager	• Interested in putting more of his people on the team • Wants feedback on his resources so they can improve	• From Iowa and follows Big Ten college sports • Enjoys travel	• Likes to call and chat or to go out and talk shop over lunch	• Maintain informality & full disclosure	• Plan for short bi-weekly meetings before work
Tom Donahue	M	-	Software Vendor	• Increase Sales of Product • Wants to use project as reference	• Can come off as arrogant and uncaring; takes relationship for granted • Is defensive about product shortcomings	• Prefers face to face communications	• Regular meetings to discuss issues; have offline discussions to build relationship	• Bi-weekly status call; publish notes and action items from the calls

Figure A-5: Stakeholder Management Tool, Partially Completed

Appendix D
Responsibility
Assignment Matrix (RAM)

The responsibility assignment matrix is often called a RACI form. RACI is an abbreviation for: Responsible, Accountable, Informed, and Consulted. An example of a completed RAM is shown in Figure A-6. This example shows one possible format for the responsibility assignment matrix. If this style doesn't work for you, feel free to use one that does.

	Project Manager 1	Project Manager 2	Program Manager	Program Office Staff
Individual Project Schedule	R/A	R/A	I	C
Program Master Schedule	I	I	A	R
Status Reporting—Project Level	R/A	R/A		
Status Reporting—Program Level	I	I	A	R
Metrics Collection—Project Level	R/A	R/A		
Metrics Collection—Program Level	I	I	A	R
Project Risk Assessment	R	R	A	C
Program Risk Management			A	R
Financial Management	I	I	A	R
Vendor Management			A	R
PM Mentoring	I	I	I	R/A

Figure A-6: Responsibility Assignment Matrix (RAM) Sample

237

Appendix E
Emotional Intelligence
Movies and Scenes

Movies are a great place to study emotions. We can observe the emotions in the performances of actors on the screen. We can also track our own emotions that occur in response to what we see on the screen.

There are nearly an infinite number of movies out there to help you observe or experience emotions. The list below provides some specific movies that can be used to explore emotional intelligence. See the following page for the title of each movie as well as a brief description of the emotions that you are likely to observe or experience.

Movie	Description of Emotions
As Good As It Gets	Jack Nicholson plays a social and emotional misfit extremely well in this entertaining movie. Emotions include anger, sadness, happiness, and fear.
Christmas Vacation	If you like to laugh at good plans and intentions gone awry, this movie will make you feel happy.
Crash	The entire movie is about exposing and confronting the biases and prejudices we have toward each other. Emotions include sadness and anger.
Hotel Rwanda	The genocide and nonsensical war in this movie is likely to produce feelings of sadness and anger in those who view it.
The Incredibles	The scene with Mr. Incredible and his boss at the insurance company is good for showing both the toxic manager as well as a loss of self-control by Mr. Incredible. The emotions include happiness, anger, and excitement, among others.
The Kid	The character played by Bruce Willis has several funny interactions in the first 15 minutes of the film. His dramatic interaction with the mayor, other clients, and his fellow travelers reveals his sarcasm and unexpressed anger. The interactions may make you feel happy, angry, or even sad.
One Flew Over the Cuckoo's Nest	This movie will take you on a roller coaster ride of emotions through sadness, happiness, excitement, tenderness, anger, and fear.
Steel Magnolias	This movie has several funny parts but overwhelmingly it is a sad film. Look for the emotions of the characters and observe whether you feel depressed by the drama.
Tommy Boy	David Spade's use of sarcasm in this movie is funny. It's used as a cover for his anger. Also, Tommy Boy (played by the late Chris Farley) provides comic relief in many scenes including one with a fan where he is saying "Luke, I am your father".
Twelve Angry Men	There are many scenes with examples of attacking and hostile behavior, lack of self-control around anger, smoothing and avoiding.
What about Bob?	This movie provides examples in which therapy patient Bob's normal and psychopathic behavior reveals character flaws, a lack of self-control, and eventually prompts an emotional breakdown in his psychologist. Look for examples of boundary issues, passive–aggressive behavior, anger, and denial.

Appendix F
Magazines and Journals
on Emotional Intelligence

There are many magazines and journals on topics related to emotional intelligence. Many popular magazines such as *Time, Newsweek,* and *PM Network* have featured articles. Here are some of the more academic journals that carry articles related to emotional intelligence:

- *American Psychologist*
- *Applied Psychology*
- *Current Directions in Psychological Science*
- *European Journal of Work and Organizational Psychology*
- *Human Resource Development Quarterly*
- *Human Resource Management Review*
- *Journal of Applied Social Psychology*
- *Journal of Managerial Psychology*
- *Journal of Occupational Health Psychology*
- *Journal of Organizational Behavior*
- *Journal of Personality and Individual Differences*
- *Personality & Social Psychology Bulletin*
- *Research on Emotion in Organizations*

The following are online newsletters related to emotional intelligence.

- **EI Consortium Newsletter**—Sign up for this free newsletter at: *http://www.eiconsortium.org/index.html*

240

- **EI Multi-Health Systems Inc**—EI Multi-Health Systems Inc. offers several free e-mail newsletters related to emotional intelligence. For more information, see *http://www.mhs.com/Intouch.asp?id=IO*
- **6 Seconds Emotional Intelligence Network**—Sign up for the free online newsletter EQ Reflections at *http://www.6seconds.org/modules.php?name =Newsletters*
- **TalentSmart**—TalentSmart offers an online newsletter at: *https://www .talentsmart.com/contactus/*

Appendix G
Books on Emotional Intelligence

The following books provide additional information about emotional intelligence.

1. *Crucial Conversations: Tools for Talking When Stakes Are High.* Kerry Patterson, Joseph Grenny, Ron McMillan, and Al Switzler. NY: McGraw-Hill, 2002.
2. *Emotional Intelligence (Life Balance).* Linda Wasmer Andrews. NY: Scholastic, 2004.
3. *Emotional Intelligence at Work.* Hendrie Weisinger Ph.D., San Francisco: Jossey-Bass, 1998.
4. *Emotional Intelligence: Why It Can Matter More Than IQ.* Daniel Goleman. NY: Bantam Books, 1995.
5. *Primal Leadership.* Daniel Goleman, Richard Boyatzis, and Annie McKee. Boston: Harvard Business School Press, 2002.
6. *The Emotional Intelligence Activity Book.* Adele B. Lynn. NY: AMACOM, 2002.
7. *The Emotionally Intelligent Manager.* David Caruso and Peter Salovey. San Francisco: Jossey-Bass, 2004.
8. *The Emotionally Intelligent Workplace.* Cary Cherniss and Daniel Goleman. San Francisco: Jossey Bass, 2001.
9. *The EQ Difference: A Powerful Plan for Putting Emotional Intelligence to Work.* Adele B. Lynn. NY: AMACOM, 2005.
10. *Working with Emotional Intelligence.* Daniel Goleman. NY: Bantam Books, 1998.

Appendix H
Training Sources for
Emotional Intelligence

■ General Emotional Intelligence Training

1. **EQ Training and Certification**—There are numerous training and certification courses offered by the 6 Seconds Emotional Intelligence Network, an organization based in San Mateo, CA. Visit their web site for the latest offerings, e-mail them at *staff@6seconds.org,* or contact by phone at (650) 685-9885.
2. **EQ Grad Course**—Susan Dunn, coach, offers an Internet course called "EQ Grad Course" to help you learn more about EQ and sharpen your EQ competencies at the same time. Course is ongoing and interactive, offering exceptional support to the learner.
3. **Emotional Intelligence for Executives**—This half-day CBT course is targeted to managers, team leaders, and project managers who want to apply the use of emotional intelligence to the organization's employees. Get more information from CBT Planet (800) 330-9111.
4. **Emotional Intelligence**—The UK-based training group called Business Learning and Conference Centre (BLCC) offers a one-day course on emotional intelligence. The target audience is managers, team leaders, and supervisors. Call the BLCC at -01383 559000 for more information.
5. **Emotional Intelligence (Parts I and II)**—The University of North Alabama offers two courses on Emotional Intelligence targeted at entry-level employees. For more information, contact Lavonne Gatlin at (256) 765-4787 (*lgatlin@una.edu*).

6. **Applying Emotional Intelligence to Critical Business Projects**—Offered by Auxilium, this two-day workshop is targeted to project managers, analysts, technical managers, and business leaders who are involved in project teams. Get more information at (800) 577-3528.

7. **Emotional Intelligence for Personal Leadership**—This is one of several courses directed to professionals and offered by the Institute for Health and Human Potential (IHHP). Contact IHHP at *inquiries@ihhp.com,* or call (705) 792-6927.

8. **Emotional Intelligence Training**—TalentSmart offers several one- and two-day workshops for emotional intelligence. Contact TalentSmart at (888) 818-7627, ext. 106.

9. **The Leadership Through Emotional Intelligence Program**—Offered by Mindspring Consulting, this course is targeted at leaders. Contact Mindspring at (828) 298-2488 or *inquiry@helpingyougrow.com.*

10. **EQ Clinic**—The Center for Applied Emotional Intelligence offers EQ Clinic, EQ Clinic for Leaders, EQ Clinic for Technical Professionals, and EQ Clinic for Teams. Contact the center at (949) 716-8103 or *info@centerforappliedei.com.*

11. **Emotional Intelligence**—The Hay Group offers a series of training programs directed at leaders at different levels in the organization: Ultimate Enterprise Leadership, Building Real Teams at the Top, Making Great Leaders, Accelerating Key Performers, and Developing First Level Leaders. Contact the Hay Group at (877) 267-8375 or use their online form at *http://ei.haygroup.com/contact_us/.*

12. **EI Skills and Assessment Program**—David Caruso, one of the creators of the MSCEIT assessment, offers on one- and two-day programs on emotional skills and asessments based on the MSCEIT. Contact David at *david@emotionaliq.org.*

13. **Emotional Intelligence Leadership Programs**—The Adele Lynn Leadership Group offers a variety of seminars as well as assessment tools. Contact them at (724) 929-5352 or online at *http://www.lynnleadership.com/contact.htm.*

14. **Leading with Emotional Intelligence: Self Awareness**—This is one of several courses offered by the Corporate Consulting Group (CCG). Contact CCG at (732) 282-9888. Other offerings include Leading with Emotional Intelligence: Self Management; Twenty-First Century Leadership: Working with Others & Building Networks; Managing Into The Future: The Leader's Role As Change Catalyst; and Building Emotional Competence: The Workshop Series.

Appendix I
Emotional Intelligence
Web Sites

There are many web sites and blogs on emotional intelligence; too many to list here. Additionally, web sites and blogs tend to come and go. Listed below are some of the top ones that I would expect to be around for at least the next few years. Use a search tool to find current offerings.

1. Consortium for Research on Emotional Intelligence in Organizations—*http://www.eiconsortium.org/*
2. The Hay Group—*http://ei.haygroup.com/default.asp*
3. Businessballs.com—*http://www.businessballs.com/eq.htm*
4. TalentSmart—*https://www.talentsmart.com/*
5. Tune Up Your EQ—*http://www.tuneupyoureq.com/*
6. The EQ Directory—*http://www.eq.org/*

■ Appendix J
Emotional Intelligence
Assessment Instruments

While there are several assessment instruments to measure emotional intelligence on the market, it is important to note that there is a great deal of controversy over the validity of these instruments.

The first three assessment instruments were created by some of the lead researchers in the field of emotional intelligence.

■ Emotional Competence Inventory 360, from Daniel Goleman

The full title of this assessment is the "Emotional Competency Inventory 360: A 360 Assessment of Emotional Intelligence Competencies." This was developed by Daniel Goleman and Richard Boyatzis based on the Emotional Intelligence Competencies. The assessment is available both for individuals to self-assess and in a multi-rater version for 360-degree assessments. The instrument is distributed through the Hay Group, one of the members of the EIConsortium.

▪ EQi, the BarOn Emotional Quotient Inventory, from Dr. BarOn

The EQi assessment was developed by Dr. Reuven BarOn based on a number of years of research. It has reportedly been used on nearly 50,000 individuals. Dr. BarOn cleverly named the competencies being measured the "BarOn Emotional Quotient Inventory." This assessment is available in individual and multi-rater versions. It is also available in a youth version.

▪ The MSCEIT, from John Mayer, Peter Salovey, and David Caruso

The MSCEIT assessment was developed by three of the original researchers of Emotional Intelligence and based on the EI model developed by Mayer and Salovey. This instrument is available in individual and multi-rater versions.

▪ Emotional Intelligence Appraisal, Me Edition

This appraisal is from Travis Bradberry and Jean Graves, authors of the *Emotional Intelligence Quickbook*. This assessment is fast and easy to take and to score. The workbook was easy enough to use to calculate your emotional intelligence score for each of the four Goleman competencies (self-awareness, self-management, social awareness, and relationship management). You can find this assessment either by searching on line or by ordering the self-scoring paper assessment from amazon.com.

▪ Index of Emotional Intelligence

This assessment is from the Adele Lynn Group. It is available in a Self-Scoring Assessment Version which consists of forty questions that take about fifteen minutes to answer. The assessment can be ordered through the Lynn Leadership store at a cost of $29.95 + shipping.

Results are provided for five major categories of EQ and ten subcategories. The five major categories are: self-awareness and control, empathy, social expertness, personal influence, and mastery of purpose/vision. Results are plotted graphically on a scale of 1 to 28.

■ SEI, Six Seconds Emotional Intelligence Assessment

Focused on self-development, the SEI is based on Six Seconds' proprietary emotional intelligence model. The test measures eight fundamental skills, such as emotional literacy, navigating emotions, intrinsic motivation, and empathy. Report comes with over twenty pages of interpretation and actionable, substantive development suggestions.

Appendix K
Results of the
2005 Survey of Emotional
Intelligence in PMs

I conducted the Survey of Project Managers in 2005 to gauge project manager awareness and attitudes regarding emotional intelligence. A subset of the responses to the survey is shown below.

Note that the respondents were asked to indicate their current level of career progression using the following scale, based on the PM career path for a previous employer. Respondents were distributed as following within the scale. This scale is somewhat arbitrary but was shown to somewhat reliably track against project management experience levels as well as overall compensation.

PM Level of Survey Respondents	Number of Respondents
Project Coordinator	5
Team Lead	4
Junior Project Manager	11
Project Manager	18
Senior Project Manager	20
Project Director	14
Program Manager	21
Program Director	16
Total Respondents	109

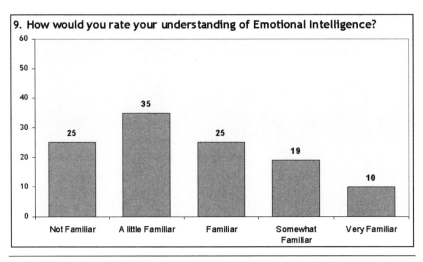

Figure A-7: Responses to Understanding of Emotional Intelligence Question.

■ Understanding of Emotional Intelligence

One of the first questions asked was regarding the level understanding of emotional intelligence concepts. The responses are shown in Figure A-7 with the majority of respondents being at least a little familiar with the concepts of emotional intelligence.

Figure A-8 shows the understanding plotted against the scale of PM progression. A positive response for this graph was a respondent who responded that they were familiar, somewhat familiar, or very familiar. Note that the understanding of emotional intelligence grows along with the PM progression. That is, as PMs move along the scale of career progression, they tend to know more about emotional intelligence.

■ Interest in Learning More About Emotional Intelligence

This question measures the level of interest about learning more about emotional intelligence. Figure A-9 shows a graph of all of the responses for this question.

The responses about interest in learning more were then plotted against the scale of PM progression to see if the interest is correlated to the level of PM experience. A positive response was considered for any respondent who an-

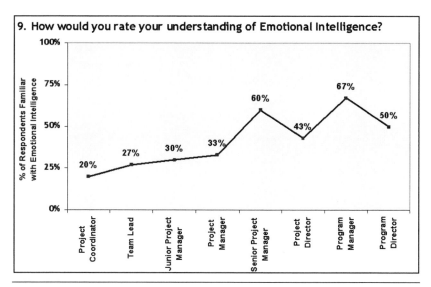

Figure A-8: Responses to Understanding Emotional Intelligence—By Level of PM Progression.

swered Agree Somewhat or Strongly Agree. Figure A-10 shows these positive responses plotted against the scale of PM progression. Note that there is a direct correlation between level of PM career progression and interest in learning more about emotional intelligence.

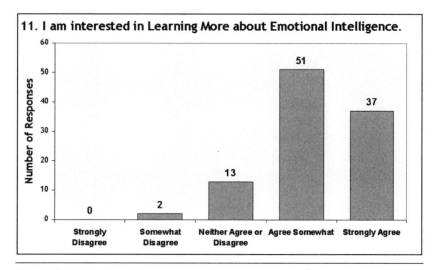

Figure A-9: Interest in Learning More about Emotional Intelligence.

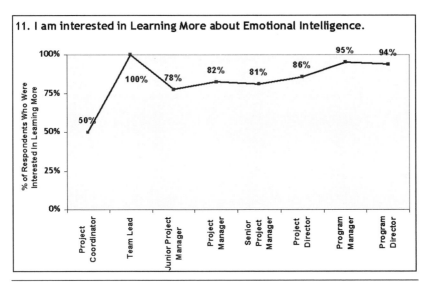

Figure A-10: Interest in Learning More about Emotional Intelligence Plotted Against Level of PM Progression.

How PMs Learn About Emotional Intelligence

When PMs were asked how they learned about emotional intelligence they gave the responses shown in Figure A-11.

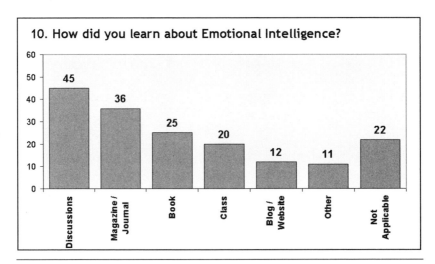

Figure A-11: How Project Managers Learn about Emotional Intelligence.

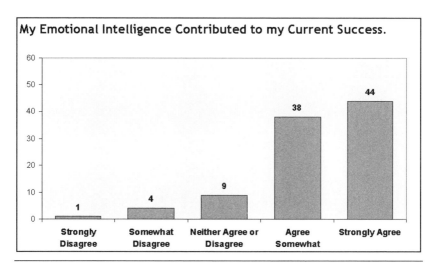

Figure A-12: Emotional Intelligence Contributed to My Current Success.

■ Emotional Intelligence Contributed to My Current Level of Success As a PM

PMs were asked if they thought that their knowledge of emotional intelligence contributed to their current success as a PM. The responses are shown in Figure A-12.

Figure A-13 shows the respondents who answered positively (Agree Somewhat or Strongly Agree) plotted against the level of PM progression.

■ Emotional Intelligence Will Contribute to My Future Success As a PM

Finally, PMs were asked if they thought that emotional intelligence would contribute to their future success as a PM. Figure A-14 shows the total responses for this question.

Figure A-15 shows those respondents who responded positively (Agree Somewhat or Strongly Agree) plotted against the scale of PM progression.

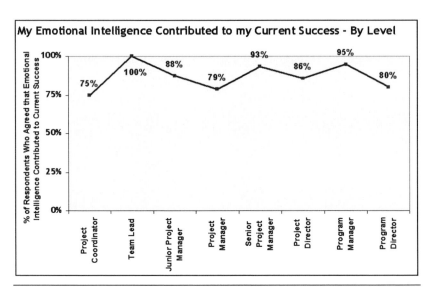

Figure A-13: Emotional Intelligence Contributed to My Current Success by Level of PM Progression.

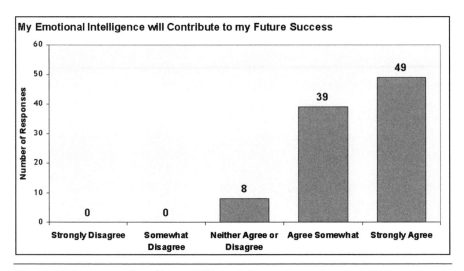

Figure A-14: Emotional Intelligence Will Contribute to Future Success.

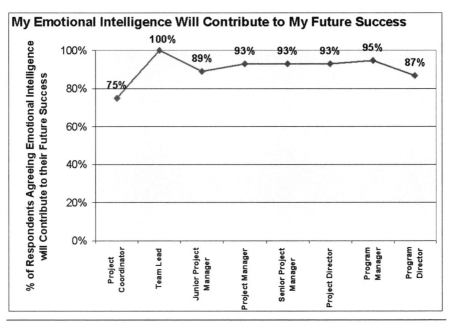

Figure A-15: Emotional Intelligence Will Contribute to Future Success—By PM Progression Level.

Anthony Mersino conducted the 2005 Survey of Emotional Intelligence in PMs by inviting visitors to the www.eq4pm.typepad.com Web site to participate. The 109 self-selected respondents consisted of visitors to the web site, which targets project managers and those interested in project management methodologies, with varying levels of expertise in project management. This sample is representative to the extent that the opinions of visitors to the web site reflect the opinions of the entire project management population, but may be too small to draw conclusions about any subset of the project management population. Thus, it is safe to draw a strong inference regarding the opinions and interests of project managers as a whole from this sample.

Index